This book is a translation into English of *La Religion grecque* by Louise Bruit Zaidman and Pauline Schmitt Pantel, one of the liveliest and most original introductions to the subject in any language.

Classical Greek religion was an amalgam of ritual practices and religious beliefs. It acquired a definite structure at the moment when one of the typical forms of political organization in the Greek world, the *polis* or 'city', came into being towards the end of the eighth century BCE. This structure was based on habits of thought and intellectual categories that differed radically from our own. It is the purpose of this book to consider how religious beliefs and rituals were given expression in the world of the Greek citizen – the functions performed by the religious personnel, and the place that religion occupied in individual, social and political life. The chapters cover first ritual and then myth, rooting the account in the practices of the classical city while also taking seriously the world of the imagination. The book is enriched throughout by quotations from original sources.

Dr Cartledge's translation amounts in many ways to a second edition of the work. He has restructured and redivided the contents of the volume, segregating some technical matter into two appendixes, and has substantially revised the bibliography to meet the needs of a mainly student, English-speaking readership.

Religion in the ancient Greek city

Religion in the ancient Greek city

Louise Bruit Zaidman
Maître de Conférences d'Histoire, Université de Paris VII
and Pauline Schmitt Pantel
Professeur d'Histoire, Université d'Amiens

translated by
Paul Cartledge
*Reader in Ancient History in the University of Cambridge,
and Fellow of Clare College*

CAMBRIDGE
UNIVERSITY PRESS

CAMBRIDGE UNIVERSITY PRESS

Cambridge, New York, Melbourne, Madrid, Cape Town, Singapore, São Paulo

Cambridge University Press

The Edinburgh Building, Cambridge CB2 8RU, UK

Published in the United States of America by Cambridge University Press, New York

www.cambridge.org

Information on this title: www.cambridge.org/9780521423571

Originally published in French as
La Religion grecque
by Armand Colin Editeur 1989
and © Armand Colin Editeur, Paris 1989
First published in English by Cambridge University Press 1992 as
Religion in the ancient Greek city
English translation © Cambridge University Press 1992
Twelfth printing 2007

Printed in the United Kingdom at the University Press, Cambridge

A catalogue record for this publication is available from the British Library

Library of Congress Cataloguing in Publication data
Bruit Zaidman, Louise.
(Religion grecque. English)
Religion in the ancient Greek city / Louise Bruit Zaidman and
Pauline Schmitt Pantel; translated by Paul Cartledge.
p.   cm.
Translation of La religion grecque.
Includes bibliographical references and index.
ISBN 0 521 41262 5 (hardback). – ISBN 0 521 42357 0 (paperback)
1. Greek – Religion 2. Cities and towns – Greece.
I. Schmitt Pantel, Pauline. II. Title
BL 785.Z3513 1992
292.08–dc20 91–39843 CIP

ISBN-13 978-0-521-41262-9 hardback
ISBN-13 978-0-521-42357-1 paperback

CONTENTS

ILLUSTRATIONS

AUTHORS' PREFACE TO THE ENGLISH TRANSLATION

The aim of this book

It may perhaps be useful for our English readers if we explain our initial motivation in writing this book. It was written under the influence of two principal and in our eyes complementary considerations, one methodological, the other pedagogical.

Pedagogically speaking, we noted that there was no recent textbook in France which dealt with ancient Greek religion. This meant that both students and anyone with a general interest in Greek antiquity had the greatest difficulty in acquiring the basic information and understanding that are indispensable for pursuing more detailed investigations within the area of religion. There was a need therefore to collect together and make generally available all such basic materials and to present them in an expository framework that raised the sorts of questions asked today by historians of religion: what is a ritual? a festival? a sanctuary? and so forth. Constant reference to different kinds of documentary evidence satisfied the need both to render the exposition more concrete and to make some fundamental texts accessible in translation to readers who might not always know Greek.

Methodologically speaking, we noted the growing gap between the textbooks that were available and the current state of scholarly research, for over the past thirty years the study of Greek religion, especially research on the myths and analysis of the pantheon, has been revitalized. Working as we were within the context of the Louis Gernet Centre for the Comparative Study of Ancient Societies, under the direction of first J.-P. Vernant and then P. Vidal-Naquet, we conceived our task as being to explain as simply as possible the chief lines of current research in the areas of rituals, myths, and polytheism. It was not at all our aim to write a grand synthesis on Greek religion – Walter Burkert's recent book (1985 [17]) is a very useful example of that genre. Rather, we wished just to provide some introductory propositions that could serve as the basis for more sophisticated readings in the above-mentioned areas. Our project, in other words, was not encyclopaedic but partial, though not, we believe, partial in the sense of biassed. Our aim was not to impose unilaterally another possibly idiosyncratic interpretation of religion in the Greek cities, but to inform non-specialists of the directions being taken by research in progress.

These two considerations give our book its twofold character, as both an introductory textbook and a pointer to new ways of approaching Greek religion. Its aim will be achieved if it spurs readers to discover for themselves all the ancient and modern authors, especially the English historians of Greek religion, who have guided us on our voyage among the rituals, myths and gods of the ancient Greeks.

Acknowledgements

In spring 1990 Paul Cartledge made us an offer we could not refuse: not only to recommend the translation of this book into English but also to do the translation himself. We accepted with enthusiasm. For in fact it is extremely rare to get the chance to have one's work translated by a colleague who is researching in the same field and who has lived for so many years on terms of intimacy with the ancient Greek world. What we did not yet suspect then was that Paul Cartledge, a latter-day hero full of *mētis*, would so feel his way into our alien prose that he would be able to supply, with great delicacy, the thousand-and-one improvements required to make it now more credible, now more accessible, and always better adapted to the needs of English-language readers. In this work of textual re-creation we admire especially the translator's precision, his conscientiousness, and, not least, his generosity of spirit, since it is no small thing to spend long months trying to get a book more widely known by giving it life in another language, at the expense of time devoted to his own research. So on the threshold of the publication of this book, which is also his book, we wish to convey to Paul Cartledge our most cordial gratitude.

TRANSLATOR'S
INTRODUCTION

Matter

O tempora! O mores! From my newspaper cuttings file marked 'Religion' I select almost at random three items appearing beneath the following headlines (in *The Independent*): (i) 'Men of stone' (26 February 1987), (ii) 'Cathedral bans statue of nude after complaints' (24 June 1990), and (iii) 'Ealing retreats on Godless syllabus' (4 April 1991).

(i) is a strange tale of ecclesiastical decay and would-be restoration obstructed by intra-sectarian feuding. The mediaeval church of St Bartholomew at Covenham, Lincolnshire, England, was derelict. A group of American Anglicans from Corona del Mar, California, USA, wished to transport the church of St Bartholomew from eastern England stone by stone and resurrect it on the West Coast. Their desire had the initial approval of the Church (of England) Commissioners but hit against the stumbling-block of the disapproval of the (US) Episcopalian Church, which successfully leaned on the Commissioners. The reason for the objection? The traditionalist American Anglicans, which included the relevant congregation of Corona del Mar, had recently decided to split from the parent Episcopalian Church because the latter was proposing to ordain women priests (as it has since done, not to mention women bishops).

The phenomenon of itinerant temples was not unknown in ancient Greece; for example, the temple of Ares originally built in the fifth century in the deme of Akharnai to the north of the city of Athens was disassembled and relocated in the Athenian Agora some four centuries later. But the phenomenon was as rare in antiquity as it is today. On the other hand, the phenomenon of women priests, so massively controversial today within certain Christian communions, was *vieux jeu* in Classical Greece (below, chapter 5). But then the Classical Greeks lacked doctrinally authoritative sacred books which could be held to have set in tablets of stone the non-eligibility of women for the priesthood, nor did they have a priesthood that was vocationally recruited and professionally trained, and that functioned within an independently institutionalized and hierarchically ordered Church.

(ii), coincidentally, also concerns Lincolnshire, although not some remote village this time but the county town of Lincoln, and more precisely its majestic Cathedral. In line with their policy of encouraging 'spiritual' art the Dean and Chapter authorized the exhibition in the Cathedral aisle – and other less conspicuous locations – of sculptor Leonard McComb's life-size 'Portrait of a Man Standing', also known familiarly as the 'Golden Man' since the statue's surface is of highly polished bronze and gold leaf. The problem (as it was soon perceived to be) was that the Golden Man is an unabashed nude. In response to public objections the Dean of Lincoln was moved to describe the statue as inappropriate for Lincoln (and presumably any) Cathedral, and the statue itself was moved to its current, almost entirely secular resting-place, London's Tate Gallery.

Had a Classical Greek time-traveller been able to witness both the controversy (and I should add that at least one Roman Catholic nun staunchly defended the original decision to exhibit the statue in Lincoln Cathedral, seeing in it somehow a representation of mankind as a whole) and the statue, he or she would have been utterly perplexed and bewildered. For here is a figure of the *kouros* type (see chapter 14), and a rather splendid specimen at that, its surface materials somewhat reminiscent of the *de luxe* gold-and-ivory cult-statues erected at Delphi, Athens and elsewhere. Surely, our traveller might have mused, there could be no more appropriate space, *mutatis mutandis*, than an Anglican cathedral for the exhibition of a *kouros* statue, and how odd that there should have been felt to be a need to encourage 'spiritual' art.

(iii) concerns a draft Religious Education syllabus drawn up by the local council of Ealing, a London borough. This failed to mention either God or the Bible or Jesus Christ, for which sins of omission it drew the ire of at least 800 Ealing residents. Led by a parent-governor of one of the schools in the locality, they took the remarkable step of formally petitioning Parliament on the grounds that the syllabus did not reflect the borough's mainly Christian religious traditions. Her Majesty's Secretary of State for Education gave them his and his Department's support; having taken legal advice, he declared himself unsatisfied that the proposed syllabus complied with the Education Reform Act 1988. Indeed, in a letter previously circulated to all chief education officers and containing the Secretary of State's guidelines he had advised that in Great Britain the religious traditions were in the main Christian.

In Classical Greece education was (except at Sparta) not an affair of state, and so not subject to state regulation and prescription. On the other hand, the idea of an atheistic religious education syllabus would have been not merely anathema but intrinsically incomprehensible to all but the tiniest handful of highly untypical Classical Greeks. If the Classical Greeks were also to be told that in Great Britain there was an established (Christian) Church, their bafflement would only increase. For although there was no 'Church' in this sense in any Classical Greek state, Classical Greek religion was as 'established', as much part of the regular political apparatus of government and of the very identity of the Greek city, as it well could be.

Such examples as these three could be multiplied with the greatest of ease. My purpose in beginning this introduction with them is to strike one of the keynotes of the book translated below. If the past as such and in general is a foreign country, and they do things differently there, this holds especially true of the Classical Greeks and their religious past. To put it another way, although Christianity developed within – and could not have developed without – the pagan Graeco-Roman empire, religion was emphatically not, in any straightforward sense, an ingredient in 'the legacy of Greece'. It is a prime merit of Dr Louise Bruit (University of Paris) and Dr Pauline Schmitt (University of Amiens) that they introduce this theme of difference right at the start of *La Religion grecque* and play variations on it throughout. The mental world of polytheistic paganism and its peculiar civic context during the Classical fifth and fourth centuries BCE are phenomena that are remarkably hard to explain or even understand in our drastically different, 'mainly Christian' society.

But that was by no means my only reason for wanting to make their book accessible to an English-language readership. Secondly, and to some most cogently, it fills a gap in the English and American market no less surely than the original did in the French market (see Authors' preface). Greek religion and – or rather, *including* – mythology (see chapter 12) were once, in the later nineteenth and early twentieth centuries, central not only to the teaching and study of the Classics in this country but also to the teaching and study of Religion *tout court*. Since the heyday of Robertson Smith and J. G. Frazer, to name only two (see further chapters 1 and 12), Classical Greek religion has been progressively marginalized (though mythology has kept its place), until it is a sign of the times that the standard handbook or textbook on the subject was written in German in 1977 and only published in English translation eight years later (Burkert 1985 [17] – all such references by author, date and number are to the Bibliography, pp. 247–67). That book, moreover, is formidably long and densely written, a tome to be consulted rather than read through, more a work of reference than an interpretative monograph. Not that it does not contain interpretation, throughout, but its many learned theses tend to be obscured by the overlay of erudition documented in the 130 pages of endnotes.

'Bruit/Schmitt', by contrast, originally appeared in late 1989 under Armand Colin's 'Cursus' imprint within the series 'Histoire de l'Antiquité' edited by François Hartog, Pauline Schmitt-Pantel and John Scheid. Attention to context being of the essence, we learn from its publication history alone that it is a 'manuel' or handbook. It was aimed, not at scholarly colleagues in the first instance, but rather at their pupils in the universities and (perhaps some) *lycées*, and at interested colleagues and students in other disciplines than 'Classics' (which in France is anyway not so rigidly departmentalized, but usually taught within some sort of 'Sciences humaines' framework at the school and undergraduate levels). This is the same kind of readership, *mutatis mutandis*, that I have in mind for this translation. At a rather paradoxical cultural moment, when Classics in the technical, philologically based sense is a shrinking asset in this country and yet interest in the Classical Graeco-Roman world has never been more intense or more widespread, there is an increasingly urgent need for the publication of books that broadcast and (in the nicest possible, French sense) vulgarize the Classical world in both exciting and critically informed ways. 'Bruit/Schmitt' seemed to me to meet all those criteria admirably.

A third reason for undertaking this translation was that the authors have a positive as well as a negative thesis to argue, and it seems to me that they argue both with equal conviction and persuasiveness. If one of the book's two main aims is to rid us of what have been described elsewhere (Price 1984: [262]: 11–15) as 'Christianizing assumptions', the other is to convince us by constant demonstration and vehemently insistent repetition that the proper context for evaluating Classical Greek religion is not the individual immortal soul (itself a concept with a history – see chapter 15) but rather the city, the peculiar civic corporation that the Greeks labelled *polis*.

Hence the title chosen for this translation: not just 'Greek Religion' but 'Religion in the Ancient Greek City'. This emphasis, too, accounts for certain deliberate exclusions from the book, most notably perhaps magic, precisely because magic is not a publicly sanctioned religious activity. However, it must at once be added that the term 'city' is or implies a theoretical abstraction (or model, or ideal type, to employ other special terminologies). For there were in empirical actuality more than a thousand separate and usually radically self-differentiated 'cities' in this sense in Classical Greece, and, traditionally but inevitably, it is the city of Athens that receives most space, since that is the source and reference-point of the great bulk of the surviving contemporary written and visual evidence. But Athens, as the authors are at pains to stress, was not in any sense a typical Classical Greek *polis*, being exceptionally large, exceptionally complex, and exceptionally democratic. Athenocentricity must therefore be resisted, but without falling into the opposite trap of excessive generalization about religion in 'Greece'. This delicate balancing act is performed by the authors with great mental agility and expository skill.

My fourth and final principal reason for translating 'Bruit/ Schmitt' is a matter of what the Germans call *Wissenschaft*, but one with cultural and indeed political ramifications beyond the confines of the academy. In terms of intellectual vitality and influence there is only one possible rival within the domain of the 'Sciences humaines' in France to the so-called '*Annales* School' of sociologically minded historians inspired by Marc Bloch and Lucien Febvre, and that is the 'Paris School' of cultural historians of ancient Greece and especially ancient Greek religion and mythology dominated for the past three decades by J.-P. Vernant. It is no accident (as they say) that both 'Schools' were crucially influenced in their origins by the work of the sociohistorical psychologist Emile Durkheim. And it is the social, or in this case specifically the civic, approach to Greek religion, originally formulated in rejection of nineteenth-century individualizing notions, that informs the present book (though not to the exclusion of other approaches: as the authors say in their Preface, they are not seeking dogmatically to impose a single line of interpretation).

English readers have increasingly of late been given versions of the work of members of the Paris School; the translations by Janet Lloyd are particularly highly recommended (e.g. Detienne 1977 [220]; Vernant 1980 [39]; Vernant and Vidal-Naquet 1988 [149]). One such, also published by the Cambridge University Press (Gordon 1981 [186]), came equipped with a helpful introduction by Richard Buxton to the School's leading ideas (which need not therefore be rehearsed here; they emerge, in any case, explicitly or implicitly, throughout the present work). But the essays collected and translated by Richard Gordon all quite clearly fell within the 'scholarly' bracket, not being aimed at an undergraduate, let alone a sixth-form or high school, audience. It is a particular virtue of 'Bruit/Schmitt' in this regard that without unduly sacrificing subtlety and complexity (or eschewing the School's coded language – see below) it has made available those leading ideas in a more popularly digestible form.

Form

All translation, it is a commonplace, is interpretation, even perhaps *mis*interpretation; at any rate, according to an Italian adage, every translator is a traducer (*traduttore traditore*). Presumably this is never more so than when, as here, translation is a threefold process: straightforwardly (relatively, anyway – see below) from the elegant French of Mesdames Bruit and Schmitt into my less than poetic but more or less accurate English version; not at all straightforwardly from the alien conceptual world of classical Greek paganism into the post-Enlightenment vocabularies of two modern European languages. The classical Greeks did not, for example, 'have a word for' religion … But at least Greek, French and English all belong to the Indo–European family of languages (unless that should turn out to be yet another nineteenth-century myth!)

The main point at issue here is that it is not at all clear whether it is possible to be true to the spirit and flavour of the original Classical Greek in which the literary texts and documentary inscriptions on which the present book is largely based were written. (Visual images raise their own, peculiar problems of 'translation': see briefly chapter 14.) Perhaps the best that any translator/interpreter of Classical Greek religion can hope to achieve is the literate equivalent of a theatrically Brechtian alienation effect. If Bruit, Schmitt and I have between us managed to get across the idea that Classical Greek religion is 'other', desperately foreign to (in particular) post-Christian, monotheistic ways of conceptualizing the divine, then perhaps we should be well enough satisfied. We may of course also congratulate ourselves on the fact that the Classical Greeks had no uniquely authoritative sacred books or texts, so that we are not confronted by the doctrinal problems faced by translators of, say, the Hebrew Bible, the New Testament or the Koran.

But the English translator of 'Bruit/Schmitt' is faced with a further problem. These authors, as we have seen, have been formed within a very specific 'school' of French scholarship. As tends to happen with such original and powerfully influential schools of thought, it has over the past forty years or so formulated, honed and refined a specialized technical vocabulary, a jargon if you like, which in addition to its overt denotational meaning carries subtle undertones and overtones of connotation for the initiated. If my translation, therefore, reads more than usually like stilted translationese, this is not solely due to my incompetence but also to my striving to do justice to the flavour and nuance of the original. Let me give just a single, apparently simple illustration.

In the penultimate sentence of the last paragraph but one I wrote 'conceptualizing the divine'. This does not, I think, read absolutely 'naturally' to a native English speaker, even to one who is inured to the esoteric vagaries of academic linguistic codes. But it does, I hope, adequately represent, that is, convey the general sense and main purport of, a French phrase much used by 'Bruit/Schmitt', namely 'penser le divin'. Their 'penser', however, is more than just 'to conceptualize': it connotes (to spell it out inelegantly) entering sympathetically, as far as someone reared in our culture (or cultures) is able, into a categorically different and conceptually alien thought-world articulated by an underlying logic of representation (see esp. Part III).

So much for the as it were 'higher-order' problems of this translation. On a more mundanely practical level the English reader should be informed – or warned – that my text is not only, or not just, an Englishing of the French original, but in some ways and to some extent more of a second edition. This is chiefly because from the very inception of the project (which was unwittingly inspired by our mutual friend and colleague Dr Annie Schnapp) I have had the enormous privilege and pleasure of working in close collaboration with the two French authors. They have not merely checked my translation for literal fidelity but also sanctioned a considerable reshaping of their original text – redivision of the whole into three, not two, parts, partial redivision and wholesale renumbering of the chapters, some reordering of sections, subsections and sentences, segregation of some matter originally in the main text into two Appendixes, amalgamation of their Glossary and Lexicon into a consolidated Index, and revamping of the Bibliography to make it answer more to the needs of a mainly undergraduate and English-speaking readership. They have also allowed me to exercise my judgement in the matter of the translations of ancient Greek texts quoted *in extenso* throughout the book – one of its most attractive features. (It should, however, be stressed that 'Bruit/Schmitt' is not a 'sourcebook' like Crahay 1966 [5] or Rice and Stambaugh 1979 [12].) These translations are sometimes more or less modified versions of what I consider to be the best or the most easily available (where available at all) published translations, duly acknowledged; otherwise they are my own.

Perhaps even more remarkably, the authors have permitted me not just to correct the few errors in the original text but also to introduce some new (usually purely illustrative) material, in cases where we all thought the additions improved either the clarity of the exposition or the force of the argument or both. The book, however, despite what they may say, remains very much the work of the original (in more than one sense) authors. Indeed, besides overseeing my labours generally, they have themselves made some specific additions to the French version, which I have silently incorporated in the translation. Anglo-French – or Gallo-English – co-operation could surely go no further than this. May it be as an omen for the success of '1992'.

It remains only to thank François Lissarrague (of the Centre Louis Gernet) for generously making available again his remarkably delicate line-drawings, Janet Lloyd and David Harvey for kindly vetting samples of the translation and reassuring me that there was a rough equivalence between it and the original, the two anonymous readers for their helpfully astringent comments on my original proposal, and, above all, the Syndics and officers of the Cambridge University Press for agreeing so readily to buy the translation rights from Armand Colin and taking care of the necessary trans-Channel negotiations.

July 1991   Paul Cartledge

LIST OF SOURCES

The following is a list of the main ancient sources on Greek religion, which are quoted at length in the course of the book. Translations are cited where used; all others are by PC.

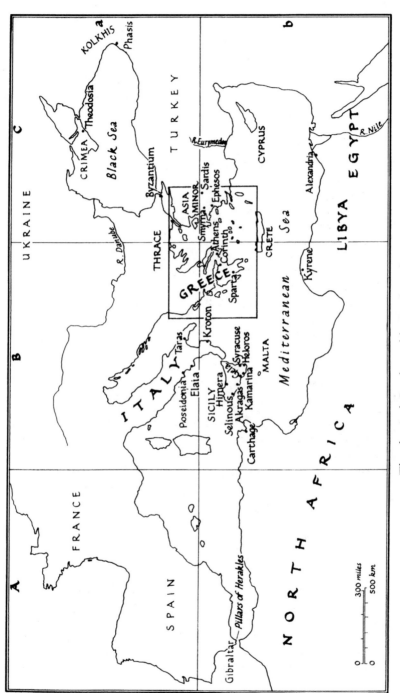

1a   The classical Greek world. (For boxed area see next page)

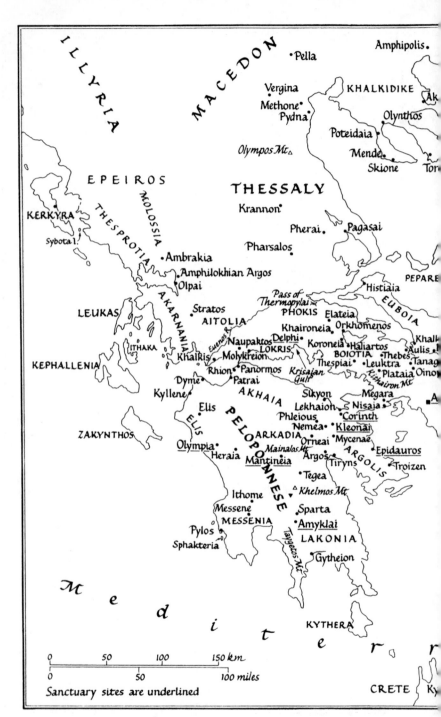

1b   Greece and the Aegean islands

PART I

Introduction: How should we study Greek civic religion?

CHAPTER I

The necessity of cultural estrangement

UNFAMILIAR TERRITORY

The study of Greek religion requires a preliminary mental readjustment: we must temporarily abandon familiar cultural territory and radically question received intellectual categories. Greek society was fundamentally different from our own, and the concepts that we employ to describe contemporary religious phenomena are necessarily ill adapted to the analysis of what the Greeks regarded as the divine sphere. Besides, the function of religion cannot be the same in a society such as ours, in which communal life is very largely secularized, and in one where religion was thoroughly intertwined with all areas of public and social interaction. We have, moreover, to disabuse ourselves of the notion of a disembodied 'essence' of religion; for only then can we treat religion as a subject for enquiry like any other, one that has a history.

The extent to which Greek religion is alien territory for us may be grasped in a preliminary way by considering the main conclusions of J.-P. Vernant's concise comparison of the beliefs of the ancient Greeks with those of a Western, still christianized culture (Vernant 1991[42]: 272–3). For 'us', the divine (in the form of a transcendent God) is external to the world, it has created the world and mankind, it is present within mankind, and it is confined, lastly, to its own sharply defined sphere within everyday life. For 'them', the Greeks, on the other hand, the gods were not external to the world: they did not create either the cosmos or mankind, but were themselves created; they had not always existed, but had usurped power; they were not eternal but only immortal; they were not omnipotent and omniscient, but possessed merely limited powers and areas of knowledge; they were themselves subject to fate, and they intervened constantly in the affairs of men. Even this rapid comparison makes it clear that we must shed all our preconceived ideas of religion before we embark on the study of the Greeks' peculiar amalgam of religious practices and beliefs.

Neither survival nor prefiguration

Besides taking that precaution, we must also avoid posing questions that hinder rather than further the understanding of the Greek world. Ancient Greek religion, among others, has been the object of two types of analysis which purport to be universally valid explanations of 'Religion' as such. First, there has been a concerted search for supposed traces of magical practices and primitive mentality surviving within the historically attested Greek pantheon, rituals and myths. This notion of 'survivals' brings with it an entourage of would-be explanations that invoke, for instance, the discredited category of totemism (the idea that originally religion was essentially a matter of groups of people identifying themselves with objects in the natural world).

Secondly, the beliefs and practices of the Greeks have been scrutinized with a view to discovering soil that was especially propitious for the growth of a monotheistic religion like Christianity. Here, the spotlight is trained on the milieux of exclusive sects and on initiation into mystery-cults. Unhappily, this conflation of religions of different kinds rests on the conviction that religions do not all have equal value, and the effect of this interpretation is to refract Greek religion artificially through the distorting prism of Christianity.

These two approaches have left their mark on a number of books, and are of great historiographical interest. Their presuppositions are those of their times. So too the view of Greek religion proposed here, which sees it as a symbolic system with its own peculiar logic and coherence, is a characteristic sign of our own, relativistic era.

4

The 'right' answers?

Two main ways of explaining the beliefs and cults of the Classical era are available in principle. One approach concentrates on their origins, the other places the emphasis rather on the way in which they functioned within a cultural ensemble that is assumed to be relatively stable, the civic community. The two approaches are not irreconcilable, but they do give different highlights and tonalities to the study of Greek religion.

The classic evolutionary model of Greek religion is that proposed by, for example, M. P. Nilsson (1925 [28], 1940 [29], 1948 [30]). This envisages Greek religion as a successful marriage between the pre-Hellenic religion of the native populations and the cults and beliefs introduced by the Greek peoples when they arrived in Greece in the course of the second millennium. Those who employ this explanatory framework are required to distinguish within each fifth-century ritual that element which goes back to the pre-Hellenic rite and that part which is 'Greek'. Each of the respective 'original sources' serves the function of explaining the ritual in question.

For example, one might on this model interpret the Greeks' ritual of bloody animal-sacrifice by tracing its origins back to the hunting practices of the Stone Age (i.e., before the third millennium). Likewise, the image of a divinity might be seen as combining both pre-Greek and Greek traits. Artemis, for example, in her rôle of 'Mistress of Animals' suggests a pre-Hellenic mother-goddess; but as 'Huntress' she appears to be an unadulterated product of the Greek newcomers. According to this model, as we said, origins function as explanations; but that necessitates the establishment of a precise chronology for the history of cults and myths, and for the most remote epochs this is largely a matter of guesswork. 'Origins-theory' also advances highly controversial explanations, such as the alleged primacy of female deities in the pre-Hellenic world and of male deities among the Greeks.

The other, functionalist paradigm of explanation rejects the idea that the origins of a cult or ritual constitute a sufficient explanation of its functioning, significance and rôle at a given moment in history. On this view the importance of the ritual of animal-sacrifice, for instance, becomes clear above all by studying the functions whose performance it guarantees and the values it symbolized for the Greek city. Or, to take the example of Artemis again, in her dual rôle of 'Mistress of Animals' and goddess of hunting she assumes the two complementary aspects of the principal function that is peculiarly hers, namely to protect the world of untamed nature.

This second approach also emphasizes the fact that Greek religious beliefs and rituals were given their characteristic structure at the moment when one of the most distinctive forms of Greek political organization was emerging – the *polis* or city (the standard translation, 'city-state', has misleading implications and will be avoided here; see further below). This holds good for the pantheon and the mythology established by Homer and Hesiod, the cult of heroes, the holy places such as temples and sanctuaries, the organization of rituals according to a sacred calendar, the great Games, and so forth. That is to say, even if the same cult-places were in continuous use from Mycenaean times into the historical era, this does not mean that the beliefs of the Mycenaeans (in so far as they can be determined) necessarily help us to understand the beliefs of Greeks who were living almost a millennium later, and, moreover, under a radically different form of social and political organization from that of the Mycenaean palace. We may be able to trace back certain details of cults and divine personages to an epoch preceding the establishment of the cities, but it is above all their function and the way in which they were reinterpreted within the new world of the Greek city that require explanation.

SCOPE OF THIS BOOK: ARCHAIC AND CLASSICAL GREEK CITIES

This book does not set out to explore either the state of religion before the emergence of the cities (the religions of the pre-Hellenic, Minoan and Mycenaean eras) or the transformations that occurred during the post-Classical, Hellenistic epoch. In the former case, there are special problems in understanding religions which existed before the appearance and diffusion of alphabetic writing, or in interpreting the religious references in the Mycenaean palace archives transcribed in the 'Linear B' syllabic script. In the latter, Hellenistic period, cults and beliefs developed with extraordinary richness and diversity from the time of Alexander the Great (reigned 336–323) onwards. The problems posed by these epochs cannot be summarized in a single chapter.

So the framework chosen for this book is the world of the Greek cities during the Archaic and Classical periods (approximately 750–330). In this context, a 'city' is an autonomous and independent political unit consisting of a territory (partly cultivated, partly wild) that includes both villages and more densely populated centres (sometimes a town), of which one acts as the capital of the whole unit for political purposes. Consider, for instance, the city of Athens – or 'the Athenians', as the state was called by the Greeks. This comprised the entire territory of Attica (some 2,500 km²), within which the urban centre of Athens was the seat of the Assembly of citizens, the city's officials and, in a word, political life in general. Cults, sanctuaries and religious practices, though, were dispersed throughout the city's territory and involved the people who lived in the country (the majority) just as much as those who lived in the town. The countryside was dotted with religious sanctuaries, mostly very modest affairs. The villages had their altars and cult-places; religious activity was a daily matter. The survival today of a few imposing temples in sometimes remote and deserted spots gives an inadequate impression of the religious landscape of the ancient Greek cities.

CHAPTER 2

Some fundamental notions

One of the problems inherent in the study of Greek religion stems from the fact that basic concepts such as the sacred, purity and pollution, and piety and impiety, had special meanings for the Greeks that do not correspond to those with which we are familiar.

THE SACRED

Any study of religion has to deal with the notion of the sacred, but in the world of the Greek cities the opposition between the sacred and the profane – which we assume to be fundamental in the area of religion – was either blurred or utterly irrelevant.

The Greek language distinguished, rather, by means of such terms as *hieron, hosion* and *hagion*, a number of concepts that we lump together under the heading of 'the sacred'. Thus *ta hiera* designated the cults and sanctuaries of the gods, but also sacrificial victims. The latter, in other words, were objects endowed by ritual with qualities that brought them into relation with the divine and thus caused them to enter the domain we label 'sacred'. These acts, these places, these objects were endowed with a power that rendered them conducive or favourable to the efficacy of the ritual. However, nothing in their intrinsic nature distinguished them from objects of everyday use, either the implements that were employed in sacrificial cooking (knives, spits, cauldrons) or the food (bread, cakes, fruit) that was transformed into sacred offerings by being deposited in consecrated places. Similarly, the *hiereus* – the priest entrusted with performing the *hiera*, the cult-acts, in accordance with the local or *ad hoc* prescriptions and prohibitions – was not for that reason in any way a holy man set apart on retreat from 'profane' life. He could continue to live within the city, in the midst of his *oikos* (household), so long as he fulfilled the obligations of his office on the appointed days.

Hosion was a term applied more especially to modes of behaviour or to actions that were in conformity with the norms governing relations between gods and men, or between men themselves. Everything that was prescribed or permitted by divine law was thus *hosion*, and the word *hosion* was often associated with *dikaion* ('just'). We might therefore be tempted to translate *hosion* as 'sanctified' or 'consecrated'. But the term could also derive its meaning from being opposed to *hieron*; in which case it signified a condition of being liberated from the sacred, desacralized, and therefore free, permitted, profane. So, for instance, *hē hosiē kre(a)ōn* meant the portion of a sacrificial victim that was regularly reserved for human consumption, the 'permitted' portion.

The third term, *hagion*, however, was applied rather to temples or sanctuaries, customs or rituals, offerings or cultic objects (whereas *hagnos* was used in this sense for human beings). It denoted a degree of ritual purity that implied withdrawal from the everyday world. It included the notion of a kind of negative respectfulness, an abstention from doing violence. It served to express an idea of prohibition.

So we must be on our guard against spurious and deceptive equivalences. Where the ancient Greek words seem to be conveying notions that are familiar to us, they may in fact be concealing quite different conceptions beneath merely apparent similarity.

PURITY AND POLLUTION

The related notions of purity and pollution also referred to religious categories that were not applied in precisely the same way as our own. At one level purity and physical cleanliness seem to be closely identified. That which is *katharon* or 'pure' is that which has been cleansed of all taint of dirt, and pollution likewise appears to have a strongly physical, material connotation.

However, it soon becomes clear that in the Classical period, if not already in Homer, the great diversity of cathartic rituals corresponded to an enormous variety of forms of pollution which can only be understood by reference to a religious world-view. *Miasma* (pollution) is no simple notion.

Consider blood, for example. On the one hand, it is the very principle of life, coursing round the human body, and a means of consecration, as when it flows out upon the altar during an animal-sacrifice. On the other hand, it becomes filth and pollution when it is spilt onto the ground or gushes out over the body of a murder-victim. For when it is mixed with dust, blood signifies murder and death. Blood, therefore, is in no sense 'impure' in itself, but it becomes so under specific conditions. Pollution consists in the establishment of a link between entities which should be kept separated and distinct. The anthropologist Mary Douglas's famous definition of pollution as 'matter out of place' (Douglas 1966[51]) seems appropriate for the Greeks.

The concept of pollution is often associated with that of the sacred, through the rapprochement of two series of terms: those attached to *agos* (another word for 'pollution') and those that we have already met in the context of *hagion*, sacred in the sense of forbidden, dangerous for men. This brings pollution into relation with one of the characteristics of the sacred: its power to inspire awe. By means of the tension between 'sacred' and 'polluted' the two polar opposites of purity and pollution can interact and be confounded. Thus the powers of death, which for mankind represents the ultimate form of pollution, were described by Aeschylus (*Persians* 628) as *khthonioi daimones hagnoi*, 'sacred daemonic powers of the earth'.

Pollution, in other words, may conceal a positive religious quality, within the framework of the ritual system and the prescriptions which govern the functioning of rituals in the world of men. To give just three examples: the bones of Oedipus, the sacrilegious being *par excellence*, might nevertheless become a source of blessings to the land that would give them a final resting-place (Sophocles, *Oedipus at Colonus* 1552–5). Secondly, it was the sacrifice of a pig, the most polluted of animals, that effected the most potent purification (*katharmos*) for the initiates of the Eleusinian Mysteries. Finally, it was one and the same god,

Apollo, who presided over both purification and pollution: he was at once the cause and the healer of disease (for example, the plague suffered by the Greeks at Troy, with which the *Iliad* begins).

In every instance, therefore, it is within the system established by Greek religious thought that we must both define the notions we encounter and study the way in which their mutual inter-′ action and transformation constitute a mode of symbolic expression with its own logical forms.

PIETY AND IMPIETY

The Greek city knew neither Church nor dogma. As a consequence Greek religious conduct, whether pious or impious, lacked the precisely defined character it could acquire in other religions. Moreover, heresy and religious persecution were in principle impossible within the Greek system, although this did not stop Greek cities from condemning people for impiety or indicating, conversely, wherein respect for the gods consisted.

Asebeia (impiety) was the absence of respect for the beliefs and rituals shared by the inhabitants of a city. The civic community could treat *asebeia* as a crime, bringing before a court those who were alleged to have demonstrated it, and condemning them. But impiety trials resulted from very different modes of behaviour, as the following selection shows:

1 Malicious damage to the property of the gods, their rituals or figural representations. For example, uprooting one of Athene's sacred olive trees was an offence tried by the Areiopagos council; and to profane the Mysteries of Eleusis or mutilate the herms erected in the civic Agora or outside private homes (as happened at Athens in 415) were capital crimes.

2 The introduction of new gods and cults not (yet) officially recognized by the city (as Asklepios, Bendis, Ammon and Adonis *were* recognized by the Athenians at the end of the fifth century). According to the first-century CE Jewish historian Flavius Josephus (*Against Apion* II.276), 'the Athenians put the priestess Ninos to death because a citizen accused her

of conducting initiations into the cults of foreign gods. Athenian law forbade this, and the penalty for the unauthorized introduction of a foreign god was death.'

3 Opinions of the gods held by certain individuals. Thus Anaxagoras was allegedly prosecuted for impiety at Athens for declaring the sun to be a red-hot stone and the moon to be made of common-or-garden earth; so too was Protagoras, who claimed to be unable to state whether the gods existed or not. But the most celebrated case is that of Socrates, whom the Athenians condemned to death in 399 for corrupting the young, undermining belief in the gods of the city and introducing new deities.

The occasions of impiety trials, therefore, were multifarious, but the motivation appears uniform. They were, it seems, the violent reaction of a civic community that felt its unity to be under threat, since religion was an integral constituent of its identity. But apart from these instances, all the more spectacular for being so rare, the Greek city was perfectly prepared to tolerate unbelief, so long at any rate as it did not give rise to acts of impiety. The enlightened circles of the Sophists, doctors and mathematicians, for example, were not persecuted, even though they did not unhesitatingly endorse the civic cults and beliefs. An anecdote concerning Perikles and Anaxagoras is in this regard paradigmatic:

There is a story that Perikles was once sent from his country estate the head of a one-horned ram. Thereupon Lampon, the diviner, when he saw how the horn grew strong and solid out of the middle of the creature's forehead, declared that the mastery of the two dominant groups in the city – which at that time were led by Thoukydides [son of Melesias] and Perikles – would be concentrated in the hands of one man, and that he would be the one to whom this sign had been given. Anaxagoras, on the other hand, had the skull dissected and proceeded to demonstrate that the brain had not filled its natural space, but had contracted into a point like an egg at that place in the cavity from which the horn grew. (Plutarch, *Life of Perikles* 6)

Accusations of impiety marked out one boundary beyond which it was impossible to proceed and still remain within the city's confines. It is more difficult, however, to grasp what the

Greeks placed positively under the heading of piety, to understand, that is, what they counted as being a pious man (*eusebēs*)
or judged to be a community that showed proper respect towards
the gods. Speaking generally, though, piety was apparently that
sentiment which the group or the individual entertained towards
certain specified obligations.

The obligations of the *community* involved above all respect
for ancestral tradition (*ta patria*). Antique rituals were performed
without the citizens knowing precisely what they meant, whereas
more recently introduced rites were sometimes decried as being
less worthy of veneration, on the grounds, for instance, that they
attributed too much importance to the banquets that followed
the animal-sacrifice. The city considered it proper for the gods to
receive their due portion, partly in material form (through scrupulous management of the gods' property, especially their sacred
areas), partly in the form of cult-honours, for the proper conduct
of which it could consult unofficial experts in ritual (*exēgētai*).
Finally, the city considered itself to be, not a divinity, but a
'concrete and living entity under the sure protection of the gods,
who would not abandon it as long as it did not abandon them'
(L. Gernet in Gernet and Boulanger 1932[24]: 295). To the unity
of the gods around a city at its moments of crisis there had to
correspond a unity of men, and the force and symbolic efficacy of
this human solidarity were expressed in collective manifestations
like the Panathenaic festival or the Athenians' public civic funeral
of their war dead.

As for the *individual*, his or her additional obligations were
manifold and multivalent. Piety was judged to be displayed
through participation in the city's cults, abundance of offerings in
sanctuaries, devotion towards kindred dead and the family's
guardian deities, financial generosity in enabling the most magnificent celebrations of public rituals (games, civic liturgies (see
p. 95), sacrifices and public banquets), and a host of other practical activities. It is hard, though, to get at the underlying personal
sentiment that animated the performance of these actions. Only
very rarely have expressions of feeling been transmitted to us.
From Euripidean tragedy we could cite Hippolytos, son of
Theseus and an Amazon, whom the playwright presents (in the
bitterly ironical words of his father) as one 'who lives in the

company of the gods, a virtuously self-controlled being innocent of all taint of evil' (*Hippolytos* 948–9); or Ion, son of Kreousa and Apollo, who from the front courtyard of his father's temple at Delphi declares 'It is a noble thing, Phoibos, this toil to which I devote myself for your sake before your temple, to honour your prophetic abode! Glorious is my task, since I bend my arms in the service of the immortal gods, not of mortal masters. And this pious toil fatigues me not at all' (*Ion* 128–35). Sentiments of closeness between man and god like that are less frequently expressed than those of distanced respect. But there were particular cults which insisted on a personal relationship between deity and mortal – those of the hero-healers, the oracular gods and the mystery religions (about whose practices and precepts we are so badly informed).

If impiety marked out one of the frontiers of piety, another was traced by the attitude of those men who lived in constant irrational dread of the gods. An excessive ritualism, a morbid recourse to interpreters of signs and portents, a panic fear of the divine – such behaviour seemed ridiculous and hardly conformable with normal Greek piety. Hence the satirical portrait drawn by Theophrastos of the *deisidaimōn* or Superstitious Man who 'will not sally forth for the day till he have washed his hands and sprinkled himself at the Nine Springs, and put a bit of bay-leaf from a temple in his mouth. And if a polecat cross his path he will not proceed on his way till someone else be gone by, or he have cast three stones across the street . . . If a mouse gnaw a bag of his meal, he will rush off to the *exēgētēs* and ask what he must do, and if the anwer be "send it to the cobbler's to be patched", he neglects the advice and rids himself of the evil by expiatory sacrifice' (*Characters* XVI.2–6).

Normal piety, therefore, was not the expression of a sentiment of intimacy between man and god. Nor was it the outward and visible sign of an inner need for spiritual transformation, let alone assimilation to the godhead (except for members of certain sects like the Orphics). Nor, however, was it straightforwardly the scrupulous observance of prescribed rituals. If we have difficulty in characterizing Greek piety, that is because the symbolic domain to which it belongs is markedly different from our own, and to judge it by Christian standards would frequently lead us badly astray. To be *eusebēs*, in sum, was to believe in the efficacy of the symbolic system that the city had established for the purpose of managing relations between gods and men, and to participate in it, moreover, in the most vigorously active manner possible.

CHAPTER 3

Sources of evidence

There are three kinds of original sources available to us for the study of Greek religion: literary texts, epigraphic documents and archaeological data.

LITERARY TEXTS

Ancient Greece had no great foundation text like the Bible, nor indeed any literature that was strictly speaking religious. Instead, the entire range of Greek literature provides us with every sort of information about religion. Rather than making a catalogue of this literature here, we shall simply cite certain works that have been especially drawn upon for the study of Greek religion.

Pride of place must go to Homer's *Iliad* and *Odyssey*. These vast epic poems, written down in the course of the eighth and seventh centuries, told the stories respectively of the Trojan War and of Odysseus' return from Troy to his native Ithaka. They constitute the earliest surviving written effort to reduce the domain of Greek religion to order, and they teem with detailed information on the pantheon, rituals and myths. Homer was 'the poet' for later Greeks, as Shakespeare is 'the bard', and his works were learned by heart as the basis of a Greek education. The vision of the world of the gods propagated in the Homeric poems formed the shared basis of knowledge for all Greeks at all periods.

Hesiod flourished in Boiotia around 700 or a little later. His two long surviving poems, the *Theogony* ('Birth of the Gods') and *Works and Days*, are indispensable sources. In the *Theogony* are related the origins of the universe and of the gods, together with such crucial myths as those describing the introduction of bloody animal sacrifice and the creation of the first woman. The *Works and Days* is largely a farmer's almanac, but it also contains descriptions of rituals and other expressions of piety, and retails myths like the 'Myth of the Races (or Ages)' (to which we shall return in chapter 12). Of Homer and Hesiod, Herodotus (II.53) said succinctly that they 'were the first to compose theogonies, and to give the gods their epithets, to allocate them their several functions, and describe their forms'.

The *Homeric Hymns* are a collection of poems composed at various dates between the seventh and fourth centuries; they are called 'Homeric' because of their epic verse-form, and not because they are now attributed to the poet (or poets?) of the *Iliad* and *Odyssey*. Each hymn is devoted to a particular deity, Demeter, Apollo, Hermes and so forth, some of whom are honoured with more than one. The poems are of very unequal importance, in some cases providing the essence of what we know of a deity's history and myths, in others a bare summary account. Here, for instance, is the entirety of the *Homeric Hymn to the Son of Kronos Most High [Zeus]*:

> It is Zeus whom I shall sing,
> The most powerful and the greatest of the Gods,
> All-seeing, mighty, who in all things accomplishes his will.
> Oft-times he converses with Thetis by his side.
> Be gracious to us, o all-seeing son of Kronos,
> O most glorious and most great one!

In the work of all the so-called lyric poets of the archaic age (700–500) it is possible to find descriptions of rituals and accounts of myths. At the end of this age and the beginning of the Classical epoch Pindar, another Boiotian, composed among other things epinician or victory odes in honour of winners at the great Panhellenic Games. His *Olympian*, *Isthmian*, *Pythian* and *Nemean Odes* form an inexhaustible repository of myths, often recast in original or idiosyncratic form.

Rather than review every single text of the Classical era (500–330), we may single out for their contributions to the study of religious practices the *Histories* of Herodotus, the tragedies of

Aeschylus, Sophocles and Euripides, and the comedies of Aristophanes (fifth–early fourth century BCE), and the fourth-century
orators (Lysias, Isaios, Demosthenes, especially) and philosophers (above all Plato and Aristotle). Two specific examples
worth mentioning are the *Bacchae* of Euripides (405), a capital
source for the cult of Dionysos, and the Athenian lawcourt
speeches of the probate specialist Isaios which contain precise
information on the cult owed to the dead.

In the Hellenistic era a literature of exegesis developed, offering compilations and descriptions of cults and rituals, accompanied by learned commentaries (*scholia*). But of this prolific
literature only a few passages have survived, especially in the
writings of Athenaeus (*c.* CE 200) and the late lexicographers. We
know, for example, that mythography, the study of myth and
myths, flourished at Alexandria, but only a few scraps of it have
come down to us in the early books of Diodorus of Sicily's
Library of History (first century BCE), in the library of 'Pseudo-
Apollodoros' (first century CE, real author unknown), and in the
scholia or learned commentaries on Classical authors.

Finally, among the works of Greek writers of the Roman
period such as Strabo (first century BCE – first century CE),
Plutarch (first–second century CE), Pausanias (second century CE)
and Athenaeus, right up to Clement of Alexandria (second–third
century CE) and the Christian authors, there is a great deal of
material relevant to the study of Greek religion. Pausanias, for
example, composed a *Periēgēsis* ('Geographical Tour') in ten
books, describing the cults and sanctuaries still in existence in
Greece in his day, together with their historical background and
the myths attached to them. A good part of our reconstruction of
the cult life of the Greek sites depends on the researches of this
indefatigably curious traveller.

EPIGRAPHIC DOCUMENTS

By the second half of the eighth century the Greeks had learned to
write an alphabetic script. Thereafter they inscribed or painted
on stone and other materials texts of all kinds, principally documents of communal importance. Thousands of these *inscriptions*
have been preserved and are constantly being unearthed by

archaeologists every year. Through these texts we are provided with religious calendars, descriptions of rituals and festivals, financial accounts of sanctuaries, rules of religious associations, dedications and thank-offerings to the gods, records of oracular pronouncements, prayers, mystical texts, and a host of other religious data.

A large number of these documents are the records of official decisions, usually taken by a city's popular Assembly. The chief purpose of these 'sacred laws' is to lay down regulations for the organization of a cult, but in a sense every law passed in Greece has a sacred character, as we shall see. Other inscriptions emanate from particular groups within the city, for instance the very numerous religious associations. Others again, such as dedications, are the product of particular individuals. In short, these texts have multiple origins, and their subject-matter affects every sphere of religious organization. Here are two examples: but for inscriptions, we would know practically nothing either of the cultic life of the Attic demes (villages) in the Classical era (see chapter 8) or of the organization of the festival of Artemis Leukophryene at Magnesia-on-the-Maeander in the Hellenistic period (Austin 1981 [66]: nos. 182, 184, 190).

ARCHAEOLOGICAL DATA

The contribution of archaeology to the study of Greek religion is doubtless the most immediately obvious. The traveller to Greece will see the ruins of a temple before s/he reads either Homer or an inscription. Excavations of sanctuaries, cemeteries and (to a smaller degree) habitation-sites, complemented by archaeological field-surveys, enable us to describe cult-places, provide knowledge of ritual practices (through the study of votive offerings, for example), and give access to figural representations of the divine – whether in sculptures and in scenes painted on vases, or on coins, which very often bore the effigy or symbol of a deity.

But although archaeology creates a religious landscape for us, it does not do so in any straightforward way. For example, ancient temples were stuccoed and painted with a variety of bright colours, and yet we contemplate them bleached a timeless white; and the votive objects, which once cluttered up the sanctuaries, we now view out of context in museums. Moreover, in order to understand funerary ritual, we have to study the manner in which a cemetery was laid out, the grave goods deposited in a tomb, and the treatment of the corpse. Happily, current archaeological practice is now more careful than it once was to preserve the total context of the individual finds and as attentive to the rituals of burial as to the objects and monuments themselves.

TWO DIFFERENT MODERN APPROACHES

Material artefacts do not speak for themselves, and the ancient texts that happen to survive require careful interpretation. The interpretation of ancient Greek religion, as of the mental structures of any alien culture, is a difficult and controversial matter. Here are two contrasting approaches from leading contemporary specialists:

1 *Jean Rudhardt (Geneva)*

THE UNDERSTANDING OF OTHERS

The chief difficulty presented by the study of religion seems to me to be that of understanding other minds [*autrui*]. God, or the gods – they are inaccessible to us, since we are historians of religion, not theologians. We study words and behaviour which express thoughts, aspirations, feelings, in short a lived experience. This lived experience belongs to a subject who feels him- or herself to have a relationship with a reality that is perceived as sacred or divine. In any other than a purely subjective way that person's experience of such a relationship is inaccessible to us. Yet, it is precisely such a relationship that constitutes the object of our study. If we approach it abstractly, we can consider institutional contexts, means of expression, and forms of behaviour or reasoning. But by so proceeding we overlook what defines them as religious, and we bypass the goal we set ourselves. That is why, no matter what importance I may attach to the study of structures that shape a people's character and outlook [*esprit*], I believe that we must go beyond studying them alone. The aim must be to gain access to the experience which is at least partially conditioned by the and expresses itself through these. The study of structural systems cannot therefore free us in any way from subjectivity; all it can do, rather, is obviate the risk that we shall attribute our own subjectivity to other people, and help us to understand them in their own terms, not the terms that our doctrine may dictate.   (Rudhardt 1981 [43]: 10)

HOW TO ACHIEVE EMPATHETIC UNDERSTANDING

On the subject of religion [the researcher] must turn him- or herself into a religious devotee and imaginatively conceptualize the religion under study in precisely the same way as the person who has practised it daily ever since learning in childhood the obligations it imposes. To achieve this empathetic identification there is no alternative to as it were becoming the pupils of those whom we wish to understand. We must watch them living and copy them in our imagination, because we cannot do otherwise. We must ape the evolutions of their thought, their affective responses, their outward behaviour. Their concepts are defined by a network of relationships – it is our task to reconstitute that network in our own consciousness. Their images owe their meaning to all the associations they conjure up – it is for us to re-establish within ourselves an analogous associational field. Their rituals are located within a complex of social behaviour – we, by taking thought, must re-create this social context in its entirety.

In sum, we must as far as possible forget our own peculiar habits of thinking in order to reconstruct – if it is Greek religion we are studying – a genuinely Hellenic mentality. The procedure may perhaps be illusory, and certainly it is always approximate, but there are no other ways of approach.

My own experience is that if we follow this path the fourth-century Athenian's religious behaviour can be made to seem intelligible. For within ancient beliefs there surges a current of meaning to which we too can open ourselves. A value is made manifest, to which – despite its alien expressions, despite everything which divides those expressions from our own concepts, habits of thought and images of reality – we may nevertheless give our adherence. However, neither this current of meaning nor this value can be defined in abstract terms without disfiguring them. For they are linked indissolubly to the lived experience through which they emerged into consciousness; and that experience can only be described in the ritual, mythic and conceptual languages that are at the same time both its expression and its instrumentality.

(Rudhardt 1981 [44]: 16)

How should we study Greek civic religion?

J.-P. Vernant (Paris)

THE DECODING OF A COMPLEX SYSTEM OF SYMBOLS

N.O.: And for you, today, what is a religion?

J.-P.V.: Take any one of the systems of signs that constitute a civiliz-ation, it doesn't matter whether it's languages, tools, institutions, the arts, or whatever. Each of these systems serves the function of mediating between men and the natural world, or between man and man. What is characteristic of all these systems is that they depend on the 'symbolic function', as psychologists call it. By which I mean that a word always 'refers to' something other than itself; for example, the word 'dog' is not a sound or a phoneme but a meaning, a concept, an instrument of thought which opens up a world of significations and at the same time enables interpersonal communication. Or consider a hammer: this isn't just the solid material object that one holds in the hand, but the mediating source of a manifold grasp on reality, coterminous with the almost infinite range of uses to which it can be put, and which others will make of it after me.

Put it another way: men have constructed a whole series of systems that enable them to transcend the data of immediate reality, to pass beyond them and by means of them aspire to a universe of signifi-cations, values, and rules by which the bonds of their community are cemented. It is by their ability to construct symbolic systems that men are distinguished from animals, which make no tools and, strictly speaking, know neither language nor sociability nor history. Now, for me, religion is one of these symbolic systems. So when the ancient Greeks say that lightning 'is Zeus', they are not operating in a very different way from the craftsman who sees in his hammer the potential for making one object or another.

The more one studies religions, the better one comes to understand that, just like tools or language, they are an integral component of the machinery of symbolic thought. Despite their diversity, they all perform the double, and mutually reinforcing, function of both giving to things a fullness of meaning which in themselves they appear to lack, and uprooting human beings from their individual isolation and embedding them in a reassuring and transcendently important community.

N.O.: Why study ancient Greek religion?

J.-P.V.: The main reason I ended up studying Greek religion is that the complexity of ancient Greek culture seemed to me to be better expressed in that area than in any other. What have always intrigued, or attracted, me in the study of a society are its heterogeneous or manifold aspects, those rays of brilliant light that are linked necessarily to its shadowy zones. Now, Greek religion, indeed Greek civilization as a whole, can only be properly understood so long as its complex cultural constituents are not reduced to just one of their components. Greek religion is a subject-area where the scholar is obliged to 'conceptualize in combination' religion *and* politics, anthropology *and* history, morality *and* daily life.

(Interview with J. P. Enthoven and J. Julliard in the Parisian
independent weekly *Le Nouvel Observateur*, 5 May 1980)

PART II

Cult-practices

CHAPTER 4

Rituals

DEFINITION

A ritual is a complex of actions effected by, or in the name of, an individual or a community. These actions serve to organize space and time, to define relations between men and the gods, and to set in their proper place the different categories of mankind and the links which bind them together.

It has often been said that Greek religion was a 'ritualistic' religion, that epithet being understood in a restrictive and depreciatory sense in accordance with the hierarchy of values we have already discussed (chapter 1). If, by contrast, one starts from the definition of 'ritual' that we have just given, Greek religion may then fairly be said to be ritualistic in the sense that it was the opposite of dogmatic: it was not constructed around a unified corpus of doctrines, and it was above all the observance of rituals rather than fidelity to a dogma or belief that ensured the permanence of tradition and communal cohesiveness. However, this Greek ritualism did not exclude either religious 'thought' or religious 'beliefs' (see Part III, below); the formalism of ritual observance, moreover, depended on a comprehensive organizing framework that structured both human society internally and its relationships with the surrounding universe.

NATURE AND PERFORMANCE

Everyday private life, no less than public civic life, was rhythmically regulated by all kinds of rituals, so that every moment and every stage of the Greek citizen's existence was intimately imbued with a religious dimension. The institution of the rituals was in all cases attributed to the direct or indirect intervention of the gods. Every failure of due observance was thought to provoke divine anger and retribution. Every modification of ritual required divine sanction. Hence one of the functions of the oracular shrines was to act as mouthpieces of the gods; the Delphic oracle, especially, played a decisive rôle in this area throughout the history of the Greek cities (chapter 11).

The observance of rituals was regulated very early on by written enactments. The multiplication of these 'sacred laws', which were inscribed on stone or bronze pillars and displayed at the entrance of temples and in other public places, was one of the characteristic phenomena associated with the emergence of the *polis* form of state in Greece from about 700 onwards. This publicity constituted one of the distinctively original features of Greek religion, in that it rendered widely accessible to all members of the community what oriental religions, for example, treated as the exclusive preserve of a priestly order.

Rituals were most often organized around a particular cult, and they varied greatly in form from one divinity and one city to another. From the simplest individual dedication of first-fruits (*aparkhai*) or the pouring of a libation (*spondē*), they were graduated on a sliding scale of complexity that culminated in the grandest civic festivals, which were typically spread out over several days.

SACRIFICE

Ancient sacrifice in modern debate

The end of the nineteenth and beginning of the twentieth centuries witnessed repeated attempts to establish a general theory of sacrifice. These coincided with the birth of a so-called 'Science of Religions' founded on the then dominant evolutionist paradigm. In the quest for a unitary definition of sacrifice within an evolutionist perspective, Robertson Smith (1894[79]) identified totemism as the elementary and primitive form of aboriginal sacrifice. On this theory, the primitive clan through the communal eating of its clan animal-totem experienced what he took to be the two essential components of the earliest conception of sacrifice, the communion meal and blood-bonding. In France, however, a different model was proposed by the sociological school of H. Hubert and M. Mauss (1964[77]), which was adopted by E. Durkheim (1912[73]). On their unitary model, sacrifice was accorded the status of a universal religious form.

The limitation of all such unitary hypotheses is that they fail to take account of the peculiar features of each religion's forms of sacrifice, its food-customs and modes of slaughter, the status of the victims, and so on. The same criticism applies to another would-be general theory of sacrifice, the anthropologically based hypothesis of René Girard (1977[74], 1987[75]), who sees in sacrificial violence the very foundational principle of all human culture.

Other current approaches include those of Walter Burkert and J.-P. Vernant. For Burkert (1983[70]) the ritual of the sacrificial meal may be traced back historically, or rather prehistorically, to the condition of man the hunter, before the discovery of agriculture. Vernant (1991[81], originally in Rudhardt and Reverdin 1981[80]), however, does not claim to offer a unitary hypothesis for sacrifice in general but prefers to 'address himself to a precisely delimited religion and society', namely that of Classical Greece, with the aim of providing material, ultimately, for 'a comparative typology of different sacrificial systems'. This same spirit of research is to be found in the collection of essays on the Greeks' 'cuisine of sacrifice' edited by M. Detienne and Vernant (1989[71]) and animates the discussion that follows here.

Sacrifice or sacrifices?

Sacrifice lay at the heart of the majority of Greek religious rituals. But since it could take varying forms, it would be more appropriate to talk of sacrifices in the plural. However, one form in particular, which may be defined as 'bloody animal sacrifice of alimentary type', predominated within the collective civic practice of the ancient city. For this simultaneously gave expression to the bonds that tied the citizens one to another and served as a privileged means of communication with the divine world. In return the gods authorized and guaranteed the functioning of the human community, maintaining it in its proper station between and at a due distance from themselves and the animal kingdom respectively.

This kind of sacrifice involved the ritual slaughter of one or more animals, a part of which was offered up to the gods by being cremated on an altar, while the remainder was consumed according to precisely fixed rules by those participating in the sacrifice. Initiated by an act of consecration, the ritual of animal sacrifice was concluded by cooking and eating. Indeed, without this strict framework of sacrificial regulation, human beings would themselves have risked sinking to the level of the beasts whenever they ate the flesh of animals.

Animal sacrifice could be prompted by many different occasions. It could be offered by an individual and give rise to a domestic feast, for example at the marriage of a son or daughter. Or it could take place in a sanctuary, on the initiative of an individual, a religious association, or a city. The sacrificer might be, as in the first of the above instances, the head of a family, or a professional *mageiros*, a sacrificial specialist employed as the occasion demanded both to sacrifice and to cook the animal. In sanctuaries it was generally the priests in charge of the sanctuary's cult who carried out the sacrifice in the name of the sacrificing group.

The animal victims varied perceptibly both in status and in number according to the wealth of the sacrificer and the importance of the occasion being celebrated. Another determining variable was the nature of the cult, which might require a particular species of animal to be sacrificed (a cow for Athene, for instance, or a pig for Demeter). In all cases, however, only domestic animals could qualify for sacrifice. Victims were thus placed on a scale of value from, at one end, a goat, pig, sheep, or even a cock (the humblest sort of offering) to, at the top end, a cow or ox, the most prestigious of all. Indeed, at the great civic festivals large numbers of cattle might need to be sacrificed (no less than 240 bulls at the Athenian Great Dionysia of 333, for example), in which case the priest would call on the services of a whole range of specialized assistant personnel.

Every day, in short, several hundred animal sacrifices were taking place in different contexts within each of the thousand and more separate political communities of the Greek world. But whatever the precise occasion may have been, they all scrupulously followed a set pattern that we are able to reconstruct from a combination of literary sources, iconographic documents (scenes on vases, sculpted stone reliefs) and epigraphic texts. In fact, all the stages of the great animal sacrifices that were performed by the Greek cities can already be found prefigured in the following passage from Homer, which describes a sacrifice of welcome for Odysseus' son Telemakhos, performed by old Nestor in his palace at Pylos. Note in particular the sharing out of the grilled entrails around the altar, once the gods have received their due portion, and the subsequent feasting of the warriors on equal portions of the huge carcase which in this instance, it is worth remarking, had been spit-roasted and not boiled:

Nestor, Gerenian horseman, was himself the first to speak: 'Dear sons, lose no time in bringing my wishes to fulfilment; before any other divinity, I desire to propitiate Athene, because she came in visible presence to the sumptuous banquet of our god (Poseidon). Let one of you go down to the plain to fetch a heifer; make sure that she comes as soon as may be, with a cowherd driving her! Let another go to the black ship of Telemakhos and bring all his comrades except for two! Let a third order the goldsmith Laerkēs to come and gild the heifer's horns! The rest of you, stay together here, but tell the serving-women to prepare a banquet in these great halls, and to bring us seats and wood and sparkling water.'

So he spoke and all set about their tasks. Up from the plain came the heifer, and from the swift ship the comrades of stouthearted Telemakhos. The smith came too, holding in his hands the tools of his craft, the anvil and hammer and shapely tongs, to work the gold. And Athene came to receive the sacrifice. Aged horseman Nestor handed over the gold, and the smith deftly worked it and gilded the heifer's horns to delight the goddess when she should see an offering so lovely. Stratios and godly Ekhephron led the beast forward by the horns, and Aretos came to them bringing from the store-room a flowery-patterned vessel that held the lustral water; in his other hand he carried a basketful of barley-groats. Nearby stood warlike Thrasymedes, with a sharp axe in his hand to fell the heifer, while Perseus held the bowl for the blood. Aged horseman Nestor began the rite with the lustral water and the barley-groats, and then addressed to Athene a long prayer, throwing the few hairs cut from the victim's head into the flames.

When they had prayed and had sprinkled the barley-groats, mighty-spirited Thrasymedes, son of Nestor, straightway took his stand beside the beast and struck her. The axe sliced through the sinews of the neck and the heifer collapsed senseless, whereupon Nestor's daughters and daughters-in-law and revered wife Eurydike, eldest of the daughters of Klymenos, raised the ritual scream. Then the young men lifted the victim up from the broad-pathed ground and held her, while Peisistratos prince of men cut her throat. The black blood gushed out, and the life departed from the bones. Then quickly they divided the flesh; at once they cut out the thigh-bones in due ritual fashion, covered them with the fat twice-folded, and laid the raw meat on top. The old king proceeded to burn these offerings on cloven wood and to pour glowing wine upon them; the young men stood round him holding five-pronged forks. When the thigh-bones were utterly consumed and they had tasted the entrails, they sliced and spitted the rest. They gripped the spits that went through the meat and roasted it thus.

Meanwhile Telemakhos had been bathed by lovely Polykaste, Nestor's youngest daughter; she bathed him, anointed him well with oil, then dressed him in a handsome cloak and tunic. He came from the bath looking like a god and went to sit by Nestor shepherd of the people.

Having roasted the outer flesh and removed it from the spits, they sat down and began to feast, and faithful serving-men attended on them, pouring wine into the golden cups.

· (Homer, *Odyssey* III.417–72, trans. W. Shewring, modified)

Technical aspects of sacrificial ritual

VOCABULARY

thuein, thusia: *thuein* is the most general verb in Greek for consecrating an offering. It embraced rituals that differed both in their procedures and in their objectives. It could be applied equally to bloody and to bloodless sacrifices, to burnt offerings and to votive objects, and to offerings intended for the gods as well as to those designed for dead mortals or heroes. Only the context, or contrast with other more specialized terms, decided its precise meaning in a particular instance.

The primary sense of *thuein*, as attested in Homer, was 'to make to burn for the sake of the gods'. Right down into the Classical era the idea of an offering mediated by fire remained present in its most common usages. The meaning of *thusia* evolved likewise. Primarily designating the act of 'throwing into the fire for the sake of the gods', it then came to mean generally 'offering to the gods'. But in the Classical epoch it was employed in everyday parlance both for the ritual of sacrifice and for the meat-banquet that followed. (For other sacrificial terminology, see pp. 37–8.)

IMPLEMENTS OF THE *THUSIA*

A whole assemblage of objects, tools and receptacles was used for the different stages of the sacrifice. Though often workaday in themselves, their rôle within the sacrificial domain endowed them with a ritual value. They may be seen depicted on several Attic vases of the Classical period, placed in close proximity to the raised altar (*bōmos*) on which the fire was lit (figs. 17, 18):

implements used for the slaughter included the tricorn basket (*kanoun*) containing the grains of barley with the butcher's knife hidden among them (and so invisible on the vases); the lustral pitcher (*loutērion*); and the basin to catch the blood (*sphageion*)

utensils for the sacrificial cooking included the table (*trapeza*) set beside the altar to serve as a butcher's block, both for the preliminary cutting-up of the carcase and for its distribution among the participants; the spits (*oberoi*) for roasting the innards and the flesh; and the cauldron (*lebēs*) in which the rest of the meat was boiled prior to its distribution.

BUTCHERY AND SACRIFICE

The Greeks did have a word for butcher in the sense of a dealer in meat (*kreopōlēs*), but their most general word was *mageiros*, which meant sacrificer, butcher and cook all in one. As Jeanne and Louis Robert once rightly remarked in their 'Bulletin épigraphique' (*Revue des études grecques* 83 (1970): 511), 'throughout antiquity there was an intimate connection between butchery and sacrifice, even for meat that was sold commercially in shops'. The sale of meat made its first appearance in the form of a simple, post-sacrificial distribution. A sacred law from Didyma (*LSAM*

[59] 54.1–3) laid down that, if it proved impossible for someone after the sacrifice to feast in the tent specially set aside for the purpose, then whoever so wished might take the meat away for it to be sold by weight.

In the stalls in a Greek market place (*agora*) one might find either the meat of animals ritually slaughtered by a *mageiros* – meat, that is to say, which had been consecrated by a first-fruits offering before the slitting of the animal's throat, and from which the gods' portion had been duly set aside (at Athens a tithe, entrusted to the *prutaneis*) – or sacrificial meat that had been allotted to the priests and resold by them. The cutting-up of the meat that was sold in the market-stalls was done on precisely the same egalitarian basis as that of the meat of victims distributed at a sacrifice.

However, the difference felt by the Greeks to exist between the two types of meat is marked in certain texts by a difference of vocabulary, as in the following passage of the 'On Marvellous Things Heard' attributed to Aristotle (*De auscultis mirabilibus* 842a33–5) apropos the behaviour of kites at Elis: 'they say that among the same people there are kites, which snatch the meat from those who carry it through the market place, but do not touch the flesh of the sacred victims'. Whereas the simple *ta krea* is used for the meat in the market place, the sacrificial meat is here described specifically as *ta hierothuta*, literally 'sacrificed in accordance with the due rituals'.

The great civic sacrifice

The most solemn form of *thusia* was that of the public sacrifices offered up by a city on the occasion of a religious festival and culminating in a civic banquet. The Panathenaia at Athens and the Hyakinthia at Sparta – to select those two states' most grandiose examples – required the slaughter of a huge army of cattle to feed the mass of citizens participating in the festival. Such sacrificial participation, at the same time as providing an occasion to eat meat, reactivated the pact between the city and its gods on which its order and prosperity depended. But for the citizens it also provided the opportunity for communal self-display and for the renewal of intracommunal ties as they shared in the distribution of the sacrificed and cooked meat.

In a stage preceding the sacrificial ritual itself a victim was chosen by a procedure of variable length and complexity. At the very least the priest had to assure himself that the victim met the criteria of 'purity' laid down (for example, a blemish on the animal's coat might be considered a sign of impurity) and conformed in all other respects to the ritual regulations.

The *thusia* proper began with a procession (*pompē*) led by the priest and the sacrificers, whereby the victim was brought to the altar. In the case of a public festival the procession was headed by the civic officials (*prutaneis* at Athens) who were to offer the sacrifice in the name of the city. Around the altar stood all those who were to participate in the act of ritual slaughter: the woman who carried the lustral water, the woman who bore the basket of grain in which the sacrificial knife was concealed, the sacrificer and his assistants, and finally the ordinary citizens in whose name the sacrifice was being made.

The priest then pronounced the customary prayers, sprinkling the victim's head as he did so with the lustral water. This act of purification was designed also to elicit the victim's 'assent' to its slaughter, which it signified by nodding its head (*hupokuptein*). Next, the priest offered up the 'first-fruits' of the sacrifice by throwing onto the altar-fire some grains taken from the basket and some hairs cut from animal's head. Without this preliminary phase of consecration the sacrifice could not proceed. The slaughterer (*boutupos*, literally 'ox-striker') was now authorized to kill the victim, first smiting it on the forehead with an axe and then cutting its throat. For the latter the animal's head had to be turned up, so that the blood might spurt out skywards and fall in a stream upon the altar and the ground. Most often, a vase was positioned to catch the blood which would then be poured over the altar. At the moment of killing, the women present let out the indispensable ritual scream (*ololugē*).

The word *thuein* ('to slaughter ritually') embraced these two operations, both the initial consecration and the throat-cutting. The third act of the sacrificial drama was the butchering and sharing out of the carcase. The *mageiros* first opened the beast's thorax in order to remove the entrails (*splankhna*: lungs, heart, liver, spleen, kidneys) and digestive system (*entera*, eaten as sausages and black puddings). Then the victim was skinned. In private sacrifices the skins went to the priest, but in public ones they were sold off for the benefit of the state's sacred treasury. Finally, there was the cutting-up of the carcase, which was done in two stages and according to two different techniques. The first stage consisted of removing the thigh-bones (*mēria*), which were placed on the altar, covered with fat, sprinkled with a liquid libation and incense, and then burnt; this was the portion allotted to the gods, since they were thought to derive sustenance as well as olfactory pleasure from the scented smoke, and it was through the smoke that communication was effected between the human and divine worlds. The second stage was the cutting-up and cooking of the remaining flesh, but before that the *splankhna*, the most vital and precious elements of the victim, were spit-roasted on the altar by the priest's assistants and shared out among the worshippers, who were thereby assured of maximal participation in the sacrifice.

The remainder of the meat was then cut up in strips into equal portions, not making any allowance this time for the different parts of the beast and their articulation. One portion, again, was reserved for the gods, though it was consumed by mortal men (at Athens by the *prutaneis*); the rest was distributed by weight. Sometimes the portions of cooked meat were distributed by lot, sometimes in accordance with the merit or status of the recipients, since, given the method of butchering, parity of weight was not incompatible with inequality of meat. Thus the distribution was strictly political, the mode of cutting up the meat corresponding significantly to the ideological model of *isonomia* (meaning both 'equality of distribution' and 'equality of political status').

These remaining parts of the flesh were either boiled in cauldrons (*lebētes*) and consumed on the spot or taken away for cooking and eating elsewhere. In this way a second circle of 'fellow-eaters' was constituted, larger than that of the original participants in the sacrifice who were privileged to eat the *splankhna*. To borrow a formula of M. Detienne (in Detienne and Vernant 1989[71]: 3), 'sacrifice derives its importance from ... the necessary relationship between the exercise of social relatedness on all *political* levels within the system the Greeks call the city. Political power cannot be exercised without sacrificial practice.'

Other types of sacrifice

The type of sacrifice we have just been examining in detail was made up of two essential elements in combination, the ritual slaughter of an animal and the eating of its flesh. A different type consisted of the slaughtering and offering of an animal that was not then consumed but was burnt whole ('holocaust'); such a sacrifice was dedicated in its entirety to the gods through the agency of the flames. This type was employed primarily for certain hero-cults or cults of the dead, which were governed by a different ritual. A particular difference was that the blood was made to flow onto a low altar (*eskhara*), or a grave, or straight onto the ground, rather than onto an altar of the *bōmos* type. Different ritual necessitated also a different vocabulary. So in these cases either a word that placed the emphasis on the slitting of the throat (*sphagizein*), or one that stressed the element of sacralization (*enagizein*), was frequently used, as opposed to *thuein*, which was reserved uniquely for the slaughtering procedure described in the previous section. A third, and quite exceptional, type of bloody sacrifice was performed annually at Patrai in honour of Artemis Laphria, as we learn from Pausanias' remarkably detailed description (vII.18.7); here both domesticated and wild animals were sacrificed, together with game-birds, and were put to the flames when still alive.

Besides these types of animal-sacrifice, the Greeks also offered blood*less* sacrifices of different materials, whether comestibles (bread with a variety of shapes and ingredients, fruits, cakes, cooked dishes, vegetables) or spices, the aroma of which was transmitted to the gods through the flames. It was in this bloodless form that the daily sacrifices in private homes were typically made. But there were also certain public cults that demanded explicitly and exclusively bloodless sacrifices, for instance that of Black Demeter at Phigaleia in Arkadia (Pausanias vIII.42.11).

Then there were numerous rituals in which bloody and bloodless offerings were combined. At Athens, for example, there were complex festivals celebrating Apollo's rôle in the vegetative cycle, in which the central place was allocated to bloodless sacrifices. In two of these, indeed, it was the bloodless offering which gave the whole festival its name. The springtime festival of the Thargelia was named for the *thargēlos* or bread specially baked for the occasion from the first flour of the year and carried in procession to the altar; and the central rite of the autumn festival of the Pyanopsia consisted in the offering to Apollo of a cooking-pot in which a kind of pottage (*puanos*) of pulses, especially dried ones, had been boiled (*hepsein*).

Finally, besides these types of sacrifice properly so called, a simple deposition of offerings might be practised. These were left on tables (*trapezai*) specially consecrated for the purpose and set up beside the altar, so that one name for them was *trapezōmata*. Or they might be deposited in a quite different sanctified spot, for example at the foot of a statue. On Delos, indeed, apart from the altar on which hecatombs (a hundred head of cattle) were sacrificed, there was a second altar reserved for these offerings, also sacred to Apollo (under the cult-title Genetōr, 'Begetter' or 'Ancestor'), on which it was absolutely forbidden to offer bloody sacrifices or to light any fire. Devotees of the Pythagorean sect were particularly enthusiastic worshippers of Apollo Genetōr, for reasons we shall now give.

Sacrificial practice among the religious sects

On the fringes of city-life there existed various sects, and it was on the issue of animal sacrifice that they chose to stake their claim to difference by ostentatiously practising bloodless sacrifice only, in the name of ritual purity. The sects in question were the Orphics and the Pythagoreans. The former set their face against the eating of meat in any guise whatsoever and took their nourishment in the perfectly pure forms of honey and cereals, the very foods indeed that they sacrificed to the gods. The Orphics thereby cut themselves off radically from all civic life, since that presupposed, as we have seen, participation in animal-sacrifice and its culminating distribution of meat. Their choice was motivated by a mystical yearning to recover that lost oneness with the gods which, so their theogonies taught them (chapter 12), mortals had once enjoyed in primordial times.

Among the sect of the Pythagoreans, two tendencies should be distinguished. One group of them agreed with the Orphics in withdrawing entirely from political life, rejecting utterly all meat-eating and offering solely bloodless sacrifices on their altars. But another group, while they abstained from eating the flesh of sheep and cattle, were prepared to accommodate themselves to the humbler offerings of goat and pig. In this way they achieved a compromise between an oppositionist religious stance and participation in civic life, which they aimed to reform from within.

At the opposite extreme from vegetarianism and abstinence from meat-eating was the *omophagia* or eating of raw flesh practised by followers of Dionysos. This ritual took the form of hunting game, tearing the victim apart (*diasparagmos*, end of chapter 12), and devouring its limbs raw. Here we find the precise inversion of all the characteristics and values of the civic sacrifice, and a total confusion of the normal boundaries between the tame and the wild, and between men and the beasts. 'Going wild' was another way of escaping from the politico-religious order of society.

In all the above cases, it is precisely in respect of sacrifice and modes of eating that the sectaries chose to express their difference. That choice tends to corroborate the central position occupied by bloody animal-sacrifice of the alimentary type in the definition of the civic community.

LIBATIONS

An important element in sacrificial rituals was the pouring of a libation (*spondē*). This could be associated with animal sacrifice, as we have seen, but it might also occur as an autonomous ritual with a rationale of its own.

Libations regularly accompanied the rituals that punctuated daily life. Hesiod, for example (*Works and Days* 724–6), evokes those performed by the pious every morning and evening. Libations also served to start off meals, as a gesture of propitiation which fulfilled the same function as the 'first-fruits' offering in animal-sacrifice. They were used too to mark an arrival or a departure, placing familiar actions under the protection of the gods who were thereby invoked as witnesses or helpers. The formulaic scene of 'the departure of the hoplite' was depicted in numerous Attic vase-paintings of the Classical period, with an old man and woman shown grouped around the young, armed infantryman, as in this typical departure scene on a *stamnos* (wine-jug) now in the British Museum:

In the centre, an armed hoplite grasps the hand of a bearded figure in a grave gesture of farewell . . . On the right, a woman holds a pitcher and a shallow bowl, ritual implements for the libation that was almost obligatory for marking a departure or return. The woman is pouring into the bowl some wine, a portion of which will be tipped out onto the ground for the gods, while the rest will be drunk by each of the participants in turn. The performance of this libation, which combines offering and sharing, marks the bonds linking each member of the group to the others and affirms the relationship that unites this group with the gods. (F. Lissarrague, 'The World of the Warrior', in Bérard *et al.* 1989[248]: 45, slightly modified)

The ritual of libation furthermore formed part of the ceremonial of the private party known as the *sumposion* (literally a 'drinking-together'). Finally, it played an important rôle in the solemn acts that were the direct concern of the civic community as a whole, such as the opening of an Assembly at Athens or the conclusion of treaties of peace or alliance between Greek states. Indeed, the plural of the word for 'libation' (*spondai*) was used by synecdoche to mean 'truce' or 'treaty'.

The libation ritual consisted in the pouring of part of some liquid on an altar or on the ground, while reciting a prayer. Most often, the liquid in question was a mixture of wine and water, such as the Greeks customarily drank (three parts water to one of wine), but depending on the ritual it might on occasion be neat wine, or milk, or a mixture of wine, water and honey. The libation most frequently depicted in vase-paintings (as above) shows a man or a woman pouring the liquid from a wine-jug (*oinokhoē*), intermediate in size between the great mixing bowl (*kratēr*) and the drinking goblet (*kulix*), into a shallow bowl of canonical ceremonial shape (*phialē*), and then from the *phialē* onto an altar or the ground. The second stage of the libation, normally, was the drinking of what remained in the *phialē*.

Sometimes, though, the libation was not followed by consumption of the liquid; for instance, in the case of the neat wine that was used to accompany the swearing of an oath, all of it was poured out onto the earth. In the *Iliad* (IV.159), in the context of an oath-ritual Agamemnon invokes 'the blood of lambs, the libations of neat wine, the clasping of hands ... '. This ritual wastage established a connection between the world of men and the dangerous world of infernal powers which were ever ready to break loose in chastisement of perjurors.

Another kind of libation that was consecrated in its totality, the *khoai* (from *khein*, 'to pour out in quantity'), was devoted especially to the dead. These libations were poured onto the earth or a burial mound with a view to establishing a bond between the quick and the dead. Since they very often excluded wine, they were known as 'wineless' (*aoinoi*, *nēphalioi*) libations. A famous example is the pure water poured by Elektra onto the tomb of her father Agamemnon at the start of Aeschylus' *Libation-Bearers* (translated below, pp. 44–5). But they could also be of milk and honey.

Sometimes *khoai* were associated with the consecrated offerings of food deposited on a tomb (*enagismata*). But certain deities too were specially honoured with them: the Muses, the Nymphs and the Erinyes (Furies). Or, as Pausanias (v.15.10) says was done once a month by the Eleians in the Altis at Olympia according to an antique rite, libations might be offered as part of a sacrifice on all the altars of a sanctuary: 'they burn frankincense with honey-kneaded wheaten cakes on the altars, and lay branches on them and pour libations of wine, except that to the Nymphs and the Despoinai ('Mistresses') and on the common altar (*koinos bōmos*) of all the gods it is the practice to pour no wine'. This last instance illustrates well the complexity of the rituals, each element of which had its special significance in contributing to the coherence of the rites as a whole, as well as in relation to the function or nature of the deities being worshipped.

PRAYER

In the unfolding of a great sacrificial drama, prayer, as we have seen (above, p. 35), initiated the act that was played out around the altar following the procession. Intoned by the priest in a loud voice, the prayer inaugurated the sacrifice proper by placing the proceedings under the auspices of the gods to whom it was being offered. There is plenty of evidence for the sacred formulas that were pronounced during the performance of rituals or as accompaniments to the chief cult-acts. In the Athenian Assembly, for example, a prayer was said over the silent citizenry before the orators addressed them from the rostrum, as we learn from Aristophanes' parodic version, placed in the mouth of a female herald in his *Thesmophoriazousai* (295–305):

Pray silence, pray silence. Pray to the two Thesmophoroi [Demeter and Persephone], to Ploutos [god of Wealth] and Kalligeneia [Demeter 'bearer of fair offspring'] . . . that this Assembly and gathering of the day may have the most beautiful and beneficial outcome . . . Address your vows to heaven and pray for your own good fortune. Hail, Paian, hail! Let us rejoice and be glad!

The crieress follows this up with curses against any men or women who should break the laws or betray the city.

Likewise, every army commander in real life addressed a solemn prayer to the gods before battle, analogous to the following prayer which Aeschylus placed in the mouth of Eteokles in his *Seven Against Thebes* (252–60):

Pray the gods above to fight with us; listen in your turn to my prayer, and modulate the sacred cry, the happy Paian, the ritual invocation of Greek sacrifices, which gives us the daring that delivers us from fear of war. As for myself, I promise to the gods of my country, to the gods of the earth, to the guardians of our homes, to the springs of Dirke, to the waters of the Ismenos, I promise, if all goes well, if the city is saved, to offer upon the altars of the gods the blood of sheep, to sacrifice bulls. I vow to do so should victory be mine; and I shall drape in our holy places the garments of our enemies, stripped, pierced through with the lance.

Again, Thucydides (VI.32), when he is describing the departure of the Athenian armada for Sicily in 415, provides us with a precise account of the ritual framework within which these prayers were offered:

When the embarkation was completed and all the necessary equipment had been stowed, the herald's trumpet commanded silence. The customary prayers made before setting sail were recited, not by each ship separately, but by the whole fleet in unison following the lead of the herald. The whole force had wine poured into mixing-bowls, and the officers and men then made their libations from goblets of gold or silver. The whole throng of the citizens and other wellwishers on shore added their prayers to those of the departing combatants. Once the paean had been sung and the libations completed, the fleet put out to sea, at first in line but then racing each other as far as Aigina.

The libation poured by the pious at the start of each day was accompanied by a prayer (again, see Hesiod, *Works and Days* 724–6), and in the same way every meal or banquet was initiated by a libation and a prayer addressed to the gods in accordance with the prescribed formulas. Every enterprise was thus placed under the protection of the gods invoked, especially Zeus, as when Hesiod recommends to the peasant about to commence his agricultural labours (*Works and Days* 465–8): 'Pray to Zeus of the Earth Below (*Khthonios*) and to pure Demeter to grant you the sacred wheat of Demeter heavy in its ripeness, at the very moment when, beginning your ploughing and taking the handles in your hand, you strike the oxen on the back as they strain at the yoke.'

Both in epic and in the theatre much space was devoted, not just to simple formulas, but to various complex forms of prayers, whether dedicatory, supplicatory, imprecatory, or votive. Even if the scenes conjured up in tragedy or epic cannot be read simply as carbon copies of the rituals and of the prayers that accompanied them, still they provide us with precious information, sometimes backed up by scenes on vases, so far as the accompanying actions are concerned. Examples include the prayer addressed to Apollo by his priest Khryses, requesting him to receive an expiatory sacrifice on behalf of the Akhaians, which preceded and ritually assured the efficacity of the sacrifice proper:

> Then hastening
> To give the god his hecatomb, they led
> bullocks to crowd round the compact altar,
> washed their hands and delved in barley-baskets,
> as open-armed to heaven Khryses prayed:
> 'Oh hear me, lord of the silver bow, . . .
> if while I prayed you listened once before
> and honoured me, and punished the Akhaians,
> now let my wish come true again. But turn
> your plague away this time from the Greeks.'
> And this petition too Apollo heard.
> When prayers were said and grains of barley strewn,

they held the bullocks for the knife, and flayed them,
cutting out joints . . .

> (*Iliad* 1.446–58, trans. R. Fitzgerald,
> slightly modified)

Another example is the long prayer addressed to Zeus Xenios
(Protector of Strangers) by the daughters of Danaos, the 'suppliant women' of Aeschylus' play of that name (630–710). These
women have fled from Egypt to Argos and they want Zeus to
reward the Argives for the aid they have been granted by them in
their hour of need. Here we find repeated the three themes which
feature in one form or other in many votive prayers: the wish
that, thanks to the gods, their children, their harvests, and their
flocks and herds may flourish and prosper. Earlier, the Danaids
on their father's advice had seated themselves in a sanctuary,
'piously holding in their left hands branches wreathed with white
wool, attributes of Zeus Protector of suppliant Strangers',
branches like those they had already placed before the gods'
altars and statues, saluting them with a prayer of supplication: 'O
Zeus, take pity on our woes, before we succumb to them
entirely!'

A final example, again from Aeschylus' *Libation-Bearers*. In a
long scene describing a funerary ritual that involved both libations and prayers (22–161), Elektra pours out the 'lustral water'
onto her father Agamemnon's tomb and rehearses the 'prescribed
formula': 'may he grant happiness to whosoever vows this offering'. But this prayer by itself is not enough for her, and with the
encouragement of the Chorus she develops at length her theme of
desire for revenge before requesting the Chorus in its turn to utter
'the prescribed lamentations and funerary paean':

ELEKTRA

Most powerful messenger between the living and the dead, O infernal
Hermes, help me and convey my message: may the subterranean spirits,
avenging witnesses of my father's death, and may Earth (Gaia) herself,
she who bears all, and having nurtured them receives anew the fertile
seed, hear my prayers. And I meanwhile pour out this lustral water for
the dead and address this appeal to my father: 'Have pity on me and on
your dear Orestes: how are we to become master and mistress in our
own home? For now we are but as vagrants, sold by the very mother

who bore us; and in exchange she has taken a lover, Aigisthos, her accomplice and your murderer. As for me, I am treated like a slave, and Orestes is in exile banished from his possessions, while they, insolent in their pride, triumph amid the spoils of your labours. I pray you that Orestes may by some chance return here; do you, father, hear my prayer. For myself grant that I may be chaster in heart, and have hands more holy, than my mother. These are my prayers for us; but, for our enemies, may there arise at last, father, your avenger, and may the slayers in turn be slain in just retribution. I cede (to those for whom vengeance is reserved). But upon the guilty alone I call down my imprecation of death; for us, on the contrary, send joy from the nether shade, with the aid of gods, and of Earth (Gē), and of Justice crowned with victory!' Such are my prayers, over which I pour here these libations. Do you crown them with the prescribed lamentations and funerary paean. (*Libation-Bearers* 124–51)

As several of our examples indicate, prayers were on each occasion accompanied by the appropriate hymns and chants: the paean intoned before battle and after victory, or funeral dirges, or the choral songs of choirs of boys and maidens at civic festivals. In short, prayer, whether in fixed ritual form or adapted to suit the individual or the circumstances, was an essential constituent of the complex of ritual as a whole, within which it was frequently combined with a libation.

CONCLUSION: READING THE COMPLEXITY OF RITUALS

By describing a selection of rituals and by analysing their functions, we have tried to show how the actions they involved can be read on several levels: *anthropologically*, in terms of the representation of space which at once separates men from and links them to the gods; *sociologically*, in that a particular image of the city was conveyed especially by the mode of distributing the sacrificial meat; *symbolically*, finally, with regard to the meanings and values attached to different methods of cooking the meat. However, every element of the rituals operated on each of these three levels simultaneously, and ritual behaviour was thus a complex unity that brought into play the entire functioning of the city and its means of self-representation.

CHAPTER 5

Religious personnel

INTRODUCTION

We saw from the preceding chapter that no special intermediary was required for the accomplishment of the principal sacred rituals, in particular the offering of sacrifice, and that there was no exclusive repository of sacral wisdom, no clergy, through whose intervention alone communication with the gods might be effected. Rather, it was open to each and every citizen, either in his or her own home or in a public sanctuary, to carry out the actions which both demonstrated piety and allowed those who practised them to affirm thereby their shared identity as Greeks (*Hellēnes*).

However, outside the sphere of private worship there were a certain number of citizens who were specially charged with religious duties entrusted to them by the city. Moreover, sanctuaries required for their functioning a range of personnel whose status varied from one religious site to another and in proportion to the shrine's popularity and perceived importance.

RELIGIOUS DUTIES DELEGATED BY THE CITY

Religious authority belonged essentially to the people or citizen body as a whole (*dēmos*), on whose behalf it was exercised by a range of personnel. The number and importance of these civic functionaries grew in the course of the fifth century, at the expense of certain ancient priesthoods. It was their job to maintain order and respect for the laws within the sanctuary enclosure (*temenos*). They organized the great religious festivals (*heortai*), in collaboration with other public officials and the relevant priests. They controlled religious finances, checking revenues and expenditure.

The office of *hieropoioi* (literally 'those who make the *hiera*' – see chapter 2) is attested in numerous cities. At Athens, for instance, they were a board of ten chosen each year by the Council of 500, with responsibility for all the major quadrennial festivals except the Great Panathenaia which had its own special board. They thus oversaw the Brauronia (in honour of Artemis), the Herakleia, the Eleusinian Mysteries and Athens' official delegation (*theōria*) to the festival of Apollo and Artemis on Delos, as well as the annual Lesser Panathenaia. Their remit included the provision of animals for the sacrifices, and the administration and policing of the festivals as a whole. In return for this they were privileged to share in the honours accorded to other officials, in particular in the distribution of the hecatomb sacrificed during the Panathenaia.

At Athens *epimelētai* ('overseers') were appointed individually for particular festivals, among others the Great Dionysia and Panathenaia. Originally, those elected were expected to pay for the processions out of their own pocket, so that being an *epimelētēs* was akin to performing a 'liturgy' (chapter 9). But by the late 330s, probably as a result of the sweeping reform of Athenian public finances presided over by Lykourgos after 338, the cost was borne by state funds. For the Eleusinian Mysteries four *epimelētai* were appointed, two of them chosen from among all Athenians aged over thirty, the other two from the two priestly families who had hereditary prerogatives in the cult of Demeter and Persephone, the Eumolpidai ('descendants of Eumolpos') and Kērykes (literally 'Heralds'). The *epistatai*, however, attested for example in the accounts of Pheidias' statue of Athene Parthenos (M/L [60] 54, A1, lines 3–4) or in a contemporary decree of the Council of 500 pertaining to Eleusis (*SEG* [61] x.24.11–13), were more narrowly financial functionaries.

The three senior Arkhons of Athens also included religious affairs in their portfolios. The King (*basileus*), who legendarily had inherited the religious functions of the old kings of Athens, was the principal religious dignitary of the Athenian state. He was charged above all with the sacrifices involved in the 'ancestral cults' (*ta patria*), the cults, that is, whose antiquity was guaranteed by tradition. These included the Eleusinian Mysteries and the Lenaia (in honour of Dionysos). Like the other Arkhons, the King had judicial functions, in his case presiding over impiety trials and arbitrating conflicts involving priesthoods. He also had overall responsibility for the religious calendar (which required a major overhaul and provoked acrimonious litigation at the very end of the fifth century: chapter 10).

Secondly, there was the Eponymous Arkhon, who had charge of the more recently established civic festivals, *ta epitheta* (literally 'those added on'), most famously the Great or City Dionysia established either during the dictatorship of Peisistratos (545–28) or, more probably, soon after the establishment of democracy in 508/7. He also had supreme responsibility for the Delian *theōria*, which was revamped in the later fifth century, the processions in honour of Zeus Sōtēr ('Saviour', no doubt instituted after the Persian Wars) and Asklepios (inaugurated in 420), and the Thargelia (a festival of Pythian Apollo).

Thirdly, there was the Polemarkh (literally 'War Archon'). As his title suggests, his religious rôle lay in the field of cults that had a specifically military application: those of Artemis Agrotera (to whom battlefield sacrifices were made) and Enyalios (a by-name of Ares), the public funeral in honour of Athenian war dead, and the festival commemorating the famous victory over the Persians at Marathon in 490. But he also presided over the sacrifices celebrating Harmodios and Aristogeiton, the heroic tyrannicides and liberators of the late sixth century.

It would be wrong, however, to give the impression that religious life was circumscribed within the physical boundaries of the city. Oracles, above all that of Pythian Apollo at Delphi, also occupied an important position. For purposes of consultation it was again the state which chose the relevant personnel from among its members: the *theōroi* (the general term for 'sacred ambassadors'), or, depending on the oracle in question, *puthioi*, *dēmiourgoi*, or *theopropoi*. Such sacred envoys are attested throughout the Greek world and were men of high status – so high, indeed, that the job of maintaining and entertaining (often magnificently, as his prestige demanded) a sacred embassy was turned into a liturgy (see p. 95) by the Athenians and entrusted to a rich man designated as the *arkhitheōros*. On the other hand, their status and prestige brought political risks, so that steps were taken to limit their powers. At Sparta it was one of the most important privileges of the two kings that 'each of them nominated two Pythioi, whose business it was to consult the oracle at Delphi, who ate with the kings [in the royal mess] and who, like them, lived at the public charge' (Herodotus VI.57).

SELECTION OF PRIESTS AND PRIESTESSES

Priesthoods and priestesshoods were tied to particular sanctuaries and cults and derived their *raison d'être* solely from their relationship to a god and the cult they performed on that god's behalf. In most cases a priest or priestess functioned like a civic magistrate, exercising a liturgical authority in parallel to the legislative, judicial, financial or military authority of the city's officials. The methods of selecting priests and priestesses make clear their affinity to the status of magistrates. Most were appointed annually, and often by lot, and at the end of their term of office they were obliged to render accounts. Into this category at Athens, for example, there fell the priests of Dionysos Eleuthereus, Asklepios and Zeus Sōtēr, and the priestesses of Athene Sōtēria and Athene Nikē. Again like magistracies, these priestly offices were typically barred to foreigners, including permanent residents, and open to all citizens (except those disqualified by some physical blemish or disability).

However, there did also exist priesthoods and priestesshoods that were the exclusive preserve of particular families or corporate descent-groups (*genē*). Holders of these positions were selected from among the relevant family members in accordance with rules of varying complexity and, in some cases, for life. Athenian examples include the priestess of Athene Polias ('City-Protecting' Athene) and the priest of Poseidon Erekhtheus, who had to be members of the Eteoboutadai *genos* and held office for life, and the male Hierophant and Daidoukhos ('Torchbearer') of the Eleusinian Mysteries, the former a member of the Eumolpidai, the latter of the Kerykes. In all other respects, however, they were just like any other citizens, equally subject to the decrees of the

Council and Assembly of Athens. Other priests, such as those of
Apollo at Delphi, were doubtless also appointed for life, but
without any stipulation of aristocratic birth. Occasionally, as at
Erythrai (*Syll.*[3] [62]: 600), the right to a priesthood was sold to the
highest bidder.

Priestly functions

We have already encountered the sacerdotal rôle of priests in our
consideration of sacrifice (chapter 4); indeed, assisting in public
or private sacrificing was their most visible function. They consecrated the victims, as we saw, pronounced the formulas of
invocation and recited prayers. The priest might personally stun
the animal and cut its throat, but he could also delegate those
functions to one or more of the sacrificers, as a priestess was
absolutely required to do, since a sacrifice did not have to be
conducted by someone holding a priestly office. In Homer, in
fact, priests never act as sacrificers but assume a more general
sacerdotal function vis-à-vis a god. This continued to be the order
of priorities in the great sanctuaries down into the Classical
period: whereas the priest or priestess assumed the overall direction of cultic ceremonies, sacrificing was delegated to resident
sacrificers.

One of the principal priestly duties was to take care of the
accoutrements of the temple and of the sanctuary to which it was
attached, with the assistance of one or more sacristans (*neōkoroi*)
in the case of the large shrines. This involved looking after the
cult-statue, which represented the deity within his or her house,
and the relevant cult-buildings. It also included administrative
responsibilities for maintaining the sanctuary as a going concern,
both financially and as a secure place of worship. But as we have
seen, the state increasingly competed in these two spheres of
operation, not least by deciding how much revenue to allot for a
sanctuary's upkeep.

Priests and priestesses, finally, were obligated to act as guardians of sacred law during their term of office, ensuring that the
laws were respected and thereby guaranteeing the perpetuation
of ancestral tradition. But even in this area it was the people as a
whole, the citizen body, which at Athens controlled the conduct

of religious cults through the decrees it passed with the assistance of the Council.

Priestly revenues

A portion of all sacrificial animals belonged to the priest or priestess by right. Like all the participating magistrates, he or she was entitled to an honorific share in the distribution of the meat; but, additionally, specific parts of the victim – which ones depended on the sanctuary in question – were more particularly set aside for them, regularly including the flesh of the thighs but often also the beast's head. They also got their share of the *trapezōmata* (chapter 4) and *theomoria* ('god's portion'), which provoked some anticlerical sarcasm from comic poets like Aristophanes (e.g. *Wealth* 676–8, on the nocturnal larceny of the priest of Asklepios at Athens: 'Then, glancing upward, I [the slave Karion] beheld the priest/ Swiping the cheesecakes and the figs from off/ The holy table ...').

Consequently the economic status of a priest or priestess varied greatly depending on the importance of the sanctuary, though on the whole remuneration seems to have been modest, except in cases like that of Erythrai in Asia Minor (above) where priesthoods were sold and purchased as a sound investment. At Miletos, for example, the priest was guaranteed a minimum salary by public decree, on the following conditions (*LSAM* [59] 52B.11–12): certain magistrates were required to make sacrifices to Asklepios on a fixed date, but should no one have sacrificed, the priest would receive a payment of twelve drachmas – by no means a fortune, since it represented little more than a week's wages for a skilled labourer. In another of Miletos's cultic regulations (*LSAM* [59]: 44.13–15) the conditions are different: 'those who have bought a priesthood shall receive all the parts of victims offered in private sacrifices, except the skin'. Here we see the origins of 'sacerdotal' meat, the meat from sacrifices that was sold in the market and provided certain priesthoods with a significant income (chapter 4).

As vicars mediating between the city and the gods, the priest and priestess were respected personages, and recognized as such by special public honours like a privileged portion of the sacrificial meat or a reserved seat in the theatre. At the same time their function did not usually confine them to a special life-style; for example, there was nothing to stop most of them from getting married, since ritual chastity was normally a temporary state and tied to an immediate ritual obligation such as arose periodically at the time of a festival. Likewise, performance of priestly duties did not as a rule require residence within a sanctuary, as is proved by the explicit exceptions.

One of Greek religion's most original features emerges from the status of priests or priestesses. Although the religious dimension was ever-present in every facet of human activity, it did not exercise a transcendent influence over it. Just like the political, legislative, judicial and other spheres of communal interaction, religion occupied a subordinate position within social life as a whole. As for religious power, in the final analysis that lay, not with a priesthood, but with the people as a whole, which exercised it through their control of religious laws, institution of new cults, financing of sanctuaries and administration of religious justice (punishment of sacrilege, and so on). Finally, as we have had more than one occasion to remark, the tendency was for central controls over priests and priestesses to multiply, and for non-priestly personnel to compete with the priesthood in performing those functions that were not narrowly sacerdotal.

Freelance religious experts

Before leaving the subject of religious specialists, three categories of practitioners may be mentioned, with whom the city might choose to deal but to whom it did not delegate any of its religious authority. First, there were the *exēgētai* or expounders of sacred laws, who do not appear to have existed in any institutionalized form before the fourth century (Isaios VIII, *On the Estate of Kiron* 39). These unelected specialists possessed a unique knowledge of the laws and might therefore be asked either to expound points of ritual or to lay down rules of purification, for example in the case of a homicide. Secondly, there were the oracle-mongers (*khrēsmologoi*, see p. 122) who knew by heart or kept written collections of oracles (not only Delphic ones), and could produce a text on demand, for a city or for a private individual, to suit almost any occasion. Thirdly, there were the diviners (*manteis*), often hereditary and often itinerant, whose skill lay in reading the entrails of sacrificial victims or interpreting such putatively divine omens and portents as chance words or the flight of birds. Their function lent itself to political exploitation, and it is no accident that the only two foreigners known to Herodotus (IX.33–6) to have been granted citizenship by Sparta were two brothers from Elis, members of the mantic family of the Iamidai, of whom one served as diviner for all the Greeks before the battle of Plataia in 479.

An ideal Platonic priesthood

At the end of his long life (427–347) Plato composed *The Laws*, a second Utopia that was both more grimly realistic and far more detailed than the one he had sketched in the *Republic* (*c.* 380). His construction of the ideal city of Magnesia in Crete in the form of a perfect theocracy went far beyond anything actually known in the Greece of his time, but his prescriptions for the priestly personnel of Magnesia were, like many of its institutional arrangements, based with modifications on those of his native Athens. *The Laws* is cast as a dialogue between a Spartan, a Cretan and an Athenian, the latter being a surrogate for Plato himself:

ATHENIAN.   We can say, then, that the temples should have Attendants (*neōkoroi*) and Priests and Priestesses. Next, there are the duties of looking after streets and public buildings, ensuring that they reach the proper standards, preventing men and animals from doing them damage, and seeing that conditions both in the suburbs and in the city itself are in keeping with civilized life. Three types of officials must be chosen: < the Priests > and the City-Wardens (as they will be called), who will be responsible for the points we have just mentioned, and the Market-Wardens for the proper conduct of the market.

Priests or Priestesses of temples who have hereditary priesthoods should not be turned out of office. But if (as is quite likely in a new foundation) few or no temples are thus provided for, the deficiencies must be remedied by appointing Priests and Priestesses to be Attendants in the temples of the gods. In all these cases appointment should be made partly by election and partly by lot, so that a combination of non-democratic and democratic methods in every rural and urban division may lead to the greatest possible feeling of solidarity. In appointing Priests, one should leave it to the god himself to express his wishes, and allow him to guide the luck of the draw. But the man whom the lot favours must be scrutinized to see, first, that he is of sound body and legitimate birth, and, secondly, that he has been reared in a family whose moral standards could hardly be higher, he himself and both his parents having always lived unpolluted (*hagnos*) by homicide and all such crimes against heaven.

They must get laws on all religious matter from Delphi, and appoint Expounders (*exēgētai*) of them; that will provide them with a code to be obeyed. Each priesthood must be held for a year and no longer, and anyone who intends to officiate in our rites in due conformity with religious law should be not less than sixty years old. The same rules should apply to Priestesses too. There should be three Expounders. The tribes will be arranged in three sets of four, and every man should nominate four persons, each from the same triad as himself; the three candidates who receive most votes should be scrutinized, and nine names should then be sent to Delphi for the Oracle to select one from each triad. Their scrutiny, and the requirement as to minimum age, should be the same as in the case of the Priests; these three must hold office for life, and when one dies the group of four tribes in which the vacancy occurs should make nominations for a replacement.

The highest property-class must elect Treasurers to control the sacred funds of each temple, and to look after the temple-enclosures and their produce and revenues; three should be chosen to take charge of the largest temples, two for the median-size, and one for the very small. The selection and scrutiny of these officials should be conducted as it was for the Generals.

So much by way of provision for matters of religion (*ta hiera*).

(*The Laws* 759A–760A, trans. T. J. Saunders, modified)

CHAPTER 6

Places of cult

SPIRIT OF PLACE

For the Greeks any location might serve as a place of cult, a sacred space (*hieron*). It was enough for it to be perceived as having a sacred character, either because of some special geographical or numinous quality (the majesty of the terrain, as at Delphi; the presence of a revered tomb) or because it contained some particular manifestation of the divine – rocks, or a tree, or a spring, for instance. Terrain that was deemed to be sacred was delimited as a *temenos* or 'cut-off' space, separated, that is, from its non-sacred surroundings. Its boundaries could be marked by pillars (*horoi*) or by a continuous boundary wall (*peribolos*). Numerous Greek sanctuaries were just such simple enclosures, containing perhaps a sacred wood, a spring, a grotto, or some other natural feature, but no permanent man-made structures. A *temenos* could harbour the cults of several different gods or be devoted to just one divinity.

The Agora of Athens (see fig. 4) is a good, if unusually well attested and cluttered, example of a *temenos*. It was a large area to the north of the Akropolis, delimited by inscribed pillars that proclaimed 'I am a *horos* (boundary-marker) of the Agora'. Here were situated a host of religious cults, funerary, heroic and divine, each with its appropriate monuments (altars and small shrines for Demeter, Zeus Phratrios, Athene Phratria, and Apollo Patrōos, the enclosure of the Eponymous Heroes, and so on and so forth). The public political buildings such as the Council Chamber and the Tholos lay outside the sacred *temenos* in the

ıl period, on its fringes, though that of course did not
...ᴄᴀıı ınat there was no place in them for religion.

SANCTUARY TABOOS

The sanctity of a sanctuary was hedged around with a series of
interdictions. It was forbidden to give birth, make love or die in a
sanctuary. No one who was in any way polluted was allowed in,
and at the entrance were placed lustral basins of holy water for
worshippers to purify themselves before crossing the sacred
boundary. Correspondingly, the sanctuary was also an inviolable
or sacrosanct space, an asylum (*asulon*, literally a place from
which plunder might not be taken). Hence sanctuaries functioned
as legally acknowledged places of refuge (or, as we say, of asylum
or sanctuary) for runaway slaves, ousted politicians on the run,
and other individuals who were being pursued. To assassinate
someone who had taken refuge in a sanctuary was considered a
heinous enough crime for the gods to inflict a scourge (a plague,
for instance) on the whole city as a punishment.

THE DISPOSITION OF SANCTUARIES

Sanctuaries were dispersed throughout a city's territory, in the
countryside no less than in the town. Those that were built on an
akropolis in the centre of an urban agglomeration, as at Athens,
were the exception rather than the rule. Nor did sanctuaries
function as the central monument of a built-up urban area in the
same way as the cathedral did in a mediaeval city. The standing
ruins one sees today, often just of temples, give a misleading
impression of what urban sanctuaries were actually like. So far
from dominating the surrounding countryside, they were tucked
away among a tangle of buildings and small streets, so that from
a distance their built structures were barely visible.

SANCTUARIES IN HISTORY

Placing sanctuaries in historical perspective allows us both to
underline the enduring nature of Greek cult-places, often stretching back to prehistoric times, and at the same time to notice just

how closely their creation and development were tied to those of the city itself.

Recent research on the territory of Greek cities in the Archaic period has stressed the importance of extra-urban sanctuaries for 'the birth of the Greek city' (de Polignac 1984 [90]). They were often positioned at the boundaries of the city's cultivated area, on the margins of forests, mountains, and uncultivated land. Here they acted both as a frontier and as a point of junction between the two kinds of terrain, the wild and the cultivated, that constituted every city's territory. But they served a more narrowly political function too, marking the limits of a city's territory in opposition to that of its often hostile neighbours. Sometimes, finally, these peripheral sanctuaries were linked to the urban centre by a 'sacred way'; these were the routes marked out for sacred processions during the great festivals, but they were also a further indication of the community's religious and civic hold on its territory.

Turning from the countryside to the town one notes that, at Corinth as at Athens, the process of urbanization took place around the sanctuaries of the city's chief deities, Athene Polias on the Athenian Akropolis and Apollo on a prominent hill at Corinth. Moreover, the earliest buildings to be constructed within the city's public space were monuments of religious cult, which progressively attracted to themselves the various administrative, judicial and political buildings, as can be seen happening around the Athenian Agora. At their origins, therefore, both the city's territory as a whole and its urban centre were organized and ordered by its sanctuaries and religious shrines.

STRUCTURES TO BE FOUND IN A SANCTUARY

Within a sanctuary there often developed a complex of cultic structures, and the great Panhellenic sanctuaries of Delphi and Olympia came to resemble veritable towns. All contained one altar (*bōmos*) or more, indispensable pieces of ritual furniture situated inside the *temenos* but never inside a temple. It was here that animal-sacrifice was conducted, and the blood of the victim made to pour out in a stream onto the altar (chapter 4). The fire-grate, in which the portions destined for the gods were burnt and those intended for humans were roasted, was placed on the stone socle surrounding the altar. In some cases the altar itself consisted of no other material than the ashes and charred bones produced by these fires, the classic example being the imposing mound that constituted the Great Altar of Zeus in the Altis at Olympia. Otherwise, it might be a pile of stones, or a hearth reached by a series of steps, or a massive block like the stone altar of Hera at the Argive Heraion (1.70 × 2.40 m). Participants in a sacrifice generally formed a circle or semi-circle around the altar, which was typically oriented at right angles to the façade of the temple (where a temple existed). The sacrificer turned to face the east, away from the temple, and the sacrificial ritual was concentrated entirely around the altar without reference to the temple behind.

The temple (*naos*), it is almost a cliché to point out, is the most spectacular surviving remnant of the ancient Greek world (see further Appendix I). Its history was no less tied to that of the city than was that of the sanctuary as a whole, inasmuch as the temple made its appearance as a distinct architectural form in the eighth century in close co-ordination with the creation of the first properly civic communities. The earliest temples were basically of mud brick with a wooden colonnade; only in the seventh century did they begin to be constructed of stone.

Yet from a strictly cultic point of view, the temple was not an indispensable element of Greek religion. Rituals, as we have said, were mostly performed outside, not inside, the temple. Indeed, it was quite rare for ordinary Greeks to be granted the right of entry to temples, which were kept locked for a large part of the year. This was because the temple typically had one precisely defined function, namely to preserve the god's cult-statue or statues and the other property dedicated to him or her. In this respect, its purpose was akin to that of the smaller buildings constructed within sanctuaries, the so-called 'treasuries' that were filled with votive offerings to the gods. Thus the Parthenon, which housed Pheidias' chryselephantine (gold-and-ivory) cult-statue of Athene Parthenos ('the Virgin'), was not used for rituals of worship; indeed, it also housed Athens' state treasury. Sometimes a sanctuary might contain two temples dedicated to the same god, possibly so that a new cult-statue for which there was no room in the original shrine could be put on display.

Not all temples, however, were designed either solely or principally as the house of a god. Some 'sanctuary temples' (Roux 1984 [89]) were built to protect a holy place and the rituals attached to it. That of Pythian Apollo at Delphi, for example, contained the Pythian hearth, the altar of Poseidon and, in its holy-of-holies (*aduton*), the oracular seat of the Pythia (see further chapter 11).

Apart from altars and temples, a sanctuary included a diversity of other structures purpose-built for worship: the treasuries already mentioned, which received sacralized dedications and were themselves votive offerings; fountain-houses, which were necessary in particular for ritual ablutions; various functional buildings such as dining-rooms and dormitories for the use of priests and pilgrims; and finally stadia or other arenas for cults that involved athletic and other competitions, such as those of Olympia and Delphi.

OTHER ARTEFACTS TO BE FOUND IN SANCTUARIES

One of the most frequent of all cult-acts was to make a dedication, so that sanctuaries were bursting at the seams with offerings of all kinds. Anything in principle could serve as a dedication, from the humblest vase given by an individual to the booty amassed by a city from a military campaign. A victorious athlete might dedicate his victor's crown, someone recovered from illness might offer a simulacrum of that part of her body which had been cured, or a city might present a standing monument. All these required the keeping of written inventories by the sanctuary's accountants, and they also required space. Not infrequently buildings were constructed simply to accommodate offerings. Alternatively, the offerings might be periodically cleared out and buried in trenches, to the great delight and joy of the archaeologists who excavate them.

Behind these offerings lay the labour of artists and craftsmen, some of whom had their workshops right by a sanctuary; in fact, the lion's share of the Greeks' artworks that have come down to us were once dedications consecrated to the gods. In order to market items for dedication and provide a variety of other goods for sale, merchants were allowed to set up their stalls on the fringes of or actually inside sanctuaries. Indeed, so flourishing a trade was done by them and other purveyors of goods and services during the great festivals that Strabo (x.5.4, c486) could describe the Panhellenic Isthmian Games, held every two years in the territory of Corinth, as 'a sort of commercial affair' (*emporikon ti pragma*). This gives a fair idea of the atmosphere of a sanctuary – a lively, colourful, noisy place, where pilgrims sometimes had a job to force their way through the crowds or even to find somewhere to gaze in admiration at the procession and catch a glimpse of the god's statue.

IMAGES OF GODHEAD

Images of the gods cannot be discussed without raising the ticklish problem of figural representation in ancient Greece (see further chapter 14). What symbolic value did images have for the Greeks, and in particular how are we to interpret what is called their 'anthropomorphism', the rendering of the gods in the image of men?

Every sanctuary, no matter how small, had its cult-image of the relevant god or goddess, around which his or her temple was built. But even though the cult-statue was in most cases the ultimate focus of rituals, it was usually kept shut up within the temple, and only taken out and handled during the great festivals. Few examples of these survive, partly because many were made of perishable wood, or had a wooden core sheathed in gold and ivory. On the other hand, we have many more examples of the host of other kinds of divine representations that populated a sanctuary in the shape of freestanding dedications, temple-decorations, statues and carvings in low or high relief. The function of these was not to play an active rôle in ritual but to recall to the worshipper's mind the divinity's attributes and history and the deities associated with him or her. The pediments of temples, for example, offered space for large compositions which often represented some aspect of the pantheon, while metopes and friezes (see fig. 21) depicted all the episodes in the lives of the gods, their battles against the Titans as well as their feasting and domestic quarrels. Everywhere the eye travelled it encountered images of the gods, deceptively familiar in their forms yet simultaneously reminding mortals how vast was the gulf in status between the human condition and the divine world.

THREE ANCIENT PERSPECTIVES ON THE SANCTUARY

(i)   This extract from *The Festival-Goers* (*thearoi*, the Doric form of *theōroi*) by the Sicilian comic playwright Epikharmos (first quarter of the fifth century) celebrates the wealth of metallic dedications on display:

> Lyres, tripods, chariots,
> brass tables, ewers, plates,
> cauldrons of bronze, mixing-bowls, spits!
> Oh! if only you wanted to,
> with these utensils hanging on their nails
> you could make quite a clatter, you really could!
> (fr. 109 ed. A. Olivieri)

(ii)   In 402 Xenophon of Athens, a rich young man of oligarchic persuasion, left his native city to seek fame and fortune in the East fighting as a mercenary for the Persian pretender Cyrus the Younger. In Asia Xenophon made a killing, financially as well as literally, and back in Greece, safely ensconced at Skillous near Olympia on an estate provided for him by King Agesilaos II and the Spartans, he devoted some of his profits to pious ends. Here is his own account:

He bought some land as an offering to the goddess in a place where Apollo [*via* his oracle at Delphi] had instructed him. A river called the Selinous ran through the land, and in Ephesos too there is a river of the same name flowing past the temple of Artemis. There are fish and shellfish in both rivers, but at Skillous there is game-hunting country too. Xenophon also used the sacred money for building an altar and a sanctuary, and thenceforth he always dedicated a tithe of the season's produce in order to celebrate a sacrifice in honour of the goddess. All the inhabitants of Skillous and the surrounding area, men and women, used to take part in the festival. The goddess [*sc.* Artemis] provided those who joined in the feast with barley-flour, bread, wine, dried fruits, and a portion both of the domesticated animals sacrificed from the sacred herds and of the wild game. The latter abounded, since

Xenophon's sons and the sons of other local people went hunting specially, and anyone who wished could join in. Wild boar, antelope and stags were caught, partly on the sacred land itself, partly on Mount Pholoē. The land lies on the road from Sparta to Olympia, about twenty stades [4 km] from the temple of Zeus. In the sacred enclosure there are meadows and thickly wooded hills, good terrain for raising pigs, cattle and also horses; plenty of fodder is available for the animals of visiting celebrants too. The sanctuary is surrounded by a grove of fruit trees providing excellent fruit in all the appropriate seasons. The temple is a small-scale reproduction of the great temple of Artemis at Ephesos, and the cult-statue is as near a likeness to the golden Ephesian original as a cypress-wood image can be. A stēlē stands by the temple, bearing the following inscription: 'This ground is sacred to Artemis. Let him who owns it and takes its produce make a tithe-offering every year. With the surplus let him maintain the temple. Whosoever fails in this duty shall not escape the goddess's notice'. (*Anabasis* v.3.7–13)

(iii)   A century later, Herodas (origin unknown) in one of his *Mimes* imagines the scene at the famous healing sanctuary of Asklepios on the island of Kos, when two fairly poor women (but not too poor to own a slave) come to present the god with his traditional offering of a cock. (Socrates' famous last words were reportedly 'We owe a cock to Asklepios'.) The women have arrived too early to be allowed into the inner chamber of the temple, so they look around at the paintings and sculptures:

KOKKALE: Don't you see, Kynno dear? Such wonderful creations! Why, you'd think a new Athene had fashioned them (saving your divine presence, my Lady). I mean, look at this naked boy here – if I scratch him, he'll show the mark, won't he? The flesh in the painting looks as though it's really warm and palpitating; and that silver fire-box – if Myellos or Pataikiskos son of Lamprion [two notorious thieves] were to see it, their eyes would pop out of their heads thinking it was the real thing. And what about the ox and the man driving it, and the woman walking beside him, and that fellow with the hook nose and the one with the curly hair – wouldn't you say that they were living and breathing, flesh-and-blood creatures? If I weren't a woman and afraid of going too far, I'd have cried out for thinking the ox was about to do me some mischief – look, Kynno, look at the way he's glaring at me sidelong out of one eye.   (Herodas, *Mime* iv.57–71)

CHAPTER 7

Rites of passage

INTRODUCTION

In this chapter we shall be discussing the rituals and beliefs relating to critical points in a person's life-cycle, that is, transitions from one life-status to another – birth, attainment of majority, marriage, death. 'Domestic (or family) religion' and 'popular religion', the labels usually employed to cover these, do not seem satisfactory to us. The former is inadequate, because the rituals in question are as much civic as domestic, and the cleavage familiar today between private and public life has hardly any meaning in a context where matrimonial and funerary rituals were a matter of concern to the community at large, not just the few individuals immediately involved. As for 'popular religion', despite its currency among historians of religion at the beginning of this century and its recent revival by English-speaking writers, the term both is excessively vague and corresponds to no ancient Greek notion. M. P. Nilsson, for example, lumped absolutely everything concerning religion under this rubric, while other exponents of the 'popular religion' category assert or assume an untenable contrast between the 'spontaneous' actions and rituals of the masses and the sophisticated religious thought of the élite.

It need hardly be added that such a conception of Greek religion is the end-product of centuries of 'Christianocentricity' and has nothing whatsoever in common with our outlook. We have adopted rather an anthropologically inspired approach that brings out the peculiar logic underlying irreducibly alien rituals and beliefs. Hence our choice of title for this chapter, which is

63

borrowed from Arnold van Gennep's *Les Rites de passage* (Gennep 1960[97]). We shall use as our expository guideline the human life-cycle, beginning with birth and ending with death.

BIRTH-RITES

Immediately following the birth of a baby, an olive-branch was fixed above the main door of the house for a boy, a fillet of wool for a girl. On the fifth or seventh day after the birth the ceremony of the Amphidromia (literally 'the running-around [*sc.* ritual]') was performed. The newborn infant was carried in a circle around the domestic hearth, the seat of the guardian goddess Hestia, and then placed directly on the ground; these rituals served to inscribe the infant within the space of the *oikos* and to attach him or her to the hearth of which s/he was a product. This was the occasion for the newborn to be officially accepted by the father and sometimes also for his or her identity and humanity to be recognized by the attribution of a name. (Not naming the child before then was a realistic response to the fair likelihood that under ancient Greek medical and sanitary conditions the infant would not survive that long.)

This ritual of incorporation within the household had its counterpart in the ritual of exposure, consequent on the father's refusal of recognition. In that event the infant was expelled from hearth and home and exposed in a distant location outside the city's cultivated territory in what the Greeks considered to be wild space (*agros*, 'open field', was cognate with *agrios* meaning 'wild'). The exposure of neonates was a central feature of numerous Greek myths, that of Oedipus, for example; here the story was set in the territory of the shepherds who pastured their flocks on the margins between different civic territories. The Oedipus story was emblematic in another way too: parents did not usually expose their infants willingly, and those at any rate who left them in an earthenware jar (*pithos*) for protection surely hoped that they might be rescued as Oedipus was. At Sparta, however, it was not the infant's father who decided whether a child should be reared but the tribal elders, representing the community as a whole; if their decision was negative, the infant was 'exposed' by being hurled to its certain death down a chasm brutally known as Apothetai, or 'the place of the throwaways'.

After a birth the household, and especially the mother and any other women who had been involved directly with the process of giving birth, had to be ritually purified. For the blood that had been shed was considered to be in this case a source of pollution (*miasma*), which is why it was forbidden to give birth in a sanctuary (chapter 6). Often it was the city which laid down regulations for purification by law, on the grounds that the pollution of one household might infect the entire civic community. The most frequently used purificatory rituals included sprinkling the mother with lustral water, bathing her in the sea or drenching her with the blood of a piglet, and the burning of incense and sulphur.

Certain deities were especially associated with childbirth: Artemis, Eileithyia, and Demeter Kourotrophos among others; to these it was customary to consecrate the clothing soiled in childbirth and the special belts worn by pregnant mothers. On the tenth day after the birth a sacrifice was held, followed by a banquet, which brought together all the members of the family and was sometimes an occasion for giving presents to the child.

ENTRY INTO THE WORLDS OF THE ADULT AND THE CITIZEN

A distinction must be drawn between the sexes here, since it was only boys who could acquire the rights of full, that is politically active, citizenship. The ceremonies marking the passage from adolescence to maturity varied from city to city. Their true significance can only be understood by placing them within a wider context of ritual practices than that of religion proper, a context usually described as 'initiation' (La Fontaine 1985[105]). But so as not to overstep the limits of this book, we shall concentrate on the religious aspects of initiation by taking the Apatouria festival as a case-study.

The Apatouria was a peculiarly Ionian festival: 'truly all are Ionians who keep the Apatouria' (Herodotus 1.147). Celebrated by those who 'have the same father' (i.e., putative common ancestor in the paternal line), it was the occasion on which new members were formally integrated into the community. In its Athenian version the festival is pretty well documented. The social framework within which it was conducted was that of the phratry, a religious and political corporation of alleged kinsmen ('blood-brothers'). Prior enrolment in a phratry was an indispensable condition of a boy's being admitted to a deme and thereby to full Athenian citizenship on reaching the age of majority (eighteen).

The festival lasted for three days during the month of Pyanopsion (roughly October–November: see chapter 10). On the first day, called *Dorpia*, the fellow phratry-members feasted together. The second day, *Anarrhusis*, was given over to sacrificing, especially in honour of Zeus Phratrios and Athene Phratria. Finally, on the third day, *Koureōtis*, young boys were admitted to their father's phratry, their change of status being celebrated by sacrifices (*koureion, meiōn*). The nature of the latter sacrifice is obscure, but the *koureion* sacrifice we know to have accompanied the boy's dedication of a lock of his hair to Artemis to signify his passage out of childhood. If an adult phratry-member had married since the last Apatouria, it was the custom for him to hold a wedding sacrifice (*gamēlia*) to inform his fellow-members of his new status and of the identity of his bride (see further below).

The difference of ritual treatment accorded to an adolescent boy and a young girl on the threshold of their adult lives was therefore blatant, and there was a corresponding difference in the myths dealing with this important transition. So far as boys were concerned, their access to the world of the citizens was marked by rituals of, on the one hand, segregation (dedication of hair to Artemis, for instance, which marked the boundary between young adulthood and childhood) and, on the other, incorporation (participation in certain communal post-sacrificial feasts, which integrated him in the civic community). The phratry acted as intermediary between family and state.

Once a young man had been enrolled on the register of his father's deme and ritually endowed with the status of 'ephebe' (literally 'on the threshold of majority') at the age of eighteen, his first action was to make a tour of all the sanctuaries of Athens. That and the oath he was obliged to swear (witnessed by no less

than eleven deities: Tod 1948[63]: 204 = Harding 1985[65]: 109A)
are exemplary proof of the fact that religion and civic life were
mutually and inextricably implicated.

THE OTHER HALF: YOUNG GIRLS

A point-by-point comparison of the ritual treatment of boys and
girls would be senseless, since no daughter of a (male) citizen
became a (full) citizen, whereas, other things being equal, every
son did. There were no collective rites of passage prescribed for
the young girls of any city (with the possible exception of Sparta).
Rather, what one does find is that a tiny and select handful were
given the temporary privilege of being in the service of a deity. A
famous and not in itself obviously funny passage of Aristophanes'
sex-war comedy *Lysistrata* succinctly describes this privileged
engagement. It is placed in the mouth of the leader of the chorus
of Athenian wives who have gone on a sex-strike and occupied
the Akropolis in an attempt to force their husbands to make
peace with Sparta; she urges the audience of citizens to 'listen, all,
for we have good advice for you':

> At the age of seven I served as one of the *arrhēphoroi*;
> at ten I pounded barley for Our Lady (Athene);
> then, shedding my dress of saffron, I served as a Bear
> for Artemis in the Brauronia festival;
> finally, having grown into a tall and comely young girl,
> I served as *kanēphoros* and wore a necklace of figs.
>
> (*Lysistrata* 642–7)

This is not, despite appearances, a description of a graded
cycle of feminine initiation. Athenian girls never became full
adult citizens. Most Athenian women will never even have served
as 'Bears' (only a few were chosen for this honorific year of
service to Artemis at Brauron), or *kanēphoroi* (basket-carriers in
the great festival processions) or *arrhēphoroi* (small girls who
helped to celebrate the Arrhephoria in honour of Athene). As the
ritual civic functions enumerated in the Aristophanic passage did
not mark the attainment of different stages in a girl's life-cycle,
they are not a parallel to the male rites of passage. What really
did count as a rite of passage for a girl was her marriage.

MARRIAGE

No ancient Greek city devised a precise legal definition of marriage. Certain types of union were privileged, but the boundary between marriage and a non-marital union was often a fine one. The rituals of the wedding-day (*gamos*) in no case constituted a sacrament, and they had no legal standing in themselves. At Athens the legal side of marriage (always *arranged* marriage) was taken care of beforehand, sometimes many years before, at the ceremony of *enguēsis*, whereby the father or other male guardian affianced or rather 'gave away' the future bride to the future bridegroom with the words 'I give you this girl for the ploughing of legitimate children'. The wedding rituals did, however, mark a change of status for both man and woman alike, although it was a far more profound change for the woman who left the paternal *oikos* and hearth for those of her husband, thereby exchanging one *kurios* ('lord and master') for another.

Wedding rituals were diverse in form and not ranked hierarchically; they were directed towards a large number of deities, each of whom had his or her precisely defined function to fulfil towards the individuals, or rather the families, concerned. On the eve of the *gamos*, sacrifices (*proteleia, progamia*) were offered by the families of the bride and groom to a range of deities considered to watch over marriage, especially Zeus Teleios and Hera Teleia, and Artemis. The bride now literally 'put away childish things' by dedicating her toys, hair-rings, and other personal tokens of her childhood, usually to Artemis. Both bride and groom took a ritual purificatory bath, for which at Athens the water was drawn from the Kallirrhoe springs in the bed of the Ilissos river southeast of the Akropolis and carried home in specially shaped jars called *loutrophoroi* ('nuptial bathwater-holders'); Attic vase-painters liked to depict the procession of women fetching the water from the fountain on vases of this shape, which might also serve as the wife's funerary urn.

On the day of the *gamos* itself both the bride's and the groom's houses were decorated with branches of olive and laurel, and the father or guardian of the bride held a sacrifice and banquet in his. The girl (usually aged fourteen or fifteen, having just reached puberty) would be veiled and wearing a wreath. In her ambiguous and liminal new status as bride (*numphē*) she would be attended by a married *numpheutria* or matron of honour, while the groom had a *paranumphos*, a sort of 'best man', to attend him. The sexes were kept rigidly segregated. A special rôle was allotted to a young boy chosen because both his parents were still living (significantly, there was a special epithet for such a fortunate boy, *amphithalēs*). Wearing on his head a wreath of thorny plants mixed with acorns, he handed round bread to the guests from a basket and formulaically pronounced 'I have banished evil and found good.' In tragic drama this ritual was represented as a harking-back to the Greeks' transition from a thorny to a smooth and cultivated life, from a life of savagery to one of milled grain, and the same agricultural symbolism was implicit in the culinary implements used for the wedding day. The bride had to bring a frying-pan to cook the barley, a child had to bring a sieve, and in front of the nuptial bedchamber there were hung a pestle and mortar. The food served at the banquet consisted of traditional dishes, including sesame cakes which were supposed to stimulate fecundity. Presents were also given.

In the early evening the bride was taken in formal, torchlit procession from the house of her father or guardian to that of her new husband. She was often conveyed on a wagon drawn by oxen or mules, and wedding songs were sung to Hymen god of marriage. At the door of the bridegroom's house his parents stood to greet their new daughter-in-law. She was given a piece of sesame-and-honey cake, a quince or a date (more fertility symbols) and performed an obligatory tour of her new home.

Within the institution of marriage the wife was the mobile element: it was she who became attached to a new hearth by being transferred to a new *oikos*. (The only exceptions were those Athenian daughters who had no surviving brothers of the same father and were known technically as *epiklēroi*, 'those who go with the inheritance'; since they acted as surrogate heirs of their father, passive vehicles for transmitting the paternal inheritance, their husbands came to live with them in their paternal *oikos* rather than *vice versa*.) The wife's physical migration and reintegration had to be marked symbolically and ritually, hence the *katakhusmata* ceremony (used also for the induction of newbought slaves), in which nuts and dried figs were showered on her head as she was led round the familial hearth (rather as a newborn was carried in the Amphidromia ceremony, above). The symbolism of fertility was predominant: the new wife's essential function was to assure the continuity of her husband's *oikos* by producing legitimate children. But the parallelism with the induction ceremonies for slaves and children should not be missed: it was also the wife's legal and political inferiority to her husband that was being ritually enacted. Now at last came the moment for the newlyweds to enter the nuptial bedchamber (*thalamos*).

On the following day further sacrificing and banqueting took place, and the couple received more presents. The final ritual seal was put on the new union, as we saw, with the *gamēlia* sacrifice and feast held during the next Apatouria festival. This was a crucial precaution in case the legitimacy and thus the citizen rights of his male offspring were ever contested. Since most weddings in ancient Greece took place in winter, one of the winter months (roughly January–February) at Athens and elsewhere was called *Gamēliōn*: it was no accident that the month in which the Apatouria fell was exactly nine months after *Gamēliōn*.

The above synthetic account is based mainly on Athenian evidence, but marriage rituals differed considerably from city to city. One of the most interesting cases we know, thanks to Plutarch (*Life of Lykourgos* ch. 15), is that of Sparta. Here brides were typically rather older than at Athens, but this did nothing to diminish the status-gap between bride and bridegroom as expressed symbolically in the wedding ritual. The bride's hair was not just cut but shaved by her *numpheutria*, she was dressed in a man's cloak and sandals, and laid down on a straw mattress in a darkened room of the bridegroom's house to await the arrival of her 'captor'. This is a classic example of what anthropologists call 'symbolic inversion': elsewhere in Greece we find brides wearing false beards, phalloi, even satyr costume, and bridegrooms dressed in women's clothes. These temporary and unique reversals of sexual rôle served to anticipate and confirm the norms of sexual differentiation and hierarchy within marriage.

There was an extremely large number of divinities concerned

with human marriage, but each of them had his or her precise function with its own underlying logic. Artemis, for example, was the goddess selected to receive the symbolic tokens surrendered by young brides as they left behind for good the 'savage' world of childhood and adolescence. Mythical narratives, such as that of Atalante and Melanion, made the point that it was as dangerous to refuse to leave the domain of Artemis as it was not to show one's gratitude towards her on departure: Atalante, an Arkadian mountain-girl and huntress, challenged all her suitors to a running-race on condition that only if she lost would she marry and surrender her virginity. For this she earned the hatred of Aphrodite, until Melanion finally beat her.

Aphrodite's function was to preside over the budding of sexual desire (*erōs*). Without her no matrimonial union could be deemed complete; on the other hand, an excess of sexual passion was thought to threaten the stability and decorum of a marriage from within, so Aphrodite had to be handled with care. Hera, frequently invoked as Teleia ('the Accomplished', 'the Achiever'), was the divine image of the maturity attained by the wife on marriage and of the legitimacy of the union; she stood for contractual reciprocity and protected the status of the lawfully wedded wife. Each of these divine powers was therefore in its own way indispensable and irreplaceable, one more proof of the logic that governed the constitution of the Greek pantheon (see further chapter 13).

In conclusion, it would be wrong to follow those modern interpreters who have seen marriage as an asymmetrical rite of passage into adulthood for the bride alone, a uniquely feminine affair. Rather, the institution of marriage was brilliantly contrived by Greek cities as a way of reproducing the citizen estate; it was a ritualized process in which both boys and girls were equally engaged. Refusal of marriage jeopardized not just the reproduction of the human species but the continuity of the civic community. That was why it was one of the favourite themes of Greek myth, involving boys such as Hippolytos (unreconstructed devotee of Artemis and recusant against Aphrodite in the play of Euripides named after him) no less than girls. In Crete, indeed, the civic embeddedness of marriage was communally and publicly demonstrated by making the initiatory cycle for boys ιte in the entry of each class of age-mates into both the ......ιαι and the civic estate simultaneously (Ephoros *F.Gr.Hist.* 70ғ149, in Strabo x.4.20, C482).

DEATH

Archaeological evidence (fig. 2), figural representations on vases and on gravestones, and written texts provide a great deal of detailed evidence about death-rituals. A burial, like a sacrifice (chapter 4), was a three-act drama. First came the laying-out ceremonial (*prothesis*). When the corpse had been washed by female kin and anointed with perfume, clothed in white garments, and wrapped in a winding-sheet, it was laid out on a bier in the vestibule of the house. In vase-paintings the head is shown garlanded with flowers and resting on a cushion, the face exposed. All around the bier stood women, relatives of the deceased, making extravagant gestures of lamentation, scarifying their cheeks, tearing their hair, beating their breasts, weeping profusely, and keening a funeral dirge (*thrēnos*). Outside the front door of the house a basin was set, filled with lustral water for mourners to purify themselves before paying their last respects.

The second act was the funeral cortège (*ekphora*), which conveyed the dead person from his or her house to the graveyard (only infants might be buried individually near the house without risking pollution). The bier was either carried by hand or transported on a wagon, the procession being led by a woman, who was followed by the men and then the rest of the women mourners; musical accompaniment was provided by players of *auloi* (a sort of oboe). At Athens, at any rate, the *ekphora* had to take place at night.

Finally, there was the burial of the corpse in the cemetery (*sēma, nekrotaphion*), a delimited space outside the inhabited area or city-walls. The body might either be inhumed or cremated on a pyre; if the latter, the ashes would be collected in a linen cloth and placed in a burial urn. Grave-goods of various kinds were deposited in and around the tomb. Their quality, quantity and arrangement provide precious information on social status and religious symbolism, though they are not easy to interpret.

2 Plan of a fourth-century ʙᴄ ᴇ tomb near Poseidonia, South Italy.
Chamber tomb (stone construction, covered, measuring 2.83 × 2.13 m).
The interior of the tomb is divided into two compartments separated
by blocks of stone. Analysis of the grave-goods (pots, iron objects,
terracottas) allows identification of one male burial (krater, skyphos,
kylix, strigil, spear . . .) and one female burial (hydria, phiale, lebēs
gamikos, miniature terracottas). Deposition rituals provide information
on both the occupation and the social status of the deceased, in some
cases enabling a better understanding of the society of the living.
Bibliography: A. Bottini and E. Greco, 'Tomba a camera dal territorio
pestano: alcune considerazioni sulla posizione della donna', *Dialoghi
di Archeologia* 8:2 (1974–75): 231–74

From funerary furniture and, where available, the remains of the corpse itself archaeologists can now tell us quite a lot about age at death, differential treatment of the dead according to gender and social status, and family-groupings.

The grave was covered over by a tumulus of earth and marked by either a large vase or a stone stēlē bearing the deceased's name. (Sparta, however, was, as often, exceptional. Only warriors killed in battle and women who died in childbed were entitled to the honour of a named gravestone.) In Attica in the seventh and sixth centuries some especially grand tombs had been marked by a greater-than-lifesize statue of a *kouros* (nude male) or *korē* (clothed female). In the Classical period sculpted reliefs or large marble *lekuthoi* (translations into stone of the clay oil-jars used both for pouring consecrated oil over the grave and as grave-goods) served the same purpose. The motive for conspicuously marking a tomb was to establish the status of the dead person in relation to the living. Hence, too, the offerings of food or of ornaments such as crowns, fillets and perfume-vases. Back at the deceased's home rites of purification had to be carried out to expunge all traces of death's pollution. The hearth-fire was extinguished and a new one lit.

Finally, on the third, ninth and thirtieth days after the burial special commemorative sacrifices and feasts were held at the tomb. Due performance of these might be used persuasively as an argument in Athenian lawsuits concerning disputed inheritance, as in this fourth-century case:

> I the adopted son with the aid of my wife, the daughter of Philonides here, tended Menekles while he lived ... On his death I buried him in a manner befitting both him and myself, and I set up a fine monument to him and performed the commemorative ceremonies on the ninth day and all the other required rituals at the tomb in the finest way I could. (Isaios II, *On the Estate of Menekles* 36)

Funerary ritual as a whole was very tightly controlled by edicts passed either by the community as such or by some subsection of it (e.g. a phratry). One of the primary tasks of Archaic lawgivers like Solon of Athens (594/3), for example, was to legislate for this area of communal life. Or consider the following regulations passed and publicly displayed on stone by the phratry of the Labyadai at Delphi some two centuries later:

No more than thirty-five drachmas' worth of grave-goods may be deposited in the tomb, whether of goods bought or of objects taken from the home. In case any of these regulations are broken, a fine of fifty drachmas shall be payable, unless one is prepared to swear an oath on the tomb [that the prescribed maximum has not been exceeded]. Beneath the corpse there may be placed only a single mattress and a single pillow. The corpse shall be transported enshrouded and in silence; there shall be no stopping on the way, and no lamentations outside the house, before reaching the cemetery. In the case of the older dead, there shall be no dirge or lamentations over their tombs; everyone shall go straight back home, excepting only those who live at the same hearth as the deceased, together with paternal uncles, parents-in-law, descendants and sons-in-law. Neither on the next day, nor on the tenth day after the burial, nor on the anniversaries of it shall there be moaning or lamentation.   (Rougemont 1977[114], nos. 9 and 9 bis)

A third example, from another fourth-century Athenian inheritance suit, demonstrates how strong and close was the interaction between supposedly private, family matters and the interests of the state in a Greek city:

All men, when they are approaching their end, take precautions on their own behalf to prevent their family-line from dying out [literally 'their *oikoi* from becoming deserted'] and to ensure there will be someone to perform sacrifices and all the other customary rituals over them. This is why, even if they die without natural issue, they at any rate adopt so as to leave children behind. Nor is this simply a matter of personal sentiment; the state also has taken public measures to see that adoption is practised, since it entrusts the (eponymous) Arkhon by law with the duty of preventing family-lines from dying out.

(Isaios VII, *On the Estate of Apollodoros* 30)

To complement the schematic, mainly Athenian picture given above we should bear in mind the diversity of local burial customs, though there was thought to be a specifically 'Greek' way of death. This view transpires from literary descriptions of funerary rituals that were clearly considered not just different but alien and deviationist – for example, the burial of Patroklos in the twenty-third book of the *Iliad*, or the funerals of Spartan and Scythian kings in Herodotus (VI.58; IV.71).

Some of the dead were more equal than others in death, notably those citizens who died in battle. A Spartan who died thus was, as we saw, exceptionally allowed a named gravestone; and in democratic Athens a collective burial ceremony was held for the war dead, immortalized for us by the Funeral Speech of Perikles in Thucydides (II.35–46) which was delivered in the late winter of 431/430 over those fallen in the first year of the Peloponnesian War. No less graphic in its non-literary way is the following law of the mid-fourth century from Thasos:

> May the superintendent of the *agora* neglect nothing ... on the day on which the *ekphora* is to occur before it has taken place. Let no one wear mourning for the heroic dead in any way for more than five days; let it not be permitted to pay them any funerary rites under pain of religious pollution; let neither the Wardens of Women, nor the Arkhons, nor the Polemarkhs give proof of negligence, and let them be ready to inflict the penalties prescribed by the laws; let the Polemarkhs and the Secretary of the Council besides have the names of the dead with their patronymic inscribed in the roll of the heroic war dead; let their fathers, mothers and children be invited on each occasion that the city sacrifices in honour of the heroic dead; let the Comptroller pay to each of them an indemnity equal to the salary paid to an official; let their fathers, mothers and children also be given places of honour at the Games; a space shall be reserved and the organizer of the Games shall set aside a bench for their use; for all those who have left male children, when they have attained their majority let them each be given by the Polemarkhs greaves, breastplate, dagger, helmet, shield and spear worth not less than three *minai*; let this equipment be given them at the Herakleia festival; for their female children, for their dowry ... when they have reached the age of fourteen ...   (Pouilloux 1954[11], no. 141)

Besides these rituals for the exceptional, heroic dead, the cult of the ordinary dead was also a central and obligatory element in the familial and civic religion of every Greek state (except, once more, possibly Sparta). In general, celebration of the dead was included as just one element in an ensemble of complex rituals; the Athenian Genesia, a festival of hoary antiquity held on the fifth day of Boedromion (late September), was therefore exceptional in being a publicly-funded celebration devoted exclusively to the commemoration of the dead. The norm is represented rather by the Anthesteria.

This was a festival of Dionysos which took place over three days on the eleventh, twelfth and thirteenth days of the month to which it gave its name, Anthesterion (roughly February–March). On the first day, called *Pithoigia*, there was a ceremonial opening of the vats containing the new wine that had been fermenting since the previous autumn. The second day, *Khoës*, was mainly given over to communal drinking and was named for the three-quart jugs from which the wine was liberally poured and quaffed; but it was also the day of the ritual marriage and sexual intercourse between Dionysos, represented by the King Arkhon, and his 'Queen' (*Basilinna*, the King Arkhon's wife) in the Boukoleion ('Ox-herd's hut'). The third and final day was the day of the cooking pots, *Khytroi*, when the mixed vegetables prepared in these vessels were offered to Hermes Psykhopompos ('Conveyor of Souls'). For this was the ghosts' high noon, when the spirits of the dead were free to return above ground from the underworld and roam among the living – who were careful to take such precautions as smearing their doorways with pitch and locking up all the sanctuaries to keep them out. When the day ended, the spirits were sent packing back to Hades again, with the cry of 'Get out, hobgoblins, the Anthesteria is over!' ringing in their phantasmal ears.

Such a complex festival is susceptible of many different explanations depending on what feature(s) one chooses to highlight. But it is reductionist to claim for it only one overriding function or meaning (fertility, celebration of plant-life), as most interpreters have done. Rather, the Anthesteria doubtless fulfilled several functions at once, social as well as religious, and the cult of the dead was inserted into a larger ritual framework that involved among other things a carnivalesque reversal of rôles.

The deities of death were as many and various as those of marriage. Thanatos ('Death'), in mythology the son of Night, was the god of death *par excellence*. Yet he was less often invoked than other deities who represented particular aspects of death. Hades, for example, was sovereign of the dead and gave his name to the underworld kingdom over which he ruled (see below). Being inflexible and indomitable he was hated both by men and by the other gods alike. By his side sat his captured bride, Persephone or Kore, daughter of Demeter and Zeus.

77

. 1ermes, eternal traveller and crosser of boundaries, was summoned at the moment of death to guide the deceased on his or her last journey. Besides these prominent members of the Greek pantheon, there were numerous other terrifying death-dealing powers to contend with, all of them, revealingly, female; these included the three Fates (Moirai), one of whom cut the thread of life; the Erinyes or Furies who exacted blood-vengeance for murder; and the Gorgon Medousa who literally petrified anyone who gazed upon her.

THE AFTERLIFE

The Greeks certainly had a graphic and often geographical conception of the world of the dead, multiple images of which they created through their rituals, myths and divine powers – Tartaros, a measureless black hole of confused space; the river Styx, the frontier from beyond which there was no return; and, far more cheerful, the Elysian Fields. But it is a quite separate question whether the Greeks believed in a different kind of future life, better or worse than their present life on earth, and whether they constructed a morality of death whereby the dead received their due deserts according to the moral code of the living. Leaving aside the beliefs of certain philosophical sects and the practice of initiates of mystery-cults (chapter 11), the question can be posed in that form only if the Greeks' religion is viewed through the distorting lens of Christianity. Every religious system has its own internal logic, and it is more fruitful to describe and attempt to understand the Greeks' way of representing the afterlife in their own terms, as belonging to an alien culture and created at a specific historical juncture, rather than reduce the Elysian Fields to Paradise and Tartaros to Hell.

THE CIVIC LIFE-CYCLE

The significant stages of the life-cycle of a Greek citizen were underlined by rites of passage. Although these did not usually possess any legal force, they symbolically marked the individual's changes of status. The context of these rituals was provided both by the family and by the civic community. Study of them sheds light on the precise functions fulfilled by the relevant deities and sometimes too on the system of representations that underlay belief in them. The citizen was a member of groups of different kinds, each of which managed its own relationship with the divine world, and within the bosom of which the citizen performed the daily round of sacrificing and praying. In the following chapter we shall be describing these different milieux of the religious life, beginning with the individual household and progressing by degrees to the level of the community as a whole.

CHAPTER 8

Settings of religious life

THE HOUSEHOLD (*OIKOS*)

'Household' is a more appropriate rendering of the Greek *oikos* than 'family', since the latter is, for us, synonymous with the restricted group of parents and children. The Greek *oikos* was something quite different, both in size and in nature. It was a complex entity embracing both people and property, bound together by common ties of kinship, residence and labour. Thus it could embrace also the unrelated persons and the slaves who lived and worked within the same unit.

The *oikos* had no legal status as such but it did possess a distinct religious identity through its performance of cults focussed on the home. Zeus Herkeios ('Guardian of the Fence or Enclosure') had his altar for sacrifice in the courtyard. Since Zeus protected the home, he also, as Zeus Xenios, oversaw the observance within it of the rules of *xenia* (hospitality, ritualized friendship). The Greek world was fundamentally governed by the institution of hospitality, which not only linked individual households within a city but provided a framework for relations between cities. The task of Zeus in yet another of his manifestations, Ktesios, was to safeguard property (*ktēmata*).

Inside the house a fire was kept constantly burning in the hearth, the seat of the goddess Hestia. It was around the hearth that the members of the *oikos* partook of the meal through which they registered their common identity; here too were enacted the rituals for the admission of newcomers (a baby, a wife, or a slave: chapter 7). Another supernatural power with a tutelary rôle in the household was the Agathos Daimōn ('Good Spirit'), a sort of *genius loci* represented in the form of a snake. The daily cult of Hestia and the other household divinities consisted of libations and prayers, but only rarely of sacrifices or any more elaborate rituals.

An *oikos* might be placed under the protection of the most heterogeneous deities, whose influence was felt everywhere from the obscurest nook or cranny of the home to the open fields. At the gates of the house there were usually to be found Apollo Agyieus, Hermes Propylaios (in the shape of a pillar) or Hekatē. Outside the house and in the fields one might salute Hermes again, by throwing a stone onto a wayside cairn. Every stream, spring, plain, wood, or cultivated field was populated with divine powers whom it was wise to conciliate. The humanizing of Nature also meant endowing it with a divine identity, though we should not imagine that the ancient Greek peasant spent more of his or her time worshipping the gods of the workaday environment than the modern countryman who *en route* to the fields passes by crosses at road-junctions, tiny votive chapels, and a thousand and one other signs of the countryside's Christianization.

The *oikos* was enmeshed in a network of groups. Some of these were official and compulsory, like the deme at Athens, but others were optional, like the cult-associations to which certain members of an *oikos* might choose to belong.

THE ATHENIAN DEME (*DĒMOS*)

A *deme* (*dēmos*) was a division of the body of citizens created at Athens by the reforms of Kleisthenes in 508/7; there were 139 or 140 of them under the new democratic dispensation. From a political point of view the deme was the basic unit of the entire constitutional structure. Among its several functions it was the source of an Athenian's citizen status and served to recruit the members of the Assembly (which any citizen was entitled to attend) and Council of 500 (to which each deme had to contribute a fixed number of Councillors each year). But it also had its own local political organization, with its own assembly, officials and, most obviously, cultic life. Demes varied greatly in size, but if we think of them as villages, wards or parishes, we shall get a better idea of the everyday framework within which civic life typically functioned.

The most concretely informative type of source on the religious life of a deme is a deme-calendar, an annual record of its obligatory religious observances. We possess examples of these from Eleusis, Teithras, Erkhia, Thorikos and the Marathonian Tetrapolis, all published on stone in the fourth century; those of Teithras and Eleusis are very fragmentary, but others yield precise information on the organization of deme-cults. They are modelled on the great calendar of sacrifices of the Athenian state drawn up by Nikomakhos and his colleagues at the end of the fifth century (see beginning of chapter 10). A similar model was employed for the cultic arrangements of other kinds of religious body, as is shown by the calendar of the *genos* of the Salaminioi (below).

Deme-calendars share certain common traits but also display local peculiarities. The Marathon calendar, for example, was constructed according to a bipartite division of the sacrifices into the annual and the biennial. Months are listed, but not days. Extremely ancient deities are mentioned, but only one living person, the *dēmarkhos* or mayor. The Thorikos calendar, on the other hand (Daux 1983 [122]), sets out the deme's cultic activities on a monthly basis, as for example under Boedromiōn (September–October):

IN BOEDROMION festival of the Proerōsia: for Zeus Polieus, a choice sheep; women acclaiming the god, a piglet bought for holocaust sacrifice; for the worshipper the priest will provide dinner; for Kephalos, a choice sheep; for Prokris, an offering-tray; for Thorikos, a choice sheep; for the Heroines of Thorikos, an offering-tray; at Sounion for Poseidon, a choice lamb; for Apollo, a choice goat; for Kourotrophos, a choice female piglet; for Demeter, a full-grown victim; for Zeus Herkeios, a full-grown victim; for Kourotrophos, a piglet ...; at the salt-marsh [?] for Poseidon, a full-grown victim; for Apollo, a piglet.

What we have here is a list of the sacrifices to be carried out within the deme, inscribed in the first half of the fourth century. The nature of the victims to be sacrificed to a particular deity is carefully specified in each case, and sometimes a price is attached too: in the month Skirophoriōn, for example, for Kephalos an ox worth 30–40 drachmas, for Poseidon a sheep worth 10–20 drachmas. The sheer number of the sacrifices and the wide range of divinities to be honoured, including many local heroes and heroines, are striking enough. But no less remarkable is the document's allusive quality, enigmatic to anyone apart from a citizen of the deme Thorikos. For not a word is breathed about the cult-places, the sacrificial procedures, the priests (apart from a single mention), the financing of the sacrifices, and many other features.

The most exceptional deme-calendar, however, is that of Erkhia, also from the first half of the fourth century (*SEG* [61] XXI.541; Daux 1963 [121]). The precision of its detail is formidable: not only months, names of divinities and victims with their prices are listed, but also days of the month, places of cult, and ritual prescriptions (e.g. an interdiction on removing sacrificed meat). The text was inscribed in five columns, each of more than sixty lines, and enumerates forty-odd separate divinities (counting the different divine epithets separately), more than fifty kinds of animal victim, and almost a score of sacrificial locations mainly in the deme of Erkhia (about 20 km east of Athens). Yet despite all that, it is still not a complete list of the sacrifices offered by the deme, but only the 'principal list of the sacrifices to be celebrated under the authority of the *dēmarkheia*', i.e. of the demarkh or mayor. The original editor of this inscription (S. Dow) emphasized that there were sure to have been many other sacrifices offered in Erkhia, by households, by cult-associations and by other deme-officials or boards, both civilian and religious.

Thanks to such documents, the cultic existence of the demes comes to life for us and seems more accessible. But interpretative problems regarding the cults also multiply. It would appear that at one particular juncture, the start of the fourth century, all the Attic demes took it into their heads to reorganize or perhaps reduce to order for the first time a mass of cultic practices which had been accumulating steadily but shapelessly since the Archaic era. In order to be able to speak of the establishment of a coherent festival programme, we would need to know what the festival calendar had looked like beforehand; but what seems to have been happening was a publication rather than a genuine reform of the sacrifices. And the reason for their publication was probably financial. The demes were finding it difficult to fund the sacrifices. The great families who traditionally had provided for cultic needs were dying out, and the deme was having to shoulder the cults' costs. Hence the detailed prescriptions regarding the price payable for the victims. But the question was, who was to pay for the sacrifices thenceforth? The answer was surely the members of the deme, who severally undertook a kind of liturgy that was apportioned to them by lot. That at least is what study of the Erkhia text suggests.

Questions are still left unanswered by these documents as to the nature of participation in the cults: for example, how wide was access to them? From other evidence we know that some, such as the Mysteries of Eleusis, rapidly acquired a general or even a Panhellenic character, whereas others remained stubbornly parochial. Yet the documents in themselves do serve to immerse us in a teeming life of local cult that we may set beside the system of civic festivals to be described in chapter 9.

So far as the relationship between deme-cults and city-cults is concerned, the first question to be asked is whether the demes held local celebrations of city-wide cults, or whether the demesmen went into Athens itself in order to participate in these festivals. The texts firmly distinguish between cults that are *dēmotelē*, common to the entire *dēmos* (citizen-body, People) of Athens, and those that are *dēmotika*, peculiar to the members of a particular deme. There is no certain trace of any local celebration in or by a deme of numerous civic festivals such as the Panathenaia, Anthesteria, Pyanopsia or Thargelia. On the other hand, other city-wide festivals were celebrated locally, for example family-oriented festivals celebrated by women only. So there was no hard-and-fast rule, and the character of a deme's participation depended on the nature of the festival concerned.

In summary, the deme provided for its residents (not all of whom were members, since deme-membership was hereditary, and citizens might change their deme of residence) a broad spectrum of cultic activities, and it was these local sacrifices and festivals that constituted the most routine feature of Athenian religious life.

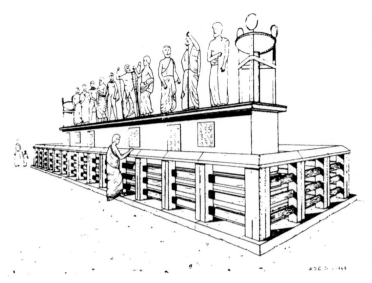

3 Athenian Agora: monument of the Eponymous Heroes. Reconstruction
drawing (by W. B. Dinsmoor, Jr) of the monument on which official
notices were posted. The Heroes are those of the ten tribes created
under Kleisthenes' democratic reform of 508/7 BCE 1 Erekhtheus (*tribe*
Erekhtheis), 2 Aigeus (Aigeis), 3 Pandion (Pandionis), 4 Leon (Leontis),
5 Akamas (Akamantis), 6 Oineus (Oineis), 7 Kekrops (Kekropis),
8 Hippothoōn (Hippothontis), 9 Aias (Aiantis), 10 Antiokhos (Antiokhis)

THE TRIBE (*PHULĒ*)

An ancient Greek tribe (not to be confused with the 'tribes' of
non-state societies studied by anthropologists) was a subdivision
of the citizen-body which varied in size and function from state to
state. An essential part of Kleisthenes' democratic reform-
package was to create ten new, geographically based tribes,
which, like all Greek public bodies, were endowed with a religious function. That function consisted in celebrating the cult of
the eponymous hero of each tribe (fig. 3) and performing rituals
connected with the conferment of citizenship.

Tribe and deme were the pre-eminent political subdivisions of
the Athenian state, and their identity as such was intimately
linked to their cultic practices. The city, however, also included
centres of religious practice that were less dependent on their

85

strictly political function, at any rate in the Classical period. The familiar catch-all rubric 'religious associations' hides a huge diversity of groups, not to mention cultic practices.

RELIGIOUS ASSOCIATIONS: GENERAL INTRODUCTION

The generic Greek term for those religious associations whose function was to pay due cult to heroes, gods or the dead was *koinon*, meaning 'that which is common'. Each *koinon* was devoted specifically to one or other divinity, for example that of the worshippers of the hero Asklepios. The internal operation of these associations demonstrates the importance of sacrifices and of the mutual sharing of sacrificial meat among the members. The figure responsible for these was the *hestiatōr* ('host', 'giver of a banquet'), and the portions allotted to men, women, sons, daughters and servants were precisely fixed. In some cases the texts also specified that the meat had to be roasted and eaten on the spot. Most of the cults performed by these religious associations were celebrated just by the small groups of devotees concerned; but the Bendideia, the festival of Bendis (see *Orgeōnes*, below), was open to the whole city of Athens. It is Athens, moreover, which provides the fullest evidence for the organization and activity of *koina*.

Phratry

The phratry (*phratria*, cognate with Latin *frater*, 'blood-brother') was an association of supposed kinsfolk who acknowledged common ancestors. It was devoted to the worship both of its own particular ancestors and of those cults common to all the phratries, especially Zeus Phratrios and Athene Phratria. The Apatouria festival, for example, was celebrated by all Ionic phratries and served, as we saw (chapter 7), to mark through a variety of rituals the incorporation of young potential citizens into the civic community. Thanks to a series of extant decrees recorded on stone, we have a precise description of the rules of incorporation laid down by the assembly of the Demotionidai phratry of the Athenian deme Dekeleia in the early fourth century:

Of Zeus of the Phratry

The priest Theodoros had this stele inscribed and set up. The priest shall receive a tithe in levy: on every *meiōn* sacrifice, a thigh, a side-cut, an ear, plus three obols of silver; on every *koureion* sacrifice a thigh, a side-cut, an ear, *plus* one *khoinix* of bread, a half-*kotylē* of wine and a drachma of silver.

Decree of Hierokles

The following resolution was passed by the members of the phratry on the proposal of Hierokles, Phormion being Eponymous Arkhon at Athens [396/5] and Pantokles of the deme Oion being chief official of the phratry [*phratriarkhos*]: 'Whichever men have not yet been adjudicated upon in accordance with the law [*nomos*] of the Demotionidai shall be adjudicated upon by the members of the phratry. They shall swear an oath by Zeus Phratrios and take their voting ballot from the altar. If anyone appears not to have been entitled to membership of the phratry but to have been admitted to it improperly, his name shall be deleted by the priest and the phratriarkh from the register kept by the Demotionidai and from the copy of same. He who introduced the one who is rejected shall be fined 100 drachmas, dedicated to Zeus Phratrios. The priest and the phratriarkh shall exact this sum or else they shall themselves pay the fine. In future adjudication shall take place after the offering of the *koureion* sacrifice, at the Apatouria, on the day called Koureōtis, and the voting ballot shall be taken from the altar...

In future victims shall be brought, both *meia* and *koureia*, to the altar at Dekeleia. Whosoever does not sacrifice upon the altar shall be fined fifty drachmas, dedicated to Zeus Phratrios. The priest shall exact this sum or else he himself shall pay the fine, except in the event of plague or war. If there be impediment of this sort, the *meia* and *koureia* shall be brought to the place designated by the priest in a published notice. Said notice shall be inscribed three days before the feast, on a whitened board at least a span in width, at the spot where the demesmen of Dekeleia congregated in town [*sc.* in the centre of Athens]. The priest shall have this decree and his tithe-levies inscribed at his own expense on a marble stēlē which shall be erected in front of the altar at Dekeleia.' *(IG* [57] ii²: 1237)

Every Athenian phratry, like that of the Demotionidai, would have had its 'Rule' (*nomos*) and its religious officials, especially a phratriarkh. In the Classical period, indeed, the phratry's rôle was primarily religious or social, since the enrolment of citizens was now the business of the deme.

Genos

The cultic activity of the religious corporation of fictive kinsmen known as a *genos* was directed towards particular sanctuaries and divinities, and its priesthoods were reserved for members of the founding families of these cultic communities. The *genos* of the Salaminioi at Athens, for example, had a rôle of special importance in organizing the Oskhophoria festival in honour of Athene Skiras (*LSS* [58] 19).

Thiasos

At Athens this term had a threefold application. It was used, firstly, of the smaller groups within a phratry, possibly organized in accordance with a law of the Periklean period, which performed the cult of Zeus Phratrios and Athene Phratria; secondly, of groups something like dining-clubs which chose a particular divinity, perhaps Agathos Daimōn, as their patron; and, thirdly, of specifically Dionysiac groups, initiates of private Dionysiac mysteries who raved through town singing and dancing with ecstatic 'enthusiasm' (see p. 198).

Orgeōnes

Associations of *orgeōnes*, upper-class in origin and mentioned already by Solon, offered sacrifices at their own expense on the altars of gods and heroes in Attica; a dozen such associations are attested, thanks to surviving decrees on stone like the following example passed and published in the fourth century by the devotees of Bendis (in origin a non-Greek goddess from Thrace) in the Peiraieus:

If any one of the *orgeōnes* who has right of access to the sanctuary wishes to offer a sacrifice to the goddess, he shall give to the priestess for a suckling animal: one drachma, one obol, the skin and the entire right thigh; for a fully mature animal: three drachmas, the skin and a thigh on the same conditions; for an ox, one drachma, one obol and the skin.

These parts of the victim shall be given to the priestess for female animals, to the priest for male ones. None shall sacrifice in the sanctuary beside the altar or he shall pay a fine of fifty drachmas.

To provide for the maintenance of the temple and the sanctuary the proceeds of the house-rentals and of the sale of water shall be devoted to the maintenance of the sanctuary and temple and to no other purpose, until the sanctuary and the temple shall be in readiness, unless the *orgeōnes* shall after a vote find another means of meeting the sanctuary's expenses. Water shall be left for the needs of the occupant. If anyone should propose a resolution contrary to the law, he shall pay a fine of fifty drachmas to the goddess and shall be excluded from the common cult (*ta koina*). The superintendents (*epimelētai*) shall inscribe on the pillar the name of him who owes this money to the goddess. The superintendents and the *hieropoioi* shall convene an assembly of the worshippers in the sanctuary to deliberate on common affairs on the second day of every month. Each of the *orgeōnes* who participates in the sanctuary shall give to the *hieropoioi* two drachmas for the sacrifice before the sixteenth day of Thargelion. But whoever is visiting Athens and is in good health but does not contribute this sum shall pay a fine of two drachmas dedicated to the goddess. So that the *orgeōnes* of the sanctuary may be as numerous as possible, it shall be permitted to anyone who wishes to take part in the sanctuary after paying the sum of [?] drachmas and to have himself inscribed thus on the pillar. Those so inscribed shall be scrutinized by the *orgeōnes*...   (*IG* [57] ii²: 1361)

Two categories of *orgeōnes* may therefore be distinguished, those worshipping heroes or heroines, and those worshipping gods or goddesses, usually of foreign extraction, such as Bendis (as here), the Great Mother (Phrygian Kybele), Dionysos or Holy Aphrodite.

Eranos

An *eranos* was a cultic association in which the ideas of reciprocity, equal contributions and mutual aid were central. Expressions of these notions ranged from a shared feast to a financial loan. The religious and social functions of an *eranos* were therefore indissociable.

Historical summary

It is sometimes hard to grasp the precise nuances which separate these groups one from another, not least because in point of ritual practice they are utterly indistinguishable. They owned and leased out land, they maintained their cult-buildings, they passed internal regulations and decreed honours to benefactors, they sought to preserve equality among their members. They were centres of sociability as much as of religious cult, and as such they played a crucial rôle in creating and confirming bonds of social solidarity. Citizens might belong to several different religious associations at once; the exception was to belong to none.

Study of these cultic associations as a vital milieu of Greek religious practice should not lead us to ignore the other functions that are sometimes, controversially, attributed to them. Most of these groups are attested as far back as the Archaic period, when they seem to have played a rôle in the creation of the Greek state that was more narrowly political as well as religious. That is not to say that their political importance declined in the Classical era, only that membership of them ceased to be a legal condition of attaining citizenship.

CONCLUSION

From the deme to the *koinon*, the principal communal structures of Greek religious life have now been surveyed in this chapter. The dominant impression we are left with is one of plagiarism. At every level of the village or the family group, the organization of these cultic associations was designed as a carbon-copy of the statewide organization. Assembly, officials, members, decrees, voting, local religious life, kinship relations – all were totally structured according to the forms governing the central admin-istration of the city. From this point of view it is hardly feasible to talk of local religious autonomy from statewide civic cult. Indeed, it might even be questioned whether the concept of 'private' cult still has any meaningful content (cf. introduction to chapter 7).

Over and above the *oikos*, the deme and the religious associ-ation there loomed the city, the community in its entirety. It was this which constituted the ultimate expression of Greek religion.

In the very process of its functioning the Greek city bore witness to the mutual implication of religion and politics, as it brought the citizens together to celebrate those great rituals, the religious festivals. Our task in the next two chapters will be to do justice to the complexity of the system within which those festivals were organized.

CHAPTER 9

Religion and political life

CITIES AND THEIR PATRON DEITIES

Every Greek city placed itself under the patronage of a god or goddess: Poseidon at Corinth, Hera at Argos, Zeus at Kos and Athene at Sparta, Tegea and Athens, to take just half-a-dozen cases. The patron divinity might bear an epithet that explicitly signalled his or her protective function, for example Polias ('Of the City') at Athens, Poliakhos ('City-holding') at Sparta; and sometimes mythical narratives told of a contest between gods for the patronage of a city. At Athens, for instance, the divine contestants were Athene and Poseidon: Athene won, but a compromise was later struck by granting both divinities space within the Erekhtheion temple on the Akropolis (see Appendix II).

Each city, too, had its heroes, sometimes founder-heroes or eponymous founder-heroes. Their cults, distinct from divine cult, had their own marked individuality from city to city, while heroic myths might also function as a way of conceptualizing the origins of a city's history (cf. chapter 13).

Religion, however, did more than just put a divine gloss on civic life. It impregnated each and every civic activity. As we saw in Part I, one of the Greek city's distinguishing marks was that it recognized no separation between the sacred and the profane, the religious and the secular, of the sort with which we are familiar. Such a dichotomy would have been meaningless to the Greeks, since in their view most human actions had a religious dimension. That was particularly the case with the collective undertakings of the community of citizens, some examples of which follow here.

THE FOUNDATION OF A CITY

Sometimes it is possible to follow in some detail the foundation of a city, as in the case of the so-called 'colonies' (*apoikiai*) founded during the Archaic period. The process involved religion in several ways. Before a site for the new settlement was chosen, the prospective founding city would consult an oracle. The sacred hearth of the new city was lit with fire taken from the hearth of the city providing the settlers. The tracing-out of the plan of the new town was preceded by sacrifices and prayers, and sacrifices were also performed after the construction of the principal buildings, which were usually oriented around an *agora* and the temple of the patron deity.

THE COMMON HEARTH (*HESTIA*)

The *hestia* of a city was located at its centre, just as the domestic hearth formed the heart of an *oikos*. Seat of the cult of the eponymous goddess Hestia, the civic hearth was often sited in the *prutaneion* or office of the city's magistrates. The flame that burned perpetually on Hestia's altar symbolized the vitality of the civic unit. Periodically it was relit from the altars that the Greeks considered to be the most pure, those of Apollo at Delphi or Delos. It was at the civic hearth that official foreign visitors, for example ambassadors, come to treat with the Council or Assembly, were received as guests and provided with a meal at public expense. The city similarly entertained those of its own citizens upon whom they had conferred the supreme honour of *sitēsis*. (Socrates optimistically demanded this honour from his judges in 399, but they decided that for him death was a more appropriate reward.)

ASSEMBLY AND LAWCOURTS

Public institutions could not function without religion. Meetings of the Assembly were opened by a sacrifice (at Athens of a piglet, whose blood was spattered over the presiding committee of the Council). 'Sacred affairs' were dealt with by the Assembly and taken first, in the presence solely of citizens. These included the consultation of oracles, the sending of sacred delegations (*theō-riai*) to the great festivals and the passing or revision of sacred laws (*hieroi nomoi*). The city's lawcourts had jurisdiction over disputes involving sacred property: at Athens, for instance, the Areiopagos council heard cases concerning damage to the sacred olive trees of Athene (e.g. Lysias VII); while impiety trials such as those of Alkibiades and Socrates were held in the popular jury-courts (*dikastēria*).

OFFICIALS

Before elected or allotted officials could take up a post at Athens they had to undergo a preliminary scrutiny (*dokimasia*) of their credentials. The questions they were asked included matters of religious cult: did they duly observe the worship of their familial Apollo Patrōos and domestic Zeus Herkeios? Once in office they regularly swore religious oaths (*horkoi*), as ordinary citizens did too when they entered on the *ephēbeia* (two years of 'national service') or acted as witnesses in a lawsuit, for instance. The procedure of oath-taking involved swearing on the victims of a sacrifice while intoning a formula that called on the gods to be witnesses and invoked divine punishment on perjurors. Some state officials' functions were partly or wholly religious (just as, *pari passu*, priests were quasi-officials: chapter 5). For example, at Athens the 'King' Arkhon had overall charge of the Eleusinian Mysteries and the Lenaia and Panathenaia festivals, directed civic sacrifices, and pronounced the religious interdict on those con-demned for impiety (*asebeia*). The Athenian Polemarkh con-ducted sacrifices to Artemis and supervised funerary games. On leaving office officials often made a dedication to the gods.

SACRED TREASURIES

The status of the Athenian exchequer or public treasury offers a good illustration of the interpenetration of religious and civic life in Classical Greece. Strictly speaking, the state of Athens had no public finances. The treasury was housed after 447 in the Parthe-non, under the protection and technically also in the ownership of Athene. But the city reserved to itself the right to utilize all the resources contained in sanctuaries for any sort of purpose, for example to finance a war. In the fifth century, from 454 onwards, one-sixtieth of the money-tribute paid by Athens' allies was devoted to Athene. This tribute-surplus and other funds were used to finance the public building programme on the Akropolis, which included the construction of the Parthenon itself (see Appendix II).

LITURGIES (*LEITOURGIAI*)

A liturgy in the technical Athenian sense (not to be confused with its modern meaning of a form of religious worship) was a compulsory financial obligation imposed on the richest Athenians and resident foreigners, the ancient equivalent of super-tax but far more honorific. Liturgies were of two main kinds, military (for Athenian citizens only) and cultic. A man liable for the liturgy of *triērarkhia* was obliged to equip and, officially, captain a warship (*triērēs*, trireme) for a year. Festival liturgies involved the financing of some aspect of the great civic festivals, for example a chorus in the dramatic competitions of the Great or City Dionysia (hence *khorēgia*) or a banquet at the Panathenaia (*hestiasis*). There were over one hundred such liturgies to be performed every year, and some rich men were more enthusiastic than others in fulfilling – or exceeding – their legal obligations, prompted by narrowly political as well as broader religious considerations.

ORACLES AND OTHER PORTENTS

Religious activity was a constant factor, not only in the functioning of institutions but also in daily political life. The most spectacular illustration of this is doubtless the consultation of oracles such as that of Apollo at Delphi before a city took any important decision, whether narrowly religious or not. But at a more humble level the Greek city was always appealing to diviners (*manteis*) and oracle-mongers (*khrēsmologoi*) for a preview of the future, an interpretation of a sacred law, or a reminder of traditional custom (cf. chapter 5). Before every military campaign and engagement diviners were charged with inspecting the entrails of sacrificial victims for any clue to the outcome of the fighting. In a famous episode during the Persian Wars, just before the battle of Plataia in 479, Pausanias and his pious Spartans stoically stood their ground under a hail of Persian arrows, refusing to advance to the fray until the sacrificial omens (*sphagia*) were propitious (Herodotus IX.61). Almost a hundred years later, at the very beginning of the fourth century, the advance of another Spartan commander was held up for no less than four days because the sacrifices (*hiera*) were considered unfavourable (Xenophon *Hellenica* III.1.17).

RELIGION AND PATRIOTISM

The question arises whether it is legitimate to talk of 'religious patriotism' and the exploitation of civic cults for the purpose of making political propaganda. Certainly, the conjunction of religion and partisan politics is clearly visible in several spheres. The cities competed with each other in interstate sanctuaries by means of rival buildings and offerings – the 'Treasuries' along the Sacred Way at Delphi are a good example; and in the international Games through the medium of the victors – for instance, any Athenian who won a crown at one of the Panhellenic Games (see chapter 11) received in perpetuity the signal honour of *sitēsis* in the *prutaneion*, a right that was inherited by his descendants. Cities also attempted to promote certain of their local cults to panhellenic status. Athens did this successfully with the Eleusinian Mysteries (chapter 11), but less so with the buildings and cults on the Akropolis (see next section), and least of all with the Panathenaia.

RELIGIOUS SPACE AND POLITICAL SPACE

The typically Greek amalgam of political function and religious function is most sharply perceptible in its physical manifestations. Two Athenian examples will serve to illustrate the various permutations. The Athenian **Agora** (literally, 'gathering-place', fig. 4) was the seat of numerous civic cults, a sanctuary precinct with its sacred enclosures, altars (fig. 5), tombs of heroes, and festivals. But at the same time it was the symbol of

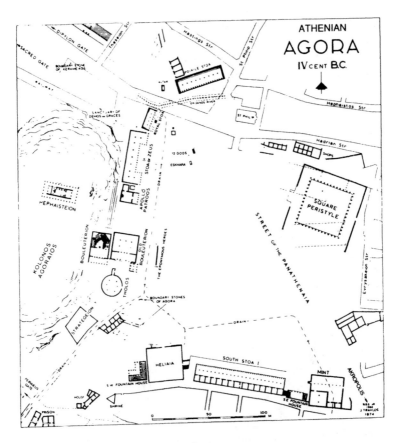

4   Athenian Agora, *c.* 300 BCE

the city of Athens' political activity; along its margins, therefore, there were eventually constructed all the buildings essential to the conduct of political life.

The history of the Athenian **Akropolis** bears more particularly on the question of religion and partisan politics raised in the previous section. It was a very ancient site of both habitation and religious cult, since at least the Mycenaean epoch (1600–1100). But the ordered arrangement of the sanctuaries on the Akropolis dates initially from the dictatorship of the 'tyrants' Peisistratos (545–28) and his eldest son Hippias (528–510). The same rulers added musical and athletic competitions to the old Panathenaic

5　Athenian Agora: altar of the Twelve Gods. Reconstruction drawing of the monument (first erected by the younger Peisistratos in the 520s BCE), taken as the point in Athens from which all distances in Attica were calculated

festival, making it famous throughout the Hellenic world. In short, the glory of Athens from the middle of the sixth century onwards would seem to be inseparably linked to a programme of religious politics. Caution, however, is required, since the intentions attributed to the tyrants by much later historians smack more of ideological construction than historical authenticity. As for the modifications of the Akropolis effected under the democracy, their historicity is undeniable, but what were their meaning and consequences?

The Akropolis was destroyed by the invading Persians in 480, and again in 479. The buildings of the Archaic era were not restored, and what survives to this day are the ruins of the Classical age, the Parthenon, the Propylaia, the temple of Athene Nikē and the Erekhtheion, which were all conceived and constructed during the second half of the fifth century (see Appendix II). But how did the Athenians themselves see the new buildings? The long description of the Parthenon sculptures in Appendix II may make it possible to grasp precisely how their iconographic programme expressed the mentality of the Athenians of the Periklean age (for once, 'Periklean' does seem to be exactly the right epithet, since he was so closely involved in the Akropolis building project). From the pediment to the metopes and frieze, themes peculiar to the mythical and real history of the Athenians were interlaced with traditional themes of mythology common to all Greeks. There are other cities for which we possess comparable sculptural complexes, but their historical context is less well known to us. Here in the Parthenon sculptures we can see better than in any other city the imprint of a civic ideology, that same ideology which was in play in the tragedies and comedies staged during the Dionysia festival (chapter 10).

Plutarch later commented in his *Life of Perikles* (12.1): 'What caused the greatest pleasure to the Athenians and contributed most to adorning their city, what most forcibly struck the imagination of foreign visitors, what alone proves that the ancient reports of Athenian power and prosperity are not lies, are the monuments that Perikles had constructed.' Should we say, then, that the Parthenon was essentially a monument to the glory of Athenian imperialism? That in our view would be to go a step too far. Caution dictates restraint. It is wise not to overinterpret documents of any kind, especially figural representations, which in any case speak a language of their own (cf. chapter 14). Still, whatever were in reality the deep-seated reasons behind the Parthenon, or the Akropolis building programme as a whole, there is no denying Plutarch's further claim that 'the monuments rose up, of an imposing size, of inimitable beauty and grace. The craftsmen strove to outdo each other by the technical perfection of their work' (*ibid.* 13.1).

WAR AND INTERSTATE TREATIES

In this chapter we have so far described only certain aspects of the mutual implication of political life and religious cult in the functioning of a Greek city. Other aspects meriting attention include the conduct of war and the establishing of peaceful relations between states.

Interstate treaties were as a rule guaranteed by the oaths sworn by the respective parties. These were the ancient, religious equivalent of our wholly secular signatures. Since the oath had a sacral value, it was accompanied either by a libation or by a sacrifice. It had binding force for the oath-taker, inasmuch as the gods were the guarantors of its observance (although, needless to say, this did not prevent breaches of treaties, alleged or genuine).

Military campaigns were the occasion for numerous rituals. Portents had to be interpreted, oracles consulted, sacrifices performed, and paeans sung. Victory necessitated rituals of thanksgiving, including the erection of a battlefield trophy (our word comes from the Greek *tropaion*) in honour of Zeus Tropaios or of Nikē, the goddess Victory herself. Such trophies began life as simple affairs, the staking of captured arms and armour to the trunk of a tree; but they came to acquire monumental form, as for example in the still largely extant stone memorial marking the famous victory of the Thebans under Epameinondas over the supposedly invincible Spartans at Leuktra in Boiotia in 371. Back home, finally, it was not unusual for a city to consecrate to a god in a sanctuary some part of the captured booty, in the form of a statue, perhaps, or a building that permanently commemorated a victory. Thus the Treasury of the Athenians along the Sacred Way at Delphi memorialized their victory over the Persians at

Marathon in 490. In short, the Greeks' ideas of warfare were permeated with what we would call religion.

CONCLUSION

We entitled this chapter 'Religion and *political* life' and not 'Religion and civic life' for one simple reason: it seems to us to be difficult to separate out those of the city's cults that are specifically and exclusively 'civic', and to isolate certain cultic practices as expressing civic communality better than others, while at the same time trying to demonstrate that the constant reference-point of every religious attitude was precisely the city. The expression 'civic cult' is therefore for us synonymous with the totality of the city's cultic practices.

By the same token, it seems to us not to the purpose to pass judgement on the spiritual content of these cults. Frequently in conventional histories of religion one reads that civic cult was but a shell without a living body or soul, that it was spiritually unsatisfying for anyone who yearned for intimate communion with the divine, that although it continued to function until the end of the Greek cities' history it did so with increasing inefficiency, like the grinding of worn gears, and that there developed alongside it more vital forms of religious belief and practice. However, to write in those terms presupposes that one has a clear idea of what religion meant for the Greeks, and more particularly that one imagines the Greeks' relationship to the divine to be comparable to that experienced by believers in a monotheistic and individualistic religion like Christianity. All such pronouncements on 'civic cult' are the product of a particular tendency within 'the history of religion', and assertions of that nature hardly help us to understand the functioning and efficacy of a system of cults within a society as different from ours as was that of ancient Greece.

CHAPTER 10

The festival system: the Athenian case

SACRED CALENDARS

Festivals in honour of the gods (*heortai* was the most general of several words used) gave a rhythm to the political and everyday life of the city. In many cities the order of the festivals was fixed in accordance with written documents generally called sacred calendars. These were lists of festivals grouped by months of the year and days of the month. In chapter 8 we looked at some Attic deme-calendars; here we shall be concerned with the festival calendar of the Athenian state as such.

This calendar, in the form in which we know it in the Classical period, dated from the time of Solon (early sixth century). It was an integral part of his lawgiving. Almost two centuries later, at the very end of the fifth century, the city commissioned a certain Nikomakhos (who was exceptionally granted citizenship despite being allegedly the son of a public slave) to reduce to order the calendar of state sacrifices. The task was duly completed and the text was inscribed on a wall within the Stoa Basileios (office of the King Arkhon) in the Agora, though Nikomakhos was still prosecuted for his pains (Lysias xxx). Only fragments of this Great Calendar of Sacrifices survive, but by combining these with other sources it is possible to reconstruct a complete Athenian festival calendar month by month (Table 1), though uncertainties of detail remain; there was, however, no popular festival in Maimakterion.

The Athenians, like the Jews among others, worked with a lunisolar calendar, attempting by various means, especially inter-

Table 1. *Principal Athenian festivals*

Festival	Month and day	Divinity
Kronia	Hekatombaion 12	Kronos
Synoikia	Hekatombaion 15–16	Athene
Panathenaia	Hekatombaion 21–9 (?)	Athene
Eleusinia	Metageitnion (?) [4 days]	Demeter
Niketeria	Boedromion 2	
Plataia	Boedromion 3	
Genesia	Boedromion 5	Gē
Artemis Agrotera	Boedromion 6	Artemis
Demokratia	Boedromion 12	
Eleusinia	Boedromion 15–17, 19–21	Demeter
Pyanopsia	Pyanopsion 7	Apollo
Theseia	Pyanopsion 8	Theseus
Stenia	Pyanopsion 9	Demeter
Thesmophoria	Pyanopsion 11–13	Demeter
Khalkeia	Pyanopsion 30	Athene
Apatouria	Pyanopsion (?)	
Oskhophoria	Pyanopsion (?)	Athene
	[Maimakterion]	
Haloa	Poseideion 26	Demeter
Theogamia	Gamelion 2	Hera
Lenaia	Gamelion 12–15	
Anthesteria	Anthesterion 11–13	Dionysos
Diasia	Anthesterion 23	Zeus
Asklepieia	Elaphebolion 8	Asklepios
City Dionysia	Elaphebolion 10–14	Dionysos
Delphinia	Mounikhion 6	Apollo
Mounikhia	Mounikhion 16	Artemis
Olympieia	Mounikhion 19	Zeus
Thargelia	Thargelion 6–7	Apollo
Bendideia	Thargelion 19	Bendis
Plynteria	Thargelion 25	Athene
Kallynteria	Thargelion (?)	
Arrhetophoria	Skirophorion 3	Athene
Skira	Skirophorion 12	Demeter
Dipolieia/Bouphonia	Skirophorion 14	Zeus

calation, to reconcile the disparate solar and lunar years, and to keep the calendar in step with the seasons. (If Aristophanic humour is to be taken seriously, the King Arkhons did not always do the most efficient job in this respect: see *Clouds* 619–23, dated 423.) The twelve lunar months were named after various divini-

Table 2. *Festivals in Hekatombaion*

Day	Festival
1	Noumenia
2	Agathos Daimon
3	Athene
4	Herakles, Hermes, Aphrodite and Erōs
6	Artemis
7	Apollo (in this month Athenians celebrated the *annual* Hekatombaia)
8	Poseidon and Theseus
11	Stated meeting of Assembly
12	Kronia
15	Biennial sacrifice
16	Synoikia
17–18	Sacrifice by *orgeōnes*
21	Sacrifices to Kourotrophos by Erkhia deme only
22	Stated meeting of Council of 500
23	Meeting of a private religious association
28	Chief day of Panathenaia

ties or festivals, differently in different cities. The Athenians' year was deemed to begin in mid-summer, the dead season of the agricultural year, and the months of their year do not coincide precisely with ours: Hekatombaion, the first, began in roughly mid-July and ended in roughly mid-August, and so on. In the Athenian calendar certain festivals were celebrated every month, others only annually. If monthly festivals and annual festivals are combined, a total of 120 days each year counted as festival-days for the Athenians, more than for any other Greek state.

Table 2 sets out the festival-calendar for one month by way of illustration; the first seven days listed were all days of monthly festivals.

These two tables give a good idea of the complexity and diversity of Athenian civic cults. Space forbids a detailed study of the festivals one by one, so we shall aim rather to bring out their general characteristics by taking certain specific examples such as the Panathenaia and the Great (or City) Dionysia. The principal moments of any festival were the procession, the sacrifice with its ensuing festal banquet, and the competitions or other ancillary features.

PROCESSION (POMPĒ)

The procession often occupied the first day of a festival. It wended its way through the city from a fixed starting-point to the sanctuary of the divine honorand, following an identical route every time. Its organization was laid down in advance, the components differing from festival to festival. The following two examples illustrate some of the possible variations.

Every four years at the Great Panathenaia, on Hekatombaion 28, the Panathenaic procession left from the Dipylon Gate, crossed the Kerameikos (Potters' Quarter) and the Agora, and entered the Akropolis through the Propylaia. It then proceeded the length of the Parthenon and finished up at the east end of the temple in front of the great altar of Zeus and Athene. It thus passed through the city's most vital points, the Agora (heart of political life) and Akropolis (its spiritual crown). Certain sequences of the procession are represented in the Parthenon frieze (Appendix II), the interpretation of which is aided (but not entirely resolved) by literary sources. The procession directly involved several sections of the citizen population: young warriors (hoplites and cavalrymen), old men, and daughters of citizens acting as Ergastinai (weavers of the *peplos*, the robe worn by Athene's olive-wood cult-statue) and Kanephoroi (basket-bearers). Resident aliens too were allotted a rôle, they and their sons carrying trays of offerings (Skaphēphoroi), their wives jars of water (Hydriaphoroi), and their daughters parasols (Skiadēphoroi). Perhaps even some of the unfree population were allowed to process. Certainly, foreigners were included, notably in the fifth century the representatives of the allied states in Athens' anti-Persian naval ?lliance, since they were treated as honorary colonists of Athens. And then of course there were the non-human participants, the cows destined for sacrifice.

The formal object of this solemn procession was to convey Athene's new *peplos*, saffron-dyed and embroidered with scenes of Athene's exploits in combat with the Giants, to the King Arkhon for him to place on Athene's *xoanon* in (eventually) the Erekhtheion (Appendix II). But it also allowed the city of Athens to display spectacularly both the hierarchy of its political organization and the unity in diversity of its population as a whole. This spectacle was aimed as much at the rest of the Athenian people as at the allied representatives present and the Greek world at large.

The procession – or rather processions – of the Great or City Dionysia were rather different. Shortly before the festival, the statue of Dionysos Eleuthereus was removed from its sanctuary at the foot of the Akropolis near the theatre and transported in procession to a temple near the Academy *gymnasion* (public exercise-ground) on the way to Eleutherai (on the borders of Attica and Boiotia). Later it was returned to its original sanctuary, whence it was taken in a new procession on the first day of the festival proper, Elaphebolion 10, to the *orkhēstra* in the middle of the theatre. The route followed is not certain, but it seems to have been a procession of conventional type, involving civic officials, representatives of different categories of the city's residents, impresarios for the plays (*khorēgoi*) dressed in their finery, bearers of offerings or of model phalli, and numerous sacrificial bulls (see p. 30). There followed a great sacrifice and banquet.

The other procession of the central day of the festival was called the *kōmos* (revel, rout), and this with its much less formal atmosphere lived up to its name. It took place at the end of the day, probably immediately after the banquet. Men carrying lighted torches and accompanied by players of *auloi* ran through the streets singing and dancing, enacting on a city-wide scale the revel (also called *kōmos*) that followed a private drinking party (*sumposion*).

The functions of these procession rituals were many and various. One was publicity: the reason for the festival was broadcast, and an invitation to join in was extended to all along the way. Other functions included renewal, a reactivation of the benefactions and virtues of the god whose statue was sometimes carried, and a reaffirmation of the sanctity of the different sites where the crowd halted, especially altars. Speaking generally, the procession served as a symbolic reappropriation of the city's space by the community. To those functions common to all processions may be added those that were specific to the festivals we have considered above. The Panathenaic procession, for example, was intended by the Classical Athenian city to give a visual representation of its unity and power and to embed its religious practice within the civic space. Every festival, we are reminded finally, was a complex system of rituals that cannot be reduced to a single interpretation.

THE SACRIFICE

Without rehearsing everything we have said earlier about the details and meanings of sacrifice in general (chapter 4), it will bear restating here that the sacrifice was a powerful ritual moment, present in every festival of the Athenian calendar. The number of the sacrificial victims, known to us through the accounts of the Treasurers of Athene, gives us a material measure of the importance of the post-sacrificial feasts. The sacrifice of a hecatomb (one hundred beasts, hence the month-name Heka-tombaion) was frequent, and the figure could rise to over two hundred victims for a single festival. The city bore the cost of these sacrifices, either directly or, as is attested for the Pan-athenaia and Dionysia, by imposing the liturgy of *hestiasis* on rich men (chapter 9). At the Panathenaia the distribution of the sacrificial meat was made in the Kerameikos among those demes-men who had participated in the procession and sacrifice.

A look down the Athenian monthly calendar (Table 1) shows that, with the apparent exception of Maimakterion, not a month passed without a massive slaughtering of beasts. A city at festival time was thus also a city that reeked with the smells of spilt animal blood and roasted or boiled animal meat, and resounded with the noise of a community eating meat, drinking wine, and making merry.

COMPETITIONS (*AGŌNES*)

Not every festival had a competition attached to it, but every competition was part of a religious festival. It is worth remem-bering that the Greeks invented the ideas of both competitive athletic games and the theatre within the (to us) alien context of religion. We shall take as our illustration of the former the Panathenaic Games, of the latter the Great Dionysia.

The Panathenaia festival had long been celebrated when, in 566, an attempt was made by Athens to produce a rival to the great Panhellenic festivals of the Olympic, Pythian, Nemean and

Isthmian Games, which had been organized into an interlocking circuit (*periodos*) in the previous decade. The attempt did not fully succeed. The Panathenaic Games remained more Athenian than Greek, although the competitions, held every fourth year during the Great Panathenaia, were opened to all Greeks. They included a contest for rhapsodes (reciters of Homeric epic verse), musical competitions of various sorts, and athletic events of the usual kinds (see the Olympics in chapter 11).

Competitors in the latter were males only and divided into three groups by age: children (up to eighteen), young men and older men. Apart from glory, they competed also for material prizes, the peculiarly Athenian Panathenaic amphoras filled with oil specially pressed from Athene's sacred olives. On one side of a Panathenaic amphora was depicted, always in the black-figure silhouette technique, Athene brandishing a sword, and alongside her an inscription that read 'Of the games (*athla*) from Athens'. On the reverse there was a scene of the particular event (chariot-race, race in armour, etc.) for which the amphora was the prize – or rather part of the prize: the winner of the boys' running race, for example, received fifty amphoras. At the Olympics all events were for individuals only, but the Panathenaic Games also included team-competitions: the dance in armour called the Pyrrhikhē, for which the prize was an ox and 100 drachmas, a torch-race, and even rowing-races (held off Cape Sounion).

FESTIVAL AND THEATRE

The Great or City Dionysia held in Elaphebolion (March–April) included three or more days of dramatic competitions. Like the Panathenaia, these attracted a wider public than just the resident Athenian population. The origins of drama are a horribly complex and controversial issue; without delving into them, we may point out that at Athens all drama (included in the Rural Dionysia in Poseideion and the Lenaia in Gamelion as well as in the Great Dionysia) was staged in honour of Dionysos. His statue stood in the *orkhēstra*, the circular space (perhaps modelled on a threshing-floor) where the chorus performed; the theatre, at first built of wood, later (from the 330s) of stone, was set within his sacred precinct; and the plays were integrated within the rituals of Dionysiac cult. The function of drama at Athens in the Classical period is another issue too complex to broach here (see further chapter 12), but some essential points that illustrate the integration of religion in civic life should be underlined.

Of the three Athenian play-festivals in honour of Dionysos the Great Dionysia was by far the most important. Competitions were held in tragedy, satyr-drama and comedy, and there was also a competition for choruses singing the special Dionysiac hymn called dithyramb. Over 1,000 Athenian citizens altogether took part as performers every year. The organization of the festival was in the charge of the Eponymous Arkhon, not the King, since this was a relative newcomer to the Athenian festival calendar. It was he who selected the poet-playwrights whose plays were to be performed, who saw to the allocation of the principal actors (*prōtagonistai*), and who appointed the impresarios (*khorēgoi*) to fulfil the liturgy of equipping and maintaining a chorus, and he finally who presided over the judging of the various keenly contested competitions.

The theatre programme began at daybreak. The spectators were in festival garb, wearing wreaths on their heads; the distinguished citizens who had been awarded front-seat precedence (*proedria*) were sitting in the front row, together with members of the Council of 500, the ephebes and the specially selected judges. A ritual purification was carried out with the blood of a sacrificed piglet, and the order of competitors was drawn up by lot. Plays went on one after the other until dusk. At the end of the whole competition three prizes had to be decided in each category of drama, for best playwright, best *khorēgos* and best actor. The following day an Assembly meeting was held, actually in the theatre (which could hold many more people than the Pnyx), to check the officials' accounts, vote honours and record the results.

The interpenetration of religion and civic life in the Great Dionysia was not confined to the organization of the festival. The plays themselves, by the themes they treated and the way they treated them, demonstrated the seamless connection between Athenian political thought and dramatic representation of myth and the gods. To put it succinctly, even though the characters of the dramas were gods, heroes or mythical figures – such as Athene, Ajax and Oedipus, or the Erinyes (Furies) – the questions raised by the plots were central to political debate in democratic Athens.

CONCLUSION

The Athenian festival-calendar, a veritable religious system, is but one example of how the Greeks organized their civic cults. But it does provide a very concrete illustration of the precise functions that festival rituals fulfilled and of the inseparability of festivals from the very definition of Greek civic life. As a microcosm of this macro-system we offer in conclusion an extract from a (substantially restored) decree of the later fourth century, governing the celebration, not of the four-yearly Great Panathenaia, but of the ordinary, annual Lesser Panathenaia:

So that with piety [...] annually, and that the procession in honour of Athene in the name of the Athenian people may be organized in the best way possible each year, and that all the necessary administrative measures relating to the festival celebrated in honour of the Goddess may be taken for always by the *hieropoioi*, let the people decree in all other respects in accordance with the Council's recommendation but adding the amendment that the *hieropoioi* shall offer as in the past two sacrifices, one to Athene Hygieia, the other in the ancient temple, that they shall distribute to the *prutaneis* five parts of meat, to the nine Arkhons three parts, to the Treasurers of the Goddess one part, to the *hieropoioi* one part, to the Generals and Taxiarkhs three parts, to the Athenian members of the procession and to the Kanephoroi as usual, and the rest of the meat to Athenian citizens; that, after having bought the sacrificial cattle with the forty-one minai raised from the new lease by agreement with those responsible for the purchase, they should immediately after the procession sacrifice these beasts near the Great Altar of Athene, keeping one of the finest for the altar of Athene Nikē; that, once the sacrifices to Athene Polias and Athene Nikē have been accomplished, they shall distribute to the Athenian People in the Kerameikos the meat of the beasts bought with the forty-one minai, as in other distributions of meat, and they shall distribute the portions by demes in proportion to the numbers of demesmen participating in the procession; that for the expenses of the procession, for the cooking, for the preparation of the great altar, for the other expenses of the festival and of the all-night celebrations (*pannukhis*), they shall be given fifty drachmas; that the *hieropoioi* appointed to run the annual Panathenaia shall celebrate the *pannukhis* in the finest way possible, in honour of the

Goddess; that they shall get the procession underway at sunrise, punishing in conformity with the laws those who do not obey orders . . .

(IG [57] ii²: 334)

CHAPTER 11

The Panhellenic cults

GENERAL FEATURES

So far in this book the emphasis has been placed squarely upon the tight nexus between religious and civic life, as we have been attempting to show how all citizens were enmeshed in the network of festivals and rituals through which they were integrated into the civic community. But the emergence of the city as a state-form and way of life was also contemporary with a truly original and highly consequential religious phenomenon, namely the appearance and development in several parts of Greece of *inter*state sanctuaries – sanctuaries, that is, whose influence and catchment-area exceeded the limits of the individual city. These served as places of meeting and exchange for Greeks coming from the farthest reaches of the Hellenic world. It was no coincidence that in this same epoch, the second half of the eighth century, the first wave of overseas migration from the Greek heartland began, chiefly to Magna Graecia (south Italy) and Sicily.

In 'Old Greece' there was now a sharp increase in archaeological sites yielding votive deposits of valuable objects – painted pottery and terracotta figurines to begin with, then objects of bronze, jewellery, and finally arms and armour. The surplus wealth that had formerly been reserved for destruction in aristocratic burials was now being diverted to the greater glory of the gods, especially those of Olympia, Delphi, Dodona and Delos, all sites which were destined to experience a Panhellenic florescence. The birth of the interstate sanctuary in the eighth century provided for centuries to come a focal assembly-point around which Greek identity could be affirmed through common religious cult as much as through common language (cf. Herodotus VIII.144.2).

In terms of their spatial layout these interstate sanctuaries were initially vast architectural complexes, located outside the immediate purlieu of a town. Around the temples and altars there arose various sorts of buildings such as the 'treasuries' set up by states or grateful individuals to receive offerings, or banqueting halls, or dormitories for overnight visitors. A *peribolos* wall delimited the sacred area. Beyond that extended the spaces set aside for the competitions in running, horse-racing and gymnastic events (see below).

What these interstate sanctuaries had in common was their Panhellenic character, since they were open to all Greeks, and for a long time only to Greeks. As a function of their respective cults and presiding deities they developed their own individual religious profiles, although several forms of cultic life could happily coexist in a single sanctuary. During the festival period, which might extend for as much as a week, considerable crowds would gather from all four corners of the Hellenic world and beyond, perhaps as many as 40,000 in the Classical stadium at Olympia, not to mention all the fringe hangers-on and fellow-travellers. Later, following the Roman conquest of Greece, non-Greeks too were allowed to participate as competitors.

These vast gatherings (*panēgureis* was the technical term) were facilitated, and sometimes indeed only made possible, by the declaration of a sacred truce (*ekekheiria*), a suspension specifically of the military hostilities that were all too regular a feature of Greek inter-city life. These truces were announced by sacred ambassadors (*theōroi* from Delphi, *spondophoroi* from Olympia and Athens) who travelled the Greek world from city to city enjoying lavish hospitality and usually inviolability (in 367 the Athenian *spondophoroi* for the Eleusinian Mysteries were seized in Aitolia 'contrary to the laws common to the Greeks': Harding 1985 [65]: 54, line 14). The truces covered the period required for the participants to congregate for the festival and return safely home. Again, they usually served their purpose, and Panhellenic sanctuaries for the most part retained their autonomy. But there were numerous politically motivated struggles for control, as between the Eleians and Arkadians over Olympia, Argos and Sparta over the Isthmian Games, and several states on several occasions over Delphi; once, indeed, in 364, fighting actually spilled into the sacred precinct at Olympia (Xenophon, *Hellenica* VII.4.28–32).

The *panēguris* was first and foremost a religious assembly, placed under the sign of the god or gods who controlled the sanctuary. The festival period was inaugurated by a solemn procession and one or more sacrifices to bind the participants together in communion; it was punctuated and closed by further rituals and sacrifices. The smooth functioning of the whole affair was assured by boards of priests assisted by numerous staff specially recruited for the occasion. Often these priests enjoyed a hereditary, aristocratic privilege. Delphi was unique in that its management was in the hands of a permanent religious league of states in central Greece, called the Amphiktiony because the states were located 'around the sanctuary'. Despite the struggles for control already mentioned, which are somewhat misleadingly known as 'sacred wars', the Delphic Amphiktiony for centuries ensured the continuous celebration of the Pythian Games every four years.

COMPETITIVE GAMES (*AGŌNES*)

The games which pitched Greek competitors against each other at regular intervals on the running track (*stadion*, whence our 'stadium') or racecourse (*hippodromos*) have often been regarded as a legacy from Homeric times; consider the funeral games of Patroklos at Troy described in *Iliad* XXIII (which had a real counterpart in those of Amphidamas on Euboia in which Hesiod competed: *Works and Days* 654–7), or those held in honour of Odysseus on Phaiakia in *Odyssey* VIII. They did, undoubtedly, encapsulate aristocratic values, but it was the whole city, not just aristocrats, which identified itself with the victory of one of its citizens at the Panhellenic games. From the beginning of the sixth century cities began to build special exercise-grounds (*gumnasia*) to encourage local athletes, and the honours they showered on home-town victors (at Athens, for example, not just a one-off 'civic reception' but lifetime dining-rights in the *prutaneion* both for the victor and for his descendants) testify to the value placed on competition and competitiveness (*agōnia*, whence our 'agony') by Greek civic ideology.

At Olympia, Delphi, Corinth and Nemea competitors and spectators gathered regularly according to a fixed four-year cycle (*periodos*, literally 'circuit') to participate in the Olympic, Pythian, Isthmian and Nemean Games, in honour respectively of Zeus (Olympia and Nemea), Apollo Pythios (Delphi) and Poseidon (at the Isthmus of Corinth). The Olympics were celebrated every four years at the height of summer (July–August), probably at the second full moon after the summer solstice, the Pythian Games in the third year of an Olympiad (a four-year period, e.g., 420–417, so in 418) towards the end of summer (August–September), the Isthmian and Nemean Games every two years, alternating with the Olympics and Pythians (e.g. 419, 417), in the spring. The same competitors might therefore compete successively at all the games in a cycle and, should they have been victorious, gain the glorious title of 'Circuit-victor' (*periodonikēs*). One such was Theogones of Thasos, a prodigious wrestler of the early fifth century whose *mana* earned him not only numerous honorific statues but also posthumous promotion to the status of hero-healer and recipient of religious worship.

The glory (*kleos*) promised to victors was that celebrated by Pindar of Thebes in his commissioned epinician ('victory') odes. In these *Olympians*, *Pythians*, *Isthmians* and *Nemeans* the victor's name was linked to that of the gods and heroes whose myths Pindar related (often giving them his own special twist). There are, for example, twelve Pythian odes, of which the first seven commemorate victors in the four-horse chariot-race, the 'blue-riband' event in the athletic competitions (though the victors did not actually drive their chariots themselves). The most successful of the victors hymned by Pindar was Hieron, tyrant of Syracuse, whose chariot won at the Pythian Games of 470 after two previous chariot victories there and a third victory won by his aptly-named stallion Pherenikos ('Victory-bringer'). Pindar's *First Pythian* thus commemorates the tyrant at the apogee of his fame, but it is also an eloquent moral and religious tract, setting before the honorand a model of comportment both for himself as sovereign ruler and for the new city of Aitna that he had just founded in Sicily. 'Only the glory of fame which they leave behind them/Proclaims men's way of life, when they die,/ In history and in song' (*Pythian* 1.93–5, trans. C. M. Bowra).

In the other five *Pythians* victors of more modest social background are celebrated; in theory, at least, the competition made available to all the glory promised to a monarch. Thus the *Eleventh Pythian*, for instance, is dedicated to a young fellow-Theban called Thrasydaios, who had won the boys' stade race (roughly 200 metres) in 474 (or 454). Pindar chooses to present him and his father as paradigms of the middling citizen:

> God help me to love beauty, yet desire
> What I may have, among men of my age.
> Having seen that the middle fortune in a city
> Abounds longer in bliss, I have no use
> For the state of tyrants.
> (*Pythian* XI.52–4, trans. C. M. Bowra)

OLYMPIA: SANCTUARY AND GAMES

The sanctuary of Zeus Olympios was situated in a fertile plain in the northwest Peloponnese, within the territory usually controlled in historical times by the city of Elis. The plain is traversed by the river Alpheios, the longest perennial river in the Peloponnese, and dotted with hills. It was at the foot of one of these, sacred to Kronos, that the sanctuary lay. The site had been occupied since the middle of the second millennium, but the sanctuary (in its original, pre-Panhellenic form) was a creation of the Dark Age, probably of the tenth century. The sacred enclosure, the *hieron*, was known as Altis after a sacred wood. It harboured the worship of several gods and goddesses, chiefly Hera and Zeus. The plentiful dedications of the Geometric and Archaic periods (*c.* 900–500) testify to the vitality of the sanctuary, whose fame grew as a result of the organization of the Games. Each generation witnessed the construction of new buildings, until by the end of the Classical period the Altis had achieved a considerable degree of complexity (fig. 6).

Two strands of foundation-myths for the sanctuary and the Games can be disentangled, one woven around a king of nearby Pisa, Oinomaos, his daughter Hippodameia and her suitor

6   The Altis at Olympia, c. 300 BCE

Pelops, the other around Herakles. Oinomaos was said to have imposed as a test on all his daughter's suitors a chariot-race against himself; but he always won, thanks to the divine horses given him by his father Ares, and the defeated claimants were summarily executed. Pelops, however, triumphed over his would-not-be father-in-law, owing to a winning combination of Hippodameia's love and the sabotaging of Oinomaos' chariot by his own driver Myrtilos. Oinomaos was thrown and killed, and Pelops (eponym of the Peloponnese, 'island of Pelops') married his Hippodameia and became king of Pisa. The Olympic rôle of Herakles, according to myth, was to mark out the sanctuary's boundary and found the games after accomplishing one of the famous Twelve Labours, namely his cleansing of the stables of bad King Augeias of Elis by diverting the course of the Alpheios.

The Olympic Games were traditionally first organized, or reorganized, in 776 and held every four years thereafter. This was a date used much later by the Greeks as an era to measure time and situate events (an event was said to have occurred in such-and-such year of such-and-such Olympiad; e.g., Sparta was barred from the Games by Elis in the first year of the 90th Olympiad, what we call '420'). But many modern scholars are inclined to doubt whether anything that could properly be called Panhellenic Games was held before the seventh century at the earliest. However, what cannot be doubted is that, once established as part of the 'Circuit', the Games continued uninterruptedly every four years until CE 394, when they were shut down for good by imperial edict of the Christian Roman emperor Theodosius I. The religious origins of the games, too, are still much debated among modern scholars, some (looking to Patroklos' games in the *Iliad*, for example) considering them to be an element of funerary ritual, others seeing them as agricultural, yet others as initiatory. We shall concentrate rather on their organization in the Classical period.

Before the festival of Zeus Olympios proper began, there was a long preparatory period, not confined to Olympia itself. In their cities the athletes, all Greek citizens, went into training, which they completed at Olympia under the eyes of the ten Eleian judges called *Hellanodikai* ('Judges of the Greeks'), who had overall responsibility for enforcing the rules. The sacred truce was announced throughout the Greek world by the *spondophoroi* (see above), so that competitors and other intending participants (official and unofficial visitors were alike called *thēoroi*), free or slave, Greek or non-Greek, might take advantage of the temporary *asulia* (freedom from reprisals: see chapter 6).

The festival lasted six days. The first was devoted to a variety of religious rituals including sacrifices at the great ash-altar of Zeus (which was composed of a mixture of sacrificial débris and water from the Alpheios, and had reached a height of seven metres by the time Pausanias saw it in the late second century CE) and other altars in the Altis. The athletes swore an oath to conduct themselves honourably, and the Hellanodikai declared the Games officially open.

The following days were given over to the several events, thirteen in all. Ten were for adults only (all competitors had to be male; women, apart from the priestess of Hera, were not even permitted to watch): *stadion* (192.27 metres = one stade), *diaulos* (two stades), *dolikhos* (long-distance, twenty-four stades), *hoplitodromos* (race in heavy armour), *pentathlon* (discus, standing jump, javelin, *stadion*, wrestling), wrestling, boxing, chariot-race, horse-race, and *pankration* (boxing, wrestling and judo combined, and almost no holds barred). Boys competed in the junior *stadion*, wrestling and boxing. The *stadion* was the senior race in two senses, being both the oldest and the most prestigious of the unaided, individual events: the winner of this received the title *Olympionikēs* and the whole Olympiad was known thenceforth as 'So-and-so's Olympiad'. The judgement of the Hellanodikai was considered sacred and therefore unquestionably final; no one, not even a distinguished Spartan like Likhas (Thucydides v.50), was immune from disqualification and a humiliating whipping at their hands.

On the sixth and last day the victors received their prize, a crown of wild olive leaves picked from trees growing in the Altis and decorated with ribbons. Victors and priests processed before the altars, sang and sacrificed. A great banquet was then served to them in the *prutaneion*.

That was the official end of the festival but further honours and ceremonies were in store for the victors. At Olympia itself they might be permitted to erect a statue, and it was commissions from this source that enabled sculptors to make great strides in the study and representation of the human body. They dedicated their olive-wreath crown in the Temple of Zeus and sacrificed to Hera (whose temple had originally been shared by Zeus, before the Eleians erected for him in the 460s and 450s a magnificent structure that later housed Pheidias' wondrous chryselephantine cult-statue). Then, their home city might organize a triumphal return, even going to the lengths of knocking down a stretch of the city wall to admit the victor, clad in purple and riding a chariot pulled by four white horses, and granting him the right to erect a statue in the city's *agora* or in a sanctuary. At Athens, as we have seen, the city's reward was *sitēsis*, one of the greatest honours it had to bestow.

The significance of these honours lay in a variety of factors. Since victory was regarded as a gift of the gods, a victor was considered to be a divine favourite and endowed with certain numinous qualities. Moreover, a citizen's victory cast its lustre over his city as a whole, and Greek cities competed fiercely with each other through the medium of their prize athletes. Competition (*agōn*) was the most highly esteemed method of measuring oneself against others, precisely because the gods themselves sanctioned it.

The odes of Pindar are, once again, the best way of gaining an understanding of these values. We quoted earlier from a couple of the *Pythian Odes*; here now is an excerpt from the ode he wrote for Alkimedon of Aigina, winner of the boys' wrestling at Olympia in 460:

> Mother of the gold-crowned Games,
> Olympia, queen of truth,
> Where diviners interpret burnt offerings
> And test the bright thunderer Zeus
> If he has any word about men
> Who long in their hearts to win great glory
> And a respite after toil.
>
> In return for reverence
> Men's prayers are fulfilled.
> O shady sanctuary of Pisa, by the wooded banks of Alpheios,
> Welcome this company and wearing of garlands.

Great is his glory for ever
Whom your glittering prize rewards.
To each man come different goods, and many
Are the paths of success
When the Gods lend aid ...

And Alkimedon by Kronion [Hill of Kronos]
Zeus made an Olympian conqueror.
He was lovely to see, and his deeds
Did not dishonour his beauty,
When he won in the wrestling and proclaimed
His fatherland, long-oared Aigina.
There Saviour Themis [Right] is honoured
At the side of Zeus, the strangers' god.
(*Olympian* VIII.1–14, 17–23, trans. C. M. Bowra,
modified)

DIVINATION AND ORACLES: THE CASE OF DELPHI

Delphi, home of the quadrennial Pythian Games, differed from Olympia, first, in that alongside the athletics it staged a musical competition of great antiquity and enormous prestige. A second point of distinction was that, whereas Olympia mostly dozed between Olympics, Apollo's sanctuary at Delphi was a constant hive of activity, thanks to its oracle. Besides the holding of games, possession of an oracle was a second major way for a sanctuary to acquire privileged Panhellenic status. The Delphic oracle was by no means the only oracular shrine in Greece to draw consultants, whether private or official, from far and wide; Herodotus alone cited eighteen oracular sanctuaries and forty-three other oracular responses in addition to the fifty-three he recorded from Delphi. But Delphi was and always had been the premier oracular shrine in the Greek world.

Divination (*mantikē*) was widely resorted to both by individuals and by states in ancient Greece, and divinatory techniques varied extremely widely too. They fell into three broad categories, unequal in prestige. First, there was cleromancy, divination by lots (*klēroi*): small pebbles or bits of wood were shaken in a vase or a bowl and drawn out. Then, secondly, there was the interpretation of signs (*sēmeia*) of one sort or another: celestial phenomena (e.g. thunder), the direction or nature of the flight of birds (the equivalent Roman procedure gives us our word 'auspices'), or sacrificial entrails (especially the liver). This required the application of specialist knowledge, acquired through professional practice. Thirdly, and most prestigiously, there was oral divination, the interpretation of divinely inspired utterance. There existed individual written collections of such oracles, kept by *khrēsmologoi* who claimed to be able to interpret them and on the strength of that claim were sometimes employed by cities. But above all there were the oracles that emanated from certain specialist sanctuaries. These shrines had a permanent staff of priests and priestesses who, using the methods peculiar to their own individual sanctuary, acted as interpreters of the divine voice. The most illustrious such sanctuaries included those of Amphiaraos at Oropos, of Trophonios at Lebadeia in Boiotia, of Apollo at Didyma near Miletos, and of Zeus at Dodona. But the greatest, the most famous and influential of all in the eyes of the Greeks, was that of Apollo Pythios at Delphi, the functioning of which we shall examine in some detail.

At the heart of Apollo's sanctuary (fig. 7) lay his temple, which was rebuilt several times and in the Classical epoch was flanked by no fewer than twenty-seven 'treasuries', a token of the esteem in which the Greek cities held this shrine. The origins of that esteem appear to lie in the crucial rôle played by Apollo as *arkhēgētēs* ('founder-leader') in the movement of overseas colonization to Sicily and elsewhere from the later eighth century onwards. But the oracle's reputation also extended beyond the Greek world, as the offerings of several non-Greek kings testify: for example, the famous silver mixing-bowl, dedicated by Croesus of Lydia, that Herodotus (1.51) claimed could hold 600 *amphorai*, or the contribution by the philhellenic Pharaoh Amasis of 1,000 talents' weight of alum towards the temple's reconstruction after a fire in the third quarter of the sixth century (Herodotus 11.180).

Tradition has preserved several thousands of Delphic oracles for us. Many of these are the product of a veritable 'industry' of oracle-fabrication, which was itself a tribute to the sanctuary's unique prestige. Others are attested by inscriptions or are cited by

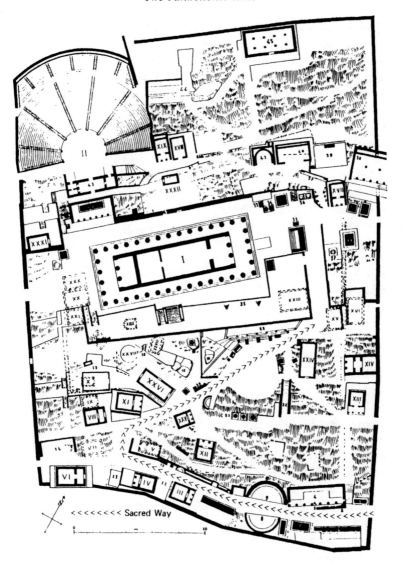

7   Delphi: the sanctuary of Apollo. I Temple of Apollo; II Theatre;
    III–XXXI Treasuries; 1–45 dedications of statues and other offerings
    by various states and individuals, Greek, Macedonian and Roman

orators, and these are the only ones whose authenticity seems guaranteed. But we shall also make use here of some oracles preserved only in the later literary tradition, since they too shed light on the Greeks' reception and interpretation of the divine word. It should be stressed that the oracles which are considered reliably authentic are the ones cast in a simple and unambiguous form, containing neither predictions nor prophecies, but only religious prescriptions. These regulated offerings, sacred contributions or the administration of divine property. They ordained sacrifices and dedications, founded new cults, gave advice on the holding of games, heroized the dead, accorded privileges, prescribed honours for a divinity, and spoke out indifferently on all matters pertaining to the gods. Legislative enactments attributed to Apollo (e.g. the so-called 'Great Rhētra' of Sparta: Plutarch, *Life of Lykourgos* 6) were certainly approved by him, although there is nothing to indicate that Delphi played a rôle in drawing them up in the first place (cf. the covenant of Ozolian Lokris regarding the foundation of a new settlement, M/L [60] 13 = Fornara 1983 [64]: 33; and the purported foundation-decree of Kyrene, M/L [60]: 5 = Fornara 1983 [64]: 18).

The oracles preserved in the literary tradition are of two kinds: 'predictive', that is purporting to foretell the predestined future, such as those which predicted the fate of Troy or of Oedipus; and 'supportive', that is serving as an 'adjunct technique of decision' (Vernant 1991 [163]: 315). Very often, in fact, the god was offered by the human consultant a choice between two options. Sometimes the response came down firmly in favour of one or other alternative, but in other cases it was couched in deliberately ambiguous or obscure terms that demanded further human exegesis. The following examples illustrate these two possibilities.

In 402 Xenophon was of a mind to join up as a mercenary under the Persian pretender Cyrus the Younger, but he piously decided, on the advice of his mentor Socrates, to consult Apollo of Delphi first: 'Xenophon went there and asked Apollo the following question: "To what god shall I pray and sacrifice in order that I may best and most honourably embark on the journey I have in mind, and return home safe and successful?"' (Xenophon, *Anabasis* III. 1.5–7). Apollo's reply, that he should sacrifice to the appropriate gods, hardly told Xenophon anything he did not already know; the response was a mere formality, since Xenophon's mind was already made up.

Our second example is the Athenians' double consultation of Delphi immediately before the battle of Salamis in 480. Uncertain how to respond to Xerxes' invasion, the Athenians appointed sacred envoys (*theopropoi*) to seek Apollo's advice:

For the Athenians had sent envoys to Delphi and were ready to consult the god; and when they had performed the customary rites about the shrine and had entered the inner hall and sat down there; the Pythia, whose name was Aristonikē, delivered the following oracular response:

Wretched ones. why sit you here? Flee and begone to remotest
Ends of earth, leaving your homes, high places in circular city;
For neither the head abides sound, nor the body;
Nor at bottom do the feet stay firm, nor the hands,
Nor does the middle remain uninjured. All is lost.
Fire pulls all down, and sharp Ares, driving his Syrian-bred horses.
Many a fortress besides, and not yours alone shall he ruin.
Many the temples of god to devouring flames he shall consign.
There they stand now, the sweat of terror streaming down them.
They quake with fear; from the rooftops black blood pours in
    deluging torrents.
They have seen the coming destruction, and evil sheerly constraining.
Get you gone out of the *aduton*! Blanket your soul with your
    sorrows.

When the Athenian envoys heard this, they were in extreme distress. They were prostrated by their calamity, foretold by the oracle. But Timon, son of Androboulos, who was as notable a Delphian as any, counselled them to take suppliant boughs and consult the oracle a second time, as suppliants. The Athenians followed his advice and said to the god: 'Lord, give us a more favourable oracle about our fatherland; reverence these suppliant boughs with which we come before you, or we will never go away from the shrine (*aduton*) but remain right here until we expire.' When they said this, the priestess (*promantis*) gave them this second response:

No: Pallas (Athene) cannot appease Zeus of Olympos
With many eloquent entreaties and all her cunning counsel.
To you I declare again this word, unyielding as adamant:
All shall be taken by foemen, whatever within his border
Kekrops contains, and whatever the glades of sacred Kithairon.

Yet to Tritogeneia shall far-seeing Zeus give a present,
A wooden wall, which alone shall abide undestroyed by the foemen;
Well shall it serve yourselves and your children.
Do not await the charge of horses and foot that come on you,
A mighty host from the landward side, but withdraw
And turn your back in retreat; on another day shall you face them.
Salamis, isle divine, you shall slay many children of women,
Either when Demeter is sown or again when she is harvested.

This second oracle seemed to be gentler than the first, and indeed it was
so. So the envoys wrote it down and returned home to Athens. When
they had left Delphi and made their report to the People at home, there
were many interpretations proposed as to its true meaning, but there
were two that clashed with each other more than all the others. On the
one hand, some of the older men said that they thought the god was
predicting that the Akropolis would be preserved. For in the olden days
the Akropolis of Athens had been fenced in with a thorn hedge, and
some therefore interpreted this hedge to be the 'wooden wall'. On the
other hand, there were those who said that the god signified the ships,
and these urged the abandonment of all else and the preparation of the
fleet.

But those who claimed that the 'wooden wall' was the ships were
baffled by the last two verses of the Pythia's oracle . . . [above]. In respect
of these lines of verse, the opinion of those who construed the ships as
the 'wooden wall' was confounded. For the oracle-interpreters [*khrēsmologoi*] took the verses in this sense: that the Athenians must prepare
themselves for a sea-battle at Salamis, which they would assuredly lose.

However, there was a man among the Athenians who at this time was
but lately come into their front ranks, whose name was Themistokles
son of Neokles. This man said that the oracle-interpreters construed the
whole matter wrongly. For if the verses had really been directed against
the Athenians, the oracle would have been couched in far less gentle
terms; instead of 'Salamis, isle divine', it would have run 'O cruel
Salamis', if its inhabitants were going to die around there. Rather, he
said, the oracle if rightly taken was really directed against their enemies,
and not the Athenians. So he counselled them to prepare for a battle at
sea, since it was the ships that were the 'wooden wall'. This was
Themistokles' explanation, and the Athenians judged it preferable to
that of the oracle-interpreters; for the latter would not have them
prepare for a sea-battle or indeed, to put it in a nutshell, lift a finger
against the enemy but advised rather that they should just leave Attica
and settle in some other country.

(Herodotus VII.140–3, trans. D. Grene, modified)

The Pythia's first message, then, unambiguously foretold catastrophe. But the terms of the second oracle, with its ambiguous reference to the 'wooden wall', provided matter for lengthy debate in the Athenian Assembly until Themistokles was able to persuade them, against the advice of the *khrēsmologoi*, that they were not incompatible with his naval policy. Since it was the citizens who ultimately were responsible for the decision to fight at Salamis, we have here a good example of how the word of the god fared when it encountered the mundane discourses of formal speeches in the Assembly and public discussion in the Agora. The divine word, that is to say, was not received as a prediction but as one of the parameters constraining human action, which was itself the fruit of secular deliberation. Divination thus appears as 'drawn into the new field of rational human discourse' (Vernant 1974 [163]: 19), which was to influence the progress of Greek political and scientific thought in Classical times and beyond.

More than one modes of consultation were employed at Delphi. But incubation (see below, under 'Epidauros') and cleromancy (the lot-oracle) were overshadowed by the prestige of the Pythia's inspired utterance. Originally the Pythia, who had to be an elderly, virgin woman from the local area, had prophesied just once a year, on the seventh of the Delphian month Bysios, Apollo's birthday. But in the Classical era solemn consultations were available once a month, also on the seventh day. It has therefore been suggested that there might have been up to three Pythias, two in post and one substitute in reserve, who prophesied in rotation to meet the huge demand. After the procedural preliminaries (ablutions, payment for the right to consult, sacrifice) had been completed under the supervision of the priests, the consultant entered the temple and participated in a second sacrifice before being allowed into the *aduton* where the priestess sat. We can only guess at the layout of the inner sanctum and the method of prophesying, but according to one modern reconstruction (Roux 1976 [161]) the Pythia descended to an unpaved area about a metre below the temple's floor level and sat on a tripod placed on the edge of a sort of well hollowed out of the earth; this hypothesis represents an attempt to reconcile the tradition of a fissure in the rock, through which the divine vapour (*pneuma*) was exhaled, with the failure by archaeologists and geologists to discover any such natural cleft in the ground. The consultants then addressed their question in a loud voice to the invisible Pythia, who, under the inspiration of Apollo, delivered the prophecy. It was the job of the priests present during the consultation to produce a written version of the response for the consultants.

Delphi, in religious terms, was the centre of the Greek world. Besides the Pythia's tripod the *aduton* contained also the *omphalos* or navel-stone symbolizing its central position in the universe ('Delphi' itself meant 'wombs'), and it was here that Apollo himself spoke to mankind. But immense though Delphi's power was within the Greek moral and religious order, it owed the duration and extent of its prestige as much to the fact that in political terms its power was strictly limited. Greek cities valued divination extremely highly, as we have seen, but Delphi most frequently contented itself with rubber-stamping decrees that had already been passed elsewhere or with responding to quite precise requests that had also been formulated outside the sanctuary. When, on the other hand, Delphi did seem to be impinging on the properly political sphere by 'medizing' or 'laconizing' (favouring the Persians or Spartans), its prestige was put into jeopardy, as in 480 and 431.

EPIDAUROS: THE HEALING POWERS OF ASKLEPIOS

The city of Epidauros in the northeast Peloponnese lay inland within a valley flanked by mountains. Here were to be found two cult-sites. The first, on the slopes of Kynortion, had been occupied since Mycenaean times and in the seventh century received a cult of Apollo Maleatas. This continued in use after the second cult, that of Asklepios, had been established at the edge of the plain towards the end of the sixth century. It was at this spot that there gradually developed the sanctuary destined to achieve Hellas-wide fame.

To begin with, Asklepios was worshipped as a hero, the son of a mortal woman (Koronis) and a god (Apollo). According to myth, Koronis entered on a marriage arranged by her father King Phlegyas, but Apollo killed the husband with an arrow. Artemis then killed Koronis in the same way, but Apollo rescued Askle-

pios from his mother's womb and he was raised by the centaur
Kheiron, under whose tutelage he became a skilled healer. In the
words of Pindar (not an epinician ode, but a sort of poetic epistle
to Hieron, composed about 474):

All who came
Bound fast to sores which their own selves grew,
Or with limbs wounded, by grey bronze
Or a far-flung stone, or wasting in body with summer fire or with
　winter,
He, loosing all from their several sorrows,
Delivered them. Some he tended with soft incantations,
Some had juleps to drink,
Or round about their limbs he laid his simples,
And for some the knife: so he set all up straight.

(Pythian III. 47–53, trans. C. M. Bowra)

So skilful, indeed, was he that he could raise men from the dead –
a talent for which Zeus struck him with a thunderbolt.
Thenceforth Asklepios was worshipped as a god. The myth-
history of Asklepios was originally set in Thessaly, but the
priests of Epidauros peddled their own versions and established
his connection with Epidauros. It was from there that his cult
spread to other cities in the fifth century, for example to Athens
in 420/19 (under the sponsorship of Sophocles).

Greeks consulted Asklepios to learn how to cure their illnesses,
as we shall see; but his sanctuary was also the site of quadrennial
games, the Asklepieia, which are comparable to other Panhellenic
festivals. Hence the presence of such structures as a theatre, a
stadium, a *gumnasion* and dormitories within the sanctuary
(fig. 8). It was, however, the healing rituals conducted by the
priests for pilgrims in search of a cure that constituted the
sanctuary's peculiar claim to fame.

The rituals began with purifications, sacrifices and ablutions in
holy water from sacred fountains. Only those who were without
stain and blemish, whether physical or moral, might enter the
shrine. Abstinence from sexual intercourse was an immediate
and absolute requirement, and, as on Delos, it was forbidden to
die or give birth within the sanctuary. The pilgrim then betook
himself or herself to the 'incubation-place' (*enkoimētērion*), which
was an *abaton* or 'no-go area' for the impure. The divinatory

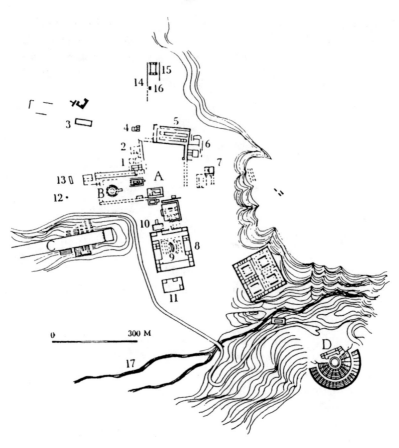

8 Epidauros: the sanctuary of Asklepios, fourth century BCE

A Temple of Asklepios.   B Tholos.   C Stadium.   D Theatre
1 Baths of Asklepios. 2 Bibliothēkē. 3 Cistern. 4 Temple of Aphrodite.
5. Stoa. 6 Baths (Akoē). 7 Temple of Apollo and Asklepios.
8 Gymnasium. 9 Odeion. 10 Propylaia. 11 Greek Baths. 12 Palaistra.
13 Palaistra cistern. 14 Sacred Way. 15 Propylaia of the Sanctuary.
16 Well. 17 Stream

procedure of incubation involved the god's appearing to the
sleeping consultant in a dream and indicating the appropriate
remedy. We have various sorts of evidence for the cures, ranging
from the *ex-voto* representations of the relevant parts of the body

that littered the shrine to detailed texts inscribed on pillars set up inside the god's temple on which, according to Pausanias (II.27.3), 'are engraved the names of men and women healed by Asklepios, with the diseases and how they were healed'. An extant example reads as follows:

Ambrosia of Athens, blind in one eye. This woman came as a suppliant to the god. Walking in the sanctuary, she mocked at certain of the cures, claiming it was unbelievable that lame and blind people should have recovered their health merely by experiencing a dream. She incubated in the sanctuary and had a dream: the god appeared right up close to her and told her that he would cure her, but that she would have to pay in sacrifice a silver pig as a memorial of her foolishness. So saying, he made an incision in her sick eye and poured in medicine. The next morning she departed, cured. (*Syll.*³ [62]: 1168.33–41)

Cures might be instantaneous, as in that case, or deferred, as when the god merely gave advice that the priests interpreted, assuming the rôle of true doctors (in competition with the practitioners of Hippokratic 'scientific' medicine, who considered the priests to be mere quacks). This combination of cures and adroit propaganda ensured the sanctuary's continued success right up to the fourth century CE, when St Jerome still thought it worthwhile to castigate those who visit 'the temple of Aesculapius to sleep on the stretched-out skins of sacrificial victims and demand from dreams the secret of the future' (*Commentary on Isaiah* XVII.65 = Edelstein and Edelstein 1945 [165]: T294).

The sanctuary as a whole comprised a great number of edifices, several times rebuilt or enlarged. Among these there is one whose function remains an enigma, a *tholos* (circular structure) with a basement in the form of a labyrinth. Archaeologists have interpreted this variously as the pit where sacred snakes lived, the tomb of a hero, or even as a representation of a mole's burrow, a proper site for the cult of a mole-god ... The sanctuary's fame and the hordes of pilgrims it attracted gradually led to its transformation from an oracular shrine for the practice of incubation into a huge complex of cures and baths where the priests of Asklepios could make a profit from the practice of their art.

In the post-Classical, Hellenistic era shrines of Asklepios multiplied, some of them, like the Asklepieion at Kos, attaining comparable celebrity to that of Epidauros. The following passage, part of the same mime of Herodas from which we quoted in chapter 6, is set in the Koan Asklepieion and provides a very lively illustration of Greek religious thought and action. Two women, Kokkale and Kynno, have come to the shrine to make a votive offering and a sacrifice; they begin by addressing Asklepios as 'Lord Paian', a title equally commonly used for Apollo:

Hail, Lord Paian, you who rule over Trikka [in Thessaly] and dwell in sweet Kos and Epidauros, and hail, Koronis, who bore you, and Apollo, and Hygieia ['Health'] whom you touch with your right hand, and hail those whose honoured altars are here, Panakē and Epio and Ieso and Podaleirios and Makhaon who destroyed the house and walls of Laomedon [king of Troy], healers of savage diseases, and all gods and goddesses who dwell at your hearth, father Paian. Come hither and graciously accept as a side-dish this cock, herald of the walls of my house, which I am sacrificing. For our resources are few and scanty, otherwise we would perhaps be sacrificing an ox or a fatted sow as a reward for healing those sicknesses which you, Lord, have cured at a stroke by laying on your gentle hands. Kokkale, dear, put the painting [the votive offering] by the right hand of Hygieia.
(Herodas, *Mime* IV.1–9)

THE ELEUSINIAN MYSTERIES

Our final example of a Panhellenic shrine has the distinguishing feature of being both an official cult-place tightly controlled by the Athenian state and a site for the expression of individual piety open to all speakers of Greek, not just Athenians. The prosperous town of Eleusis was an independent community to begin with, but at the beginning of the sixth century or possibly even the end of the seventh it was absorbed into the state of Athens. In the process the sanctuary of the Two Goddesses (Demeter and Persephone) and the Mysteries celebrated therein passed into the control of the Athenian 'King' Arkhon, who had overall responsibility for traditional cults.

The two local aristocratic families of the Kerykes and Eumolpidai were allowed to retain their hereditary priestly prerogatives, but that did not hinder the city of Athens from exercising a more or less direct influence over the life of the sanctuary and the organization of the cult. From the end of the sixth or beginning of the fifth century the emoluments of the Eleusinian priesthood were centrally regulated (the Hierophant – see below – was probably granted a financial allowance from public funds), and the rules to be followed in certain sacrifices were laid down, with the Council of 500 meeting the day after the Mysteries to adjudicate possible breaches. During the third quarter of the fifth century a board of *epistatai* was established centrally to keep accounts of the sanctuary's property, and there are documents showing that throughout the fifth and fourth centuries the Athenian state maintained a special interest in the Eleusis shrine.

Another piece of evidence to the same effect is the successful speech written and published by the politician Andokides in his own defence in 399 against a charge of sacrilegiously placing a suppliant's branch in the Eleusinion (sanctuary of Demeter and Persephone) at Athens itself during the celebration of the Mysteries:

We were returning from Eleusis; the information [*endeixis*] had been lodged. The King Arkhon according to tradition presented himself before the Presidents [*prutaneis*] of the Council to make his report on the conduct of proceedings at Eleusis. The Presidents said they would introduce him to the full Council and told him to summon Kephisios and myself to attend at the Eleusinion where the Council was obliged by a law of Solon to sit on the day following the Mysteries. We duly attended, and when the Council was in session, Kallias son of Hipponikos [a member of the Kerykes and Andokides' chief accuser] stood up in his ceremonial robes and announced that a suppliant's branch – which he displayed – had been placed on the altar. The city-herald [Eukles, below] then asked who had placed it there, but no one replied. I was there, though, and in full view of Kephisios. When no one replied, Eukles here, who had come out to enquire, went back inside. Call Eukles for me. Eukles, are the facts as I state? Do you testify. [Evidence of Eukles.] I told the truth, then, as has been testified, and the truth of the situation is quite the opposite of what my accusers claim. They, as you will recall, have stated that the Goddesses themselves caused my wits to go astray and made me place the branch in the sanctuary in ignorance of the law, in order to punish me. But I, gentlemen, maintain that, even if every word of the prosecution's allegation were true, I was rather saved than punished by the Goddesses. Suppose that I really had laid the branch there and then had not replied to the herald's proclamation: would it not have been I myself who was bringing about my own destruction by placing the branch, and would it not have been by my silence – a piece of good fortune for which I clearly had the Goddesses to thank – that I was saved? For if the Goddesses had indeed willed my destruction, I ought surely to have done the reverse, that is, made a confession even though I had not actually deposited the branch. As it was, I neither replied nor had I in fact placed the branch. So when Eukles reported to the Council that no one had confessed, Kallias stood up again and declared that a law of our ancestors condemned to death without trial anyone who placed a suppliant's branch in the Eleusinion; it was his father Hipponikos who had once interpreted the law in that sense, and he, Kallias, understood that it was I who had placed the branch. Forthwith Kephalos here jumped up and said: 'Kallias, most impious [*anosiōtatos*] of mankind, first you offer an exegesis of the law, something which is not legitimate (*hosion*) for you as a member of the Kerykes. Then you speak of an ancestral law [enjoining the death-penalty] when the pillar beside you prescribes a fine of 1,000 drachmas for placing a suppliant's branch in the Eleusinion. Finally, you say it was Andokides who put it there – but who told you that? Summon him before the Council so that we too may hear this allegation.' The text on the pillar was then read out, and Kallias was unable to say who his source was. It thus became evident to the Council that it was he himself who had placed the branch.   (*On the Mysteries* 11–16)

According to the *Homeric Hymn to Demeter*, most of which dates from the period before the Athenian takeover, the Mysteries were founded by Demeter herself when, during her prolonged wanderings in search of her daughter Persephone (or Korē), she stopped a while at Eleusis as a guest of King Keleos. In her honour the people of Eleusis constructed a great sanctuary, and Demeter taught them the sacred rituals for alleviating her mourning and celebrating her power:

With sharp pangs pain gripped her heart, and she tore the bands covering her ambrosial hair with her own hands. A dark cloak she threw around her shoulders and sped like a wild bird over land and sea in search of her. But none was willing to tell her the truth, neither god nor mortal man; nor did any bird of omen come to her as a messenger bearing true news. For nine days, then, queenly Deo wandered ceaselessly over the earth with flaming torches in her hands, so grief-stricken that she refused ambrosia and the sweet draught of nectar nor would bathe her body in water ...

[The Sun god finally tells her that Hades has abducted Persephone, with the consent of his brother Zeus. She is received in the home of Metaneira and, being entrusted with the royal infant Demophon, she tries to render him immortal by rubbing him with ambrosia and concealing him in the fire. But she is caught in the act by the queen, who breaks the spell]:

But lovely-crowned Demeter was angry with her, and with her divine hands she snatched from the fire the dear son whom Metaneira had borne unlooked-for in the halls and hurled him onto the ground, raging with anger in her heart. And straightway she addressed deep-girdled Metaneira thus: 'Ignorant, senseless humans, who never foresee your destiny, whether good or ill! You in your folly have wrought incurable harm. For – and I swear the oath of the gods, by the unappeasable Styx – I would have made your dear son deathless and ageless all his days and endowed him with imperishable honour. As it is, he can in no way evade death and the fates. Yet shall an imperishable honour be his always, because he sat upon my knees and slept in my arms. When the years revolve and he is in his prime, the sons of the Eleusinians shall wage continuous war and dread strife with one another. But I am that Demeter who receives honour, the greatest source of wealth and joy to immortals and mortals. Come, let the whole people build me a great temple and an altar beneath it, at the foot of the akropolis and its high wall, on a prominent hill above Kallikhoros. I myself will found my Mysteries, that hereafter you may piously perform them and render my heart propitious.' So saying, the goddess changed her stature and form, thrusting away old age. Waves of beauty spread around her, and a delightful fragrance wafted from her perfumed clothes, and from her immortal flesh a beam of light shone afar, while golden tresses fell down onto her shoulders, so that the solid house was filled with radiance as if lit by lightning.

[The following day, King Keleos summons his people]:

So calling to assembly his numberless people, he bade them build for thick-tressed Demeter a rich temple and an altar on a prominent hill. And they made haste to obey and hearkened to his words, doing as he commanded. And the temple grew great as the divine will desired. Now when they had finished it and were quit of their heavy task, every man returned to his home. But golden-haired Demeter sat there apart from all the blessed gods and remained, pining for her deep-girdled daughter. Thus she caused for mankind the most terrible and cruel year of all over the much-nurturing land. The earth would not even bring forth the seed, since well-crowned Demeter kept it hidden. Many a curved plough was drawn over the soil by the oxen in vain, and much white barley fell fruitlessly upon the earth. Thus would she have destroyed the whole race of mortal men with cruel hunger and robbed those who occupy Olympos of their glorious honour of offerings and sacrifices, had not Zeus noted and marked this in his heart.

(*Hom. Hym. Dem.* 40–50, 251–80, 296–313)

[Zeus then intercedes with his brother Hades and secures his permission for Persephone to return to her mother on earth for a part of each year; but the remainder of the year she must spend down below in the Underworld with her captor-husband.]

The chief priest of the Mysteries was the Hierophant (*hierophantēs*), who had to be a member of the *genos* of the Eumolpidai. His principal function accorded with the etymology of his title: it was to show (*phainein*) the sacred objects (*hiera*) at the culminating point in the ceremonies. But he also presided over all the other most solemn moments of the ritual, beginning with the recitation of the formula that threw the Mysteries open to all Greek-speakers and barred from them 'murderers and non-Greeks'. Next to him, the priestess of Demeter, who had to be of the *genos* of the Philaïdai, occupied the cult's most ancient and prestigious position; indeed, she disputed with him the right to perform certain of the sacrifices. The *daidoukhos* ('Torchbearer') accompanied the Hierophant in the opening ceremony of the Mysteries; he had to be a member of the *Kerykes* ('Heralds') *genos*. The same *genos* provided the fourth most important functionary, the 'Altar-Priest', who supervised the completion of the ritual. These four, like some of their assistants, held their positions for life, and in return they received important privileges such as *proedria* (the right to an honorific front-row seat in the theatre) and remuneration, on a scale commensurate with the ever-increasing fame of the Mysteries in the course of the fifth and fourth centuries.

The Mysteries followed a complex ceremonial pattern, divided into several stages located at different places and occupying two separate moments of the year. Every person who could speak some Greek, male or female, free or slave, provided only that his or her hands were not sullied (through the commission of some crime, especially murder or sacrilege), could become a candidate for the status of *mustēs*, that is, an initiate of the Mysteries of Eleusis. He or she thereby embarked on a long period prepara-

136

tory to induction, with the guidance of *mustagōgoi* and under the surveillance of the cult's *epimelētai*. This preparation consisted of a multiplicity of ritual actions, including fasting and retreats, undertaken with the encouragement of the initiates of the preceding year and under the eyes of the participants in the festivals.

The first stage was accomplished in spring, in the month of Anthesterion, when the Little Mysteries were held at Agrai near the central area of Athens. These represented the first grade of initiation, an indispensable preliminary to presenting oneself for the Great Mysteries at Eleusis itself. They were presided over by the King Arkhon, assisted by the religious personnel of Eleusis and members of the sacerdotal families, and culminated in the solemn sacrifice for the Two Goddesses that accompanied the ritual ablutions of the would-be *mustai* in the River Ilissos.

The Great Mysteries took place six months later, in Boedromion, and lasted for ten days. First, the *hiera* were transported in round boxes (*kistai*) from Eleusis to the Eleusinion at the foot of the Akropolis of Athens. At least in the Classical period this solemn procession was accompanied by ephebes (eighteen- and nineteen-year-olds doing compulsory 'national service'), but the procession itself, like the Little Mysteries, may have originated as early as Athens' incorporation of Eleusis and symbolized the imposition of central control. The arrival of the *hiera* was solemnly notified to the priestess of Athene Polias before an assembly of magistrates and priests in the midst of a huge crowd.

The Mysteries properly speaking began at the full moon on the next day, Boedromion 15, which was called *Agurmos* ('Gathering', *sc.* of the initiates and initiands) or *Prorrhēsis* ('Proclamation', viz., that of the official opening by the Hierophant assisted by the Torchbearer). Those deemed to be qualified were then admitted within the Eleusinion after being purified. The following day was named *Halade Mustai* ('To the sea, initiands!') after the shout that accompanied its principal ritual, the procession of the initiands to the sea at Phaleron where they each sacrificed, burned and scattered the ashes of a 'scapegoat' pig to cleanse them of their pollution. They then took a purificatory dip in the sea, dressed themselves in new clothes and crowned their heads with myrtle-wreaths before returning in procession to the city, where yet another purificatory sacrifice was held.

O 1 Boedromion 19 the *hiera* were taken back again to Eleusis in the most solemn of all the Eleusinian processions, and participants were spaced out all along the twenty kilometres that separated Athens from Eleusis. At its head was carried the statue of Iakkhos (a by-form of Dionysos), followed by the wagon carrying the *hiera*. Then came the priestly personnel, the candidates for initiation, the members of the Areiopagos and the Council of 500 and other magistrates, and behind them the citizens ordered by tribe and deme. Bringing up the rear was a crowd of onlookers attracted by the festival's reputation. The goal of the procession was the Hall of Initiation (*Telestērion*), which in the fifth century could accommodate up to 3,000 people on its benches. It was *inside* this building – unusually for a Greek ritual but *de rigueur* for a mystery-cult (*mustēria* means 'secret things') – that the Mysteries proper took place.

Only duly prepared *mustai* were eligible to participate in the ceremonies, which lasted for three days. They began with a solemn sacrifice to Demeter and Korē within the enceinte of the *peribolos* wall; to this were admitted only last year's initiates, who together consumed the sacrificed flesh on the spot. A ceremonial formula reported by the Christian writer Clement of Alexandria marked the entry of the initiands into the *Telestērion*: 'I have fasted, I have drunk the *kukeōn* [a potion of water, barley-groats and mint with which Demeter had consented to break her fast in the palace of King Keleos], I have taken from the *kistē* [box] and after working it have put it back in the *kalathos* [open basket]'. Behind this enigmatic declaration many interpreters have wanted to see the manipulation of model genitals, but if we are to believe Theophrastos (as cited by Porphyry, *On Abstinence* ii.6.2; cf. Delatte 1954 [170]), it was perhaps rather a mill that was in question, symbol of the blessings brought by Demeter that gave mankind access to the life of 'milled grain'.

With the entry of the *mustai* into the Hall of Initiation began the part of the ceremonies about which there was a rule of absolute secrecy. Since the ancients scrupulously adhered to this rule of silence, all modern attempts at reconstruction are based on the calculated indiscretions of Christian writers or the allusive and metaphorical remarks of philosophers like Plato. Perhaps what happened was that dramatic representations involving

Demeter, Korē and Zeus led up to the final climactic ceremony, the *epopteia* ('viewing'), in which the *hiera* were brought out of the Anaktoron (a sort of chapel within the *Telestērion*) and shown by the Hierophant to the *mustai*. The identity of these 'sacred things' has caused a great deal of ink to be spilled. Were they objects related to Demeter's 'gift' of the ear of wheat? Or models connoting sexual fertility? Or *xoana* (ancient aniconic statues carved from wood)? Despite the ingenuity of modern hypotheses and reconstructions, we shall no doubt never know the answer for certain. On the next day, the festival ended with a final *panēguris*.

The value of the initiation process in the eyes of the Greeks, apart from the significance of each of its stages, doubtless lay in its long period of preparation and in the progression towards the final revelations in the Hall of Initiation. These revelations consisted partly of visions and partly of oral instruction, that is, interpretations or homilies delivered by the Hierophant; together they constituted the *aporrhēta*, the 'unrepeatables'. But what sort of 'revelation' did this secret initiation entail? The *Homeric Hymn to Demeter* culminated in the promise of a different and happier afterlife for initiates: 'Blessed is he who, among the earthbound men, has been privileged to see these mysteries. But he who has not been initiated into the sacred rituals and does not participate in them has no like destiny, once he is dead, among the watery darkness' (479–83). On the other hand, Aristotle (as cited by Synesius, *Orations*, p. 48) affirmed that 'initiates are not required to learn anything; rather, they receive impressions and are put into a certain frame of mind, after having been suitably prepared.' Initiation in the Mysteries, then, apparently did not involve instruction of a dogmatic nature, but was rather a process of internal transformation, founded upon the emotional experience of a direct encounter with the divine. One of Plutarch's characters expresses himself thus (*On the Obsolescence of Oracles* 22 = *Moralia* 422C): 'I heard these marvellous things, precisely as one does during the initiatory rituals of the Mysteries, except that there was no demonstration, no visible proof of their formulas.'

These revelations were of course addressed individually to each of the *mustai*, but they also concerned the community of initiands as a whole that was gathered in the *Telestērion* and united by its shared experience; and, moreover, they reached out to embrace the wider community of all past initiates. The exaltation of the newly initiated was further reinforced by the mass gathering of the populations of Athens and Eleusis as a whole, assembled in their constituent bodies, and by the presence of all those who had come from outside Attica to participate in the festival. Thus the initiation, so far from separating the new *mustai* from their broader social context, was itself sustained and valorized by that external matrix.

Nor were the Eleusinian Mysteries a unique phenomenon within the Greek religious tradition. Both the secrecy, which contributed so much to the prestige of Eleusis, and the idea of mysteries itself, that is, the notion of gaining access to revelations denied to non-initiates, could be experienced in other cults, for example in the mysteries of Dionysos or of the Great Mother (Phrygian Kybele). As for the mystical dimension of the personal encounter with the godhead and the accompanying revelations, that may be compared to the religious experience involved in Dionysiac worship, on the one hand (chapter 13), and Orphism, on the other (chapters 4 and 12), even if these three means of approaching the divine were by no means equal in their status or identical in their objectives. The particular *éclat* of the Eleusinian Mysteries, therefore, was doubtless due to the importance of the ancient cult of Demeter, which the Athenian state celebrated with such pomp, no less than to the experience of mystic emotion, which was itself as much a collective as an individual phenomenon.

This civic context of the ritual must be kept firmly in mind if we are not to distort the meaning and value of mystery-cults for the Greeks. What must be avoided at all costs is treating them as if they were a religion apart, 'other' than the civic religion, and endowed with a spirituality of a superior kind, on the grounds that, from the standpoint of modern western civilization, the religious attitudes of the initiates appear closer to those held by spiritual monotheists. For it is that perspective which has so often led to false interpretations of the Eleusinian Mysteries, as indeed of other aspects of ancient Greek religion.

PART III

Systems for representing the divine

CHAPTER 12

Myths and mythology

DEFINITIONS OF MYTH AND MYTHOLOGY

What is labelled collectively as 'myth' can, in the context of ancient Greece, assume the most diverse forms depending on the way it is preserved and represented. On one level, for example, there are the myths of the specialist ancient mythographers or the scattered fragments collected in lexicographers' glosses. At another level, there are the literary reworkings of myth to be found in epic, tragedy and lyric poetry. Or, thirdly, there are compositions with an explicitly theological purpose such as theogonies (divine genealogies). Then, finally, there are the figural representations (to be considered in chapter 14). It is this mass of disparate discourses that modern mythologers attempt to decipher, using a variety of methods and procedures (see next section).

The very concept of myth has been transmitted to us by the Greek tradition itself. At an early period *muthos* meant any 'spoken word' and so belonged to the general category of *logos* or 'that which is said'. But *logos* progressively came to mean not only that, but, more specifically, persuasive utterance that appealed to the rational intelligence and to the concept of 'truth'. Thus an opposition developed between *logos*, in this sense of rational discourse, and *muthos*, which now bore the twofold connotation of untruth and irrationality.

The emergence of writing helped to precipitate and sharpen this conceptual dichotomy. With the transition from a purely oral tradition of discourse to various types of written literature, a new way of thinking became established that is attested from the last quarter of the fifth century onwards in medical treatises, historical narratives, forensic orations and philosophical tracts. Within the framework of these different kinds of written discourse *logos* was considered synonymous with demonstrative rationality and as such counterposed to myth. It was Athens that witnessed the triumph of this intellectual *démarche*. Thucydides, for example, equated the 'mythical' (*muthōdes*) with the fabulous and totally excluded it from his historiography in his single-minded quest for the truth (1.21.1, 22.4). The same antithesis reappears in Plato's account of the education of his ideal philosopher in the *Republic* (522A8), where the *muthōdes* is presented as the proper sphere of the poets and is opposed to the *alēthinoteroi logoi* ('more veridical discourses') of the 'scientific' disciplines.

In the same period, though, the originally purely oral myths were recorded in works of written literature. Homer and Hesiod were the first to establish for the Greeks 'a kind of canonical repertory of stories about the Powers of the Beyond' (Vernant 1980 [39]: 193), and it was on this repertory that the elegiac, lyric and tragic poets drew unstintingly while simultaneously endowing the traditional myths with a new function and meaning. Pindar, for example, gave myth the status of a paradigm, a benchmark against which the particular competitive exploit that his ode was celebrating could be measured and evaluated. The tragic poets, for their part, drew upon the mythical past in order to pit it against the present and, through the medium of the characters on stage, create an occasion for communal, civic debate. Each of their dramas problematized and called into question one or other aspect of the human condition, so that in their hands the heroes of myth ceased to be Pindaric 'paradigms' and became instead objects of contestation and the bases for an enquiry into social values that was unceasingly renewed from one play to the next.

Consider Sophocles' Oedipus, for example, in *Oedipus Tyrannus*: here is a man with a double identity, the very image of man in search of himself. Or take the Orestes of Aeschylus' *Oresteia* trilogy: through the prism of his personality is refracted the debate on Justice and Law, and through the medium of his story the old and the new gods are both invoked and challenged. A third and final example is Sophocles' *Antigone*, which dramatizes the controversy over the relationship between divine justice and temporal power by means of the struggle between the epony-mous heroine and the ruler of Thebes. Other texts from the same period purport to present straightforward transcriptions of the multiple versions of these same orally transmitted myths, with the upshot that eventually, in the Hellenistic and Roman eras, we find genuine mythographic manuals being composed, like the 'Library' (*Bibliotheca*) of pseudo-Apollodoros [55].

'Mythology' is a term best reserved strictly to designate 'a unified, narrative, corpus of stories' (Vernant 1980 [39]: 197), as distinct from the collections of more or less co-ordinated stories assembled by ancient mythographers. Hesiod's *Theogony*, for example, which puts forward an ordered general overview of the human and divine universe, falls under this definition, as does his 'Myth of the Races (or Ages)' in the *Works and Days* (see below). By analysing the narrative organization of the myth and the semantic and symbolic relationships that constitute it, the modern mythologer can decipher its multiple meanings.

Hesiod's *Theogony* is both rooted in the oral poetic tradition and an original and learned creation. But it was presented by its author as a revelation of didactic theology inspired by the Muses whose prophetic mouthpiece he was. Of other Greek theogonies we possess only fragments, but they do at least enable us to discern the contours of a vast submerged continent of multiple, partly overlapping, partly contradictory, versions engaged in a sort of internal dialogue of mythical thought. One example is the Orphic theogony attested both in late accounts of the birth of the gods and mankind and in a commentary that was compiled in the second half of the fourth century and discovered on papyrus in a tomb at Derveni in Macedonia (see below).

READINGS OF MYTHOLOGY: A HISTORICAL CONSPECTUS

From the end of the eighteenth century attempts had been made to sketch out a rough programme for a 'Science of Myth'. This project was given a new lease of life towards the end of the nineteenth century, when grand mythological theories of would-be universal scope began to be produced. Within the framework of the British anthropological school of E. B. Tylor and Andrew Lang, for example, J. G. Frazer proposed a general theory founded on a comparison of Greece and Rome with so-called primitive civilizations; according to this, the explanation of myths was to be sought in the function they had of representing natural forces such as the life and death of vegetation.

These sweeping generalizations provoked a reaction from the Germanic school of historical philology, then dominated by L. Deubner and the Swede M. P. Nilsson. Their philological approach construed the variant mythical narratives and discourses as a haphazard accumulation of disparate and discontinuous elements, the function of which was to explain a particular religious ritual in accordance with the relevant historical or geographical circumstances. Between the two World Wars followers of this school collected and classified the data, thereby providing indispensable aids to further work. But their general approach had the effect of reducing mythology to a mere agglomeration of heterogeneous stories. Hence the development of a contrary interpretative tendency, the concern of which was to discover ways of deciphering myths that would do justice to the coherence underlying their superficial variety and complexity. By this means it was hoped to gain access to the secret springs of meaning of which they were the vessels and thereby to illuminate the mentality to which they bore witness. Researchers of diverse backgrounds and with different perspectives have devoted themselves to this project throughout the twentieth century.

One approach, for instance, focusses on the distant roots of Greek mythology and religion. Thus W. Burkert [178] traces the origins of sacrificial myths and rituals as far back as the Old Stone Age, while others like P. Lévêque [190] look to the more recent Aegean Bronze Age or Mycenaean past of Greece. Another approach aims to set Greek mythology and religion within an Indo-European framework; and even if Greece may be a special and essentially marginal case, G. Dumézil's [182] conception of Indo-European 'tri-functionality' (rulership, warriorhood, fertility) has proved fruitfully applicable to certain Greek rituals and cycles of myth, for example the legends of Herakles, the

Hesiodic 'Myth of the Races' (below), and the theology of Apollo (chapter 13).

Within the past twenty to thirty years the emphasis has been shifted rather onto the status and function of Greek mythology and religion in the historical, that is, Archaic and Classical, periods; here the leading exponents are, on the one hand, J.-P. Vernant and M. Detienne, and, on the other, J. Rudhardt. This new direction taken by scholarly research derives its impetus and sustenance from French sociology and anthropology, especially that of M. Mauss and, with reference to ancient Greece, L. Gernet. But here too Dumézil's contribution has been utterly decisive. Behind the different religious systems of the Indo-European peoples he has discerned profound structural ana-logies; and by analysing myths within a comparativist framework he has brought to light structures of mentality that govern ways both of representing the universe and of organizing society. Myth, seen within such an interpretative framework, acts as a system of symbols and, like language, 'conveys various modes of classifying facts – by co-ordinating, grouping and opposing them, various ways of recognizing both resemblances and differences, in short ways of organizing experience' (Vernant 1980 [39]: 222).

Claude Lévi-Strauss [191–2] continued and extended the researches of Dumézil, advocating a new method of analysis that was inspired originally by the discipline of linguistics. He thereby both brought out the 'logic of the concrete' at work in the myths and related the myths to their cultural and ethnographic context:

Rather than undertake hasty comparisons and throw oneself into specu-lations on origins, it is better to proceed to the methodical analysis of myths, defining each one by the totality of its attested variants, and eliminating all preconceived ideas. Only in this way can we hope to reach a stage where man and his works take their place as objects of positive knowledge. But to do so, one should apply a very strict procedure, which is reducible to three rules:

1   A myth must never be interpreted on one level only, for any myth consists in an *interrelation* of several explanatory levels.
2   A myth must never be interpreted individually, but in its relation-ship to other myths which, taken together, constitute a transforma-tional group.
3   A group of myths must never be interpreted on its own, but by

reference (*a*) to other groups of myths; and (*b*) to the ethnography of the societies in which they originate. For, if the myths transform each other, a relationship of the same type links (on a transverse axis) the different levels involved in the evolution of all social life. These levels range from the forms of technological and economic activity to the systems of ideological representation, and comprehend economic exchanges, political and familial structures, aesthetic expression, ritual practices, and religious beliefs.

Relatively simple structures are thus reached, from the transformations of which are created myths of various types. In this way, anthropology is a modest collaborator in the elaboration of that *logic of the concrete* which seems to be one of the major concerns of modern thought, and which shows us to be closer to – rather than farther from – forms of thought very foreign to us in appearance.

These myths can no longer be described as prelogical. Their logic is alien, but only to the extent that Western thinking has long been dominated by too narrow a logic.

('Comparative religions of nonliterate peoples' (1960), in Lévi-Strauss 1977 [191]: 61, with my corrections and modifications)

Lévi-Strauss's ethnographic reading of mythology in general has been nuanced and applied specifically to Greece by among others Marcel Detienne. Here is an extract from a recent essay of his:

'Mythology' is not a simple matter. In Greece and elsewhere the *Odyssey* sets the tone, with its air of knowing that it's very boring always to be hearing the same stories. There is a place, too, for all opinions. Demosthenes, mantled in the dignified robes of a Funeral Orator, can announce to the Athenians to general satisfaction that through their exploits they are entering the realm of myth. A century earlier Herodotus, decked out in the brand new garb of the Ionian 'scientific' historian, can chuck 'myth' on the rubbish-heap, but without renouncing any of the traditional tales, let alone the genealogies of the divine powers. But there is more still to mythology than that, and our own, very local [*sc.* French] model of 'double reading' can lead us to it.

Since Lévi-Strauss and Dumézil, there have essentially been two methods of perceiving and so analysing mythology – either as a narrative genre organized by certain narrative modes, or as a system of representation that constantly oversteps the bounds of narrative by reason of its singular nature *qua* mythology. In brief, Lévi-Strauss and Dumézil make the same choice as Plato, deciding that mythology is basically a structure of thought, a *chose mentale* [in Italian in original] over and above the narrative clothing in which it happens for the moment to be invested. It's even probable that the philosophical author of the *Timaeus* would have been interested in the (very linguistic) theory of A.-J. Greimas, for whom mythology is a semantic code capable of 'generating' the totality of mythical stories, whatever their form.

More certain is the fact that there simultaneously existed in Greece, quite independently of Plato's philosophical project, a mythology-as-framework of thought and a mythology-as-field of knowledge. On the one hand, there was a system of thought which functioned as a more or less tightly fitting integument from one end of Greek culture to the other. This invites one to read the culture as a whole, with its beliefs, fields of knowledge, practices, and different types of stories, to read them in correspondence with each other, in their modes of interrelationship, with their categories, their modes of logical organization, to read them, moreover, in a unitary manner without being too impressed by the short term and its often artificial constraints. Then, as well as – or rather *within* – mythology-as-framework of thought, there is a mythology-as-field of knowledge with its different spheres of operation: Odysseus, the local historians of Athens, the philosophers, and the 'mythographers' (lexically, the mythographers *par excellence*) cited by Diodorus of Sicily. This mythology-as-field of knowledge was inhabited, and for a long time, by history-as-memory with its narrative forms like 'archaeology' (*arkhaiologia*, tales of antiquity), the funeral oration, the foundation myths – a field, to conclude, that was marked out and bounded by people who claimed to be the real professionals in the 'writing up of myths'. So what we have here is an indigenous way of conceptualizing mythology – with just this one difference, that those 'natives' are also our informants. That Greek way of thinking must be taken on board and integrated into the, that is our, analysis of myths. ('La double écriture de la mythologie', in Detienne 1989 [181]: 185–6)

Applying the structural and 'ethnographic' analysis advocated by Lévi-Strauss and Detienne to Greek myths has led to the elaboration of a range of readings specially adapted to the different forms of mythic discourse. Corpora have been established in which all versions and variants of related myths are set side by side, whatever their source or period, and with these has been integrated information drawn from other areas of Greek culture as well. In this way, by their researches on the conceptual faculty of *mētis*, 'cunning intelligence', Vernant and Detienne have explicated the mode of operation of a certain type of divinities (Detienne and Vernant 1978 [219]). To give a further example, through his study of the rituals and representation of Adonis Detienne has sought to reconstruct the basic categories informing the Greeks' mythic universe, their alimentary, sexual and agricultural codes, their practices of sacrifice, marriage and agriculture (Detienne 1972 [220]). When applied to specific works of literature this method has enabled their underlying mythical content to be deciphered, as for example in Vernant's exegesis of the Hesiodic 'Myth of the Races' (1983 [40]: 3–32) or P. Vidal-Naquet's study of the metaphors of corrupted sacrifice in the *Oresteia* ('Hunting and sacrifice in Aeschylus' *Oresteia*', in Vernant and Vidal-Naquet 1988 [149]: 141–59).

This progressively refined methodology has of late been extended profitably beyond literary texts to other topics of research within the general area of myth, both in France and abroad. A large-scale enquiry, addressed simultaneously to myths and to ritual practices, has demonstrated the central place occupied by animal sacrifice both in the institutions of the Greek city and in the Greeks' mental outlook (Detienne and Vernant 1989 [71]). Other studies (cited in the Bibliography) have used myths as a medium for exploring the themes of marriage and the status of women, of the youth and their admission to membership of the civic community, and of death. These studies, by reason of their content and the problems they address, necessarily deal with the relationships between myth and politics, and between myth and history, huge questions that we can only touch upon here. Besides these, there have been special studies of the structures of the polytheistic system as a whole and of the leading divinities. The aim in all cases has been to use the relevant myths as a means of uncovering the complex structure which informs their modes of operation. In parallel to these varied projects research has been conducted into the very notion of myth and mythology, starting with their origins among the Greeks and taking the story right up to the modern theories which have renewed our understanding of the subject.

To conclude this brief historical conspectus of modern interpretations of Greek myth, we can do no better than quote from P. Ellinger's recent review article [184]:

In the course of all these researches myth ceased to be some incomprehensible relic from the depths of the dim and distant past, or

something charged with a mysterious power that one might from time
to time evoke. It came instead to be seen as constituting the basic
categories and major articulations of a conceptual framework through
which the Greeks were enabled to get a grasp on reality in the mundane
as well as in the momentous aspects of their life . . . scholars ceased to be
interested in myths for and in themselves . . . what interested them
rather were the problems that were being posed through the medium of
myths, the implicit thoughts which were being developed therein, the
dominant articulations of a system of collective representations, that
highly structured mental cement . . . which served to bind together the
most heterogeneous stories and social phenomena.

COSMOGONIES AND THEOGONIES

The Greeks had several cosmogonic myths, accounts of the
genesis of the *kosmos* or universe which told of the progressive
emergence from chaos of an ordered world. Only fragmentary
traditions have come down to us of the majority of these myths;
there was one, for example, which regarded the aquatic powers
Okeanos and his sister-wife Tethys as *the* primordial divinities,
the very beginning of the world; whereas another attributed that
rôle to Nux (Night). Later, towards the end of the seventh
century, the Spartan poet Alkman sought to effect a reconciliation in his cosmogony by linking the theme of primordial
waters to that of originary Night. But the most ancient of the
completely extant cosmogonical texts to propound a systematic
ordering of the universe is Hesiod's *Theogony*, which he composed in Boiotia around 700 BCE together with another long
poem entitled *Works and Days*.

Hesiod's Theogony

The *Theogony* is a rigorously constructed composition and tells
the story of the generations of gods and their struggles for
suzerainty. In his preface (lines 1–115) Hesiod claims supernatural inspiration from the Muses, who have, he says, revealed
to him the Truth of 'what has been, what is, and what will come
to be'. He then describes the time of the primordial gods, thus
presenting a true cosmogony:

First, then, came the Abyss, and then broad-breasted Earth, secure seat for ever of all the immortals who occupy the peaks of snowy Olympos and misty Tartara in the recess of the broad-pathed earth; then Erōs, handsomest among the immortal gods, dissolver of limbs, who overcomes the reason and purpose in the breasts of all gods and all men.

Out of the Abyss came forth Nether Gloom and black Night, and from Night in turn came Upper Air [Aithēr] and Day, whom she bore after intimate union with Nether Gloom. Earth bore first of all one equal to herself, starry Heaven, so that he should cover her all about, to be a secure seat for ever for the blessed gods; and she bore the long Mountains, charming haunts of the goddesses, the Nymphs, who dwell in mountain glens; and she bore also the undraining Sea, with its furious swell, but not in sweet union of love. But then, bedded with Heaven, she bore deep-swirling Okeanos, Koios and Kreios and Hyperion and Iapetos, Thea and Rhea and Themis and Memory, golden-wreathed Phoebe and lovely Tethys. After them the youngest was born, crooked-scheming Kronos, most fearsome of children, who loathed his lusty father.

And again she bore the proud-hearted Kyklopes, Thunderer, Lightner, and Whitebolt stern of spirit, who gave Zeus his thunder and fashioned his thunderbolt. In all else they were like the gods, but a single eye lay in the middle of their forehead. They had the surname of 'Circle-eyes' because of this one circular eye that lay in their forehead. And strength and force and resource were upon their works.

And again there were born of Earth and Heaven three more sons, great and stern, not to be spoken of, Kottos and Briareōs and Gyges, overbearing children. A hundred arms sprang from their shoulders, unshapen lumps, and fifty heads grew from the shoulders of each of them upon their strong bodies. And strength boundless and mighty was upon their great form.

For all those that were born of Earth and Heaven, these were the most terrible of children, and their own father detested them from the beginning. As soon as each of them was born, he hid them all away in a cavern of Earth, and would not let them up into the light; and he rejoiced in the wicked work, did Heaven, while huge Earth was tight-pressed inside, and groaned. But she planned a nasty scheming trick. Without delay she created the element of grey adamant, and fashioned a great sickle and showed it to her dear children, and spoke to give them courage, sore at heart as she was:

'Children of mine and of an evil father, if you are willing to obey, we could get redress for your father's cruelty. For it was he who first plotted ugly deeds.'

So she spoke; but they were all seized by fear, and none of them uttered a word. But the great crooked-scheming Kronos took courage, and soon replied to his good mother:

'Mother, I would undertake this task and accomplish it – I am not in awe of our unspeakable father. For it was he who first plotted ugly deeds.'

So he spoke, and mighty Earth rejoiced. She set him hidden in ambush, placed the jagged sickle in his hands, and revealed the whole stratagem to him.

Great Heaven came, bringing on the night, and, desirous of love, he spread himself over Earth, stretched out in every direction. Then his son reached out from the ambush with his left hand and with his right he took the huge sickle with its jagged teeth and quickly cut off his own father's genitals, and flung them behind him to fly where they might. They were not released from his hand in vain, for all the drops of blood that flew off were received by Earth, and as the years revolved she bore the powerful Erinyes and the great Giants in gleaming armour with long spears in their hands, and the nymphs whom they call Meliai over the boundless earth.

As for the genitals, just as he first cut them off with [his instrument of] adamant and threw them from the land into the surging sea, even so were they carried on the waters for a long time. About them a white foam grew from the immortal flesh, and in it a maiden was reared. First she approached holy Kythera; then from there she reached sea-girt Cyprus. And out stepped a modest and beautiful goddess, and grass began to grow all round beneath her slender feet. Gods and men call her Aphrodite, because she was formed in foam, and Kytherea, because she approached Kythera, and Cyprus-born [Kyprogenēs], because she was born in wave-washed Cyprus, and 'genial' [a pun on *philommēdēs*, 'genital-loving', and *philomeidēs*, 'laughter-loving'], because she appeared out of genitals.

Love and fair Desire attended her birth and accompanied her as she went to join the family of the gods. And this has been her allotted province from the beginning among men and immortal gods – the whisperings of maidens, smiles, deceptions, sweet pleasure, intimate love, and tenderness.

As for those children of great Heaven, their father who begot them railed at them and gave them the surname of Titans ('Strainers'), saying that straining tight in wickedness they had done a terrible thing, and that he had a title to revenge for it later.

(*Theogony* 116–210, trans. M. L. West, modified)

The first time period of Hesiod's cosmogony is that of Khaos (the Abyss), Gaia (Earth) and Erōs (Love, power of regeneration).

Khaos and Gaia give birth to further powers without the need for intercourse between them. From Khaos alone, for example, there issue forth Erebos (Nether Gloom) and Nux, and from Gaia come Ouranos (Sky, Heaven) and Pontos (Sea) . . .

The second time period of the cosmogony is inaugurated by the sexual union of Ouranos with Gaia, who conceives the twelve Titans (the youngest being Kronos) and Titanesses, the three Kyklopes and the three Hundred-Armers. However, Ouranos tries to prevent his children from seeing the light of day by continuously covering Gaia and forcing her to secrete her children in the nethermost depths of her being. So Gaia devises a ruse. She fashions a sickle and entrusts it to Kronos, who uses it to castrate his genitor. Thenceforth Ouranos is eternally separated from Gaia and confined to the roof of the world, and with that the generation of the primordial beings is completed. The world can now be set in order.

The action of Kronos had further consequences. First, the birth of Aphrodite: Ouranos' severed penis fell into Pontos and, mingling there with marine foam, produced Aphrodite ('foam-born'). Then, we get three groups of divine powers, the offspring of drops of Ouranos' blood which had impregnated Gaia: the Erinyes (Furies), the Giants, and the Meliai (Nymphs of the ash-trees). With the mutilation of Ouranos struggle and violence, on the one hand, and persuasion and love, on the other, found a place in a world where time was unblocked, and the struggle for power among the gods could commence.

Between the creation of the primordial divinities and the establishment of the last generation of gods there occurred an episode of prime importance, which comprehended the appearance of the Titan Prometheus, the institution of bloody animal-sacrifice and the definition of the status of mankind. This tale is as it were the coping-stone of the whole text (for an analysis, see the section on myths of sacrifice, below).

The third act of the theogonic drama is the struggle for power among the gods. The children of Ouranos and Gaia enter the stage and pair off into brother-sister couples, which in turn procreate divine powers. Pre-eminent among these Titan pairings is that of Kronos and Rhea who hold sway over the other gods. To prevent any of his children succeeding to his throne Kronos devours them as they are born: Hestia, Demeter, Hera, Hades, Poseidon. But the last-born, Zeus, escapes, and again (cf. Gaia, above) it is the feminine exercise of cunning intelligence (*mētis*) that proves essential for success. In place of Zeus, Rhea gives Kronos a stone to swallow; Zeus survives, grows up and compels his father to vomit up the rest of his children.

Before achieving the definitive conquest of supreme power Zeus and the generation of his 'brothers' are obliged to fight the Titans for supremacy. The latter are struck down by thunder-bolts, and the monstrous Typhon is hurled down into Tartaros below. The Olympian gods bestow the throne on Zeus, who distributes their several honours and inaugurates a reign of peace and justice (though later, post-Hesiodic traditions recount further upheavals). Zeus then marries Metis, the deified cunning intelligence, but, to ensure that no future son of his should dethrone him as he had his father Kronos, he swallows his wife when she is pregnant with Athene. He thereby controls all the *mētis* necessary for the exercise of his suzerainty. At the conclusion of the *Theogony* the cosmos, the world of the gods and the world of mankind are all definitively established, and the universe according to Hesiod may be graphically represented in the form of a family-tree (fig. 9).

Hesiod's *Theogony* invites comparison to cosmological tales with similar themes that are to be found in the Near East. But one of its peculiarities is that it lays the emphasis less on the genesis of the world than on the setting up of a hierarchy of divine powers. This balance of emphasis may be linked with the struggles for monarchic power in the real world of humans at the time (the Dark Age) when these great tales were being created. In any study of the invention of symbolic systems like these cosmogonies and theogonies, the historical context that moulded their elaboration has to be given due weight.

Uncanonical theogonies

Orphic theogonies are represented by a small corpus of complete or fragmentary accounts, the most important of which is pre-served on a papyrus roll found in a tomb at Derveni not far from Thessalonikē in 1962 (West 1983 [205]: 75ff.). This bears the

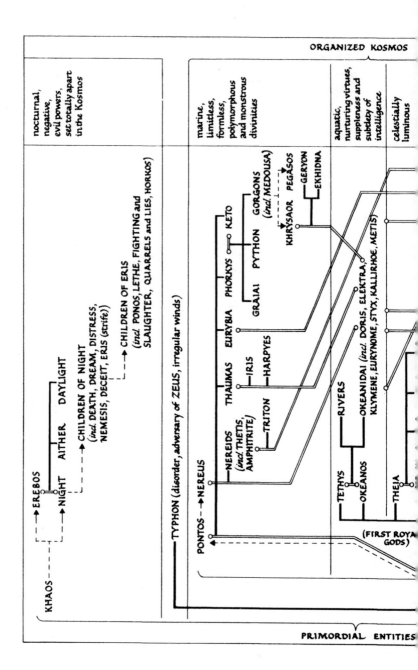

ORGANIZED KOSMOS

nocturnal, negative, evil powers, set totally apart in the Kosmos

marine, limitless, formless, polymorphous and monstrous divinities

aquatic, nurturing virtues, suppleness and subtlety of intelligence

celestially luminous

KHAOS

EREBOS

NIGHT   AITHER   DAYLIGHT

CHILDREN OF NIGHT
(incl. DEATH, DREAM, DISTRESS,
NEMESIS, DECEIT, ERIS (strife))

CHILDREN OF ERIS
(incl. PONOS, LETHE, FIGHTING and
SLAUGHTER, QUARRELS and LIES, HORKOS)

TYPHON (disorder, adversary of ZEUS, irregular winds)

PONTOS → NEREUS

NEREIDS (incl. THETIS, AMPHITRITE)

TRITON

THAUMAS

IRIS

HARPYES

EURYBIA

PHORKYS

KETO

GRAIAI   PYTHON

GORGONS (incl. MEDOUSA)

KHRYSAOR   PEGASOS

GERYON

EKHIDNA

RIVERS

OKEANIDAI (incl. DORIS, ELEKTRA,
KLYMENE, EURYNOME, STYX, KALLIRHOE, METIS)

TETHYS

OKEANOS

THEIA

(FIRST ROYAL GODS)

PRIMORDIAL ENTITIES

9   Hesiod's genealogy of the gods

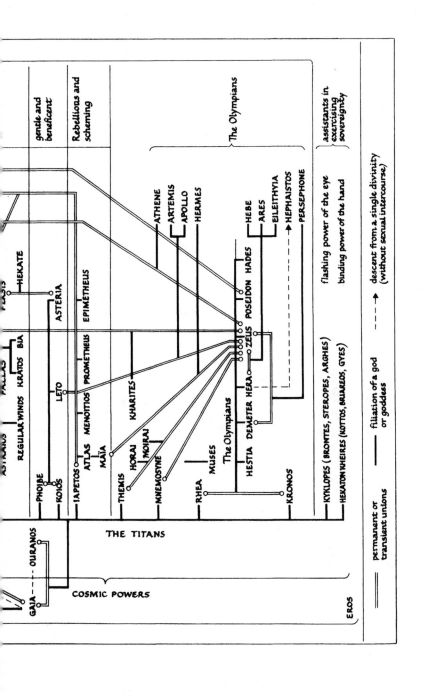

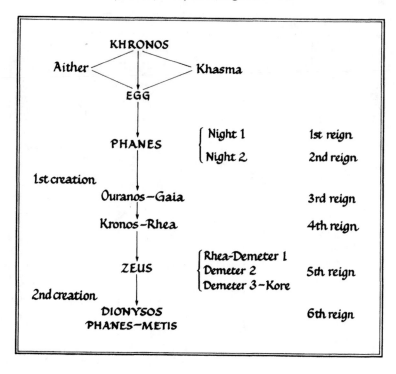

10   Orphic cosmogony

lengthy text of a philosophico-religious treatise written in the later fourth century. Orphic 'thought', however, or elements of it, can be traced back at least to the sixth century, since when the followers of Orpheus had been practising what they themselves called the 'Orphic life' (*bios Orphikos*). Evidence of their style of life is provided by three bone tablets found at Olbia on the northern shore of the Black Sea and dated to the beginning of the fifth century BCE (discovered in 1978, cf. West 1983 [205]: 17–20).

Orphic theology was constructed in opposition to Hesiodic cosmogony and theogony and contested their canonical status. It provided a rationale for those recusants who invoked the legendary figure of Orpheus as a counter-ideal to the civic model of politico-religious observance. Whereas Hesiod's theogony had proceeded from chaos to order, Orphic cosmogonies (more than one version of which existed, with several more or less important variants) situated a primordial power, either Time or Night, at the origin of the world (fig. 10).

Out of this primordial power there emerged an egg which gave birth in turn to Phanes (the Brilliant One) or Erōs (Sexual Love). This egg was a perfectly complete whole. But the subsequent history of the world was one of piecemeal subdivisions and successive corruptions linked to the appearance of sexual reproduction. In multiplying, the divine couples became separated from and opposed to each other. This process of degeneration reached a nadir with the murder of Dionysos and the appearance of the human race (see below). Orphic cosmogony thus debouched into an anthropogony, the function of which was to anathematize as murder the killing of all living beings. Only by abstaining from all murder, and therefore from bloody animal-sacrifice, could those mortals who opted for the Orphic way of life effect a reconciliation with the gods. This was a life synonymous with purity but it also entailed a radical separation from those Greeks who pursued the conventional civic way.

THE HESIODIC MYTH OF THE RACES

Through this myth we have the opportunity to watch a living mythic tradition of thought in operation. Vernant's structuralist analysis (1983 [40]: 3–33), the main lines of which we shall follow here, enables us to see that Hesiod was using an ancient myth, that of the metallic races or ages, as a vehicle for his own reflection upon the society of his day. By transforming the myth's organization Hesiod was able to introduce into it a picture of what in his eyes threatened to destroy the human species:

If you like, I will summarize another tale for you, well and skilfully – be sure you take it in – telling how gods and mortal men have come from the same source.

Of gold was the race of men that the immortals who dwell on Olympos made first. They were in the time of Kronos, when he was king in heaven; and they lived like gods, with carefree heart, removed from toil and misery. Vile old age did not affect them either, but with hands and feet ever unchanged they enjoyed themselves in feasting, freed from all ills; and they died as if overcome by sleep. All good things were theirs, and the grain-giving ploughland yielded its fruits of its own accord in unstinted plenty, while they at their leisure lived off their fields in contentment amid abundance. Since the earth covered up that race, they have been called divine spirits (*daimones hagnoi*), by great Zeus's design, good spirits on the face of the earth, watchers over mortal men, bestowers of wealth. Such is the kingly honour that they received.

A second race after that, much inferior, the dwellers on Olympos made of silver, resembling the gold one neither in body nor in disposition. For a hundred years a boy would stay in the care of his good mother, playing childishly at home. But when they were full grown and reached the full measure of their prime, they lived but a little time, and in suffering, because of their witlessness. For they could not refrain from abusive crimes against each other, and they would not serve the immortals, or sacrifice on the sacred altars of the blessed ones, as is laid down for men wherever they dwell. They were put away by Zeus son of Kronos, angry because they did not offer honour to the blessed gods who occupy Olympos. Since the earth covered this race up too, they have been called the mortal blessed below the earth, second in rank, though they too still have honour.

Then Zeus the father made yet a third race of men, of bronze, not like the silver in anything. Out of ash trees he made them, a terrible and fierce race, concerned with the woeful works of Ares and with deeds of violence, no eaters of grain, their unyielding hearts being of adamant; unshapen hulks, with great force and indescribable arms growing from their shoulders above their mighty bodies. Bronze was their armour, bronze their houses, and with bronze they laboured, as black iron was unknown. They were laid low by their own hands, and they went to the dank house of chill Hades leaving behind no names. Mighty though they were, black death seized them, and they left the bright sunlight.

After the earth covered up this race too, Zeus son of Kronos made yet a fourth one upon the rich-pastured earth, a juster and more noble one, the godly race of the heroes who are called demigods, our predecessors on the boundless earth. And as for them, evil war and fearful fighting destroyed them, some before seven-gated Thebes, in the Kadmean land, as they battled for the flocks of Oedipus; and others war led in ships over the great gulf of the sea to Troy on account of fair-tressed Helen. There some of them were enshrouded by the consummation of death, but to some Zeus the father, son of Kronos, granted a life and home apart from men, and settled them at the ends of the earth. These live with carefree heart in the Isles of the Blest, beside deep-swirling Okeanos: happy heroes, for whom the grain-giving ploughland yields its honey-sweet fruits thrice yearly.

Oh, would that I were not then among the fifth men, but either had died earlier or been born later! For now it was a race of iron, and they will never cease from toil and misery by day or night, in constant distress, and the gods will give them harsh troubles. Yet even they shall have good mixed with the ills. But Zeus will destroy this race of men too, when at birth they turn out grey at their temples. Nor will father have common bond with children nor children with father, nor guest with host nor comrade with comrade, nor will a brother be as dear to brother as in former times. Soon they will cease to respect their ageing parents, and will rail at them with bitter words, the wretches, in ignorance of the gods' retribution. Nor will they repay their ageing parents for their nurture, replacing justice with violent hands. One will sack another's city, and there will be no thanks for the man who abides by his oath or for the righteous or worthy man; but instead they will honour the miscreant and the criminal. Law will lie in strong hands, and decent shame shall be no more. The villain will harm the better man by telling crooked tales, and swearing an oath upon them. Envy who exults in misfortune with a face full of hate will everywhere dog men in their misery. Then verily, veiling their fair faces with white robes, off to Olympos from the wide-pathed earth will depart Decency and Right-eous Indignation to join the family of the immortals, abandoning mankind. Those grim woes will remain behind for mortal men, and there will be no help against evil.

(*Works and Days* 106–201, trans. M. L. West, modified)

The traditional version of the myth told the story of the successive races of mankind which had peopled the earth before our age and then disappeared: the golden race, then the silver and the bronze races, and finally the race of iron, following each other in order of ever more pronounced and apparently inexorable degeneration. But this orderly sequence of decadence was dis-turbed by Hesiod's inserting a race of Heroes between the bronze race and the iron (that is, ours). This modification of the struc-ture of the myth entailed an essential alteration of its meaning. For the races now appeared opposed to each other in two groups of two, in the form of justice (*dikē*) opposed to excess (*hubris*): that is, the golden race was opposed to the silver, the bronze to the heroic. In the first pairing it is *dikē* that triumphs, but in the second it is *hubris*. That left the race of iron, itself subdivided into two: first, the race as known to Hesiod, a time of intermingled *dikē* and *hubris* and one of choice, but, secondly, a looming threat of the impending triumph of *hubris* and misfortune in a world turned upside down where 'nothing will be any longer as it was in days past' (*Works and Days* 184). The meaning of the lesson which Hesiod drew from the myth, for the benefit not only of his brother Perses but also indirectly of the great lords of the land (Askra within the territory of Boiotian Thespiai), thus becomes clear: 'Hearken to Justice, do not let excess wax strong' (213).

In these three successive pairings there can also be discerned that functional tripartition which G. Dumézil has shown to permeate the religious thought of the Indo-European peoples. The races of gold and silver display the characteristics of royalty, as is symbolized by the very metals that define the races. The Good King who dispenses justice and considers himself a scion of Zeus is succeeded by the impious kings of the race of silver who are avatars rather of the Titans. In their turn the men of the race of bronze are characterized by their martial comportment; this corresponds to the behaviour of the Giants, who in the myths of their struggle with the Gods for supreme power are represented as revolting against the sovereignty of Zeus and being vanquished by him. Then, over against the race of bronze there rises up the race of Heroes, which is also a martial race; but, as it incarnates the model of the ideally just warrior, it is on that account transported by Zeus to the Isles of the Blest.

Finally, there comes the race of iron, marked by ambiguity and ambivalence, for which good and evil are inseparable companions. Men of this unhappy race know suffering and death, and they must earn their bread from the soil by the sweat of their brow:

For the gods keep men's livelihood concealed: otherwise you would easily labour enough even in a day to provide you for a full year even without working. Soon you would stow your rudder up in the smoke [above the hearth], and the business of oxen and toiling mules would disappear.

But Zeus concealed it, angry because Prometheus' crooked cunning had tricked him. He therefore devised grim cares for mankind; he concealed fire. But the noble son of Iapetos stole it back for men from resourceful Zeus in a hollow fennel-stalk, eluding the eye of thunder-rejoicing Zeus. In anger Zeus the cloud-gatherer addressed him:

'Son of Iapetos, clever above all others, you are glad at having stolen fire and outwitted me – a great calamity both for you yourself and for men to come. To set against the fire I shall visit them with an affliction in which they will all delight as they embrace their own destruction.'

So saying, the father of men and gods laughed out loud; and he bade renowned Hephaistos at once to mix earth with water, to add in a human voice and strength, and to model upon the aspect of the immortal goddesses the fair lovely form of a maiden. Athene he bade teach her crafts, to weave the embroidered web, and golden Aphrodite to shower charm around her head, and painful desire and limb-wearying cares; and Hermes the guide and Argos-slayer he charged to put in the mind of a she-dog and a deceitful nature.

So he ordered, and they all obeyed the lord Zeus son of Kronos. At once the renowned Ambidexter [Hephaistos] moulded from earth the likeness of a modest maiden by the design of the son of Kronos, and the owl-eyed goddess Athene dressed and adorned her. The Graces and the lady Persuasion put necklaces of gold about her body, and the lovely-haired Seasons [Horai] garlanded her about with spring flowers. Pallas Athene arranged all the adornment on her body. In her breast the guide and Argos-slayer contrived lies and wily stratagems and a deceitful nature by deep-thundering Zeus's design; and he also put in a voice, did the herald of the gods, and he named this woman Pandora ['Allgift'] because all the dwellers on Olympos made her their gift – a calamity for bread-eating men.

When he had completed the vertiginous, unnegotiable trap, the father sent the renowned Argos-slayer, swift messenger of the gods, to take the gift to Epimetheus. But Epimetheus gave no thought to what Prometheus had told him, never to accept a gift from Olympian Zeus but to return it lest some ill afflict mortals: he accepted, and only realized when the evil was already his.

For formerly the tribes of men lived on earth remote from ills, without harsh toil and the grievous sicknesses that bring deadly fates to men. But the woman unstopped the jar and scattered them all, bringing grim cares upon mankind. Only Hope remained there within her secure dwelling, under the lip of the jar, and did not fly out, because the woman put back the lid in time by the providence of cloud-gathering Zeus who wears the aegis. But the rest, numberless troubles, roam among men: full of ills is the earth, and full the sea. Diseases visit men by day, and others by night, uninvited, bringing ill to mortals, silently, because Zeus the resourceful robbed them of speech. Thus there is no way to evade the design of Zeus.

(*Works and Days* 43–105, trans. M. L. West, modified)

Pandora, the model Woman, is here presented as the cause of mankind's ills, since it is she who opened the jar in which they had hitherto been confined. But Pandora is also the symbol of humanity's 'mixed-up' quality of life, a 'beautiful evil', as Hesiod describes her in the *Theogony* (555, see below). For she stands for the function of fecundity, both the production of food, inasmuch as she is a creature of the earth, and the reproduction of the human species. Mankind, tiller of the soil in the age of iron, is thus presented with a choice: either to submit to the order of *dikē* or to abandon itself to *hubris* and the inevitable triumph of evil.

The three functions of sovereignty, martial activity and fecundity, which are incarnated respectively by the King, the Warrior and the Farmer, are in Hesiod subordinated to an overarching tension between the forces of Dikē and Hubris. It is that tension which ultimately controls the entire Hesiodic version of the myth, giving it its most innovatory aspect and deepest originality. The place accorded by Hesiod to Dikē, Justice, the daughter of Zeus, is his answer to the problems thrown up by the social upheavals of his own day, the turn of the eighth and seventh centuries. The triumph of Dikē over Hubris is a matter of equal concern to the small farmer Perses, Hesiod's brother, and to the lords whose task it was to make the rule of justice prevail. As for the warrior's function, Hesiod keeps that at a distance and gives only a small hint of it in his representation of Eris ('Strife'). The latter can be either the bad kind of strife which provokes conflicts like that between himself and Perses over their paternal inheritance (see the prologue of the *Works and Days*), or the good strife which enables and permits the triumph of Dikē.

In sum, by breathing fresh life into an old myth so as to adapt it to the living realities of his own time, Hesiod has given it a new resonance. And by taking Hesiod's myth of the races as an example we have been able to show two things: first, how a structural analysis that takes into account the different levels of a myth can do justice to a complex totality; and secondly, how every myth is a living and pliable creation which may itself in its turn become an element in a yet more complex elaboration.

MYTHS OF SACRIFICE

The problem of sacrifice occupied a crucial position in Greek religion, and at its centre lay the myth of Prometheus, the object of which was to define the relationship between mankind and the gods. In chapter 4 we demonstrated the essential place of sacrifice within Greek religious ritual. Here by way of illustration we have chosen to show how some myths of sacrifice functioned.

(i) The separation of men and gods

Let us look first at the Hesiodic version of the Prometheus myth as presented in the *Theogony*, which, as we have seen, is repeated in part in the Pandora myth of the *Works and Days*:

For when the gods and mortal men were in dispute at Mekone, he [Prometheus] had a large ox cut up and served so as to deceive Zeus. For men he laid out meat and entrails rich with fat on the hide, covering them with the ox's stomach, while for Zeus he laid out the ox's white bones carefully arranged for a cunning trick by covering them in glistening fat. Then the father of men and gods said to him:

'Son of Iapetos, most conspicuous among all the lords, my good sir, how unfairly you have divided the portions!'

So chided Zeus, whose resource is unfailing. But crooked-scheming Prometheus answered him, smiling gently and intent on deceit:

'Zeus, greatest and most glorious of the eternal gods, take then whichever of the portions the spirit in your breast bids you.'

He spoke, meaning trickery; but Zeus, whose resource is unfailing, recognized the trick and did not mistake it, and he meditated evil in his heart for mortal men, which was to come to pass. With both hands he took up the white fat; and he grew angry about the lungs, and wrath entered his mind when he saw the white ox-bones set for a cunning trick. Ever since that, the tribes of men upon earth have burned white bones for the immortals on aromatic altars. In great ire cloud-gathering Zeus addressed him:

'Son of Iapetos, clever above all others, my good sir, then you are still intent on deceit.'

So said Zeus in his anger, whose resource is unfailing. And after that, with his anger ever in his mind, he would not grant to the ash-trees the power of unwearying fire for mortal men who dwell on earth. But the noble son of Iapetos outwitted him by stealing the far-beaconing flare of unwearying fire in a hollow fennel-stalk. And it stung high-thundering Zeus deep to the spirit and angered him in his heart, when he saw the far-beaconing flare of fire among mankind.

At once he fashioned an affliction for mankind to set against the fire. The renowned Ambidexter moulded from earth the likeness of a modest maiden, by design of the son of Kronos. The owl-eyed goddess Athene dressed and adorned her in an incandescent garment; down over her head she drew an embroidered veil, marvellous to behold; and around her head she placed a golden diadem, which the renowned Ambidexter made with his own hands to please father Zeus. On it were wrought many designs, marvellous to behold, all the beasts that the land and sea nourish. Many of them he included, wonderful designs, like living creatures with voices of their own – and much charm gleamed out.

But when he had created the beautiful evil as the cost of a blessing, he led her out where the other gods and men were, and she rejoiced in the finery bestowed on her by the owl-eyed daughter of a stern father. Both immortal gods and men alike were seized with wonder when they saw that vertiginous, unnegotiable trap. For from her is descended the race of women, a great affliction to the mortal husbands with whom they dwell, no fit partners for accursed Poverty but only for Plenty. As the bees in their sheltered hives feed the drones, those fellow-hatchers of evil deeds, and while they busy themselves from sunup to sundown making the white honeycomb, the drones stay inside in the sheltered skeps and heap the labour of others into their own bellies, even so as a bane for mortal husbands did high-thundering Zeus create women, fellow-hatchers of dire deeds.

And he gave them a second bane as the cost of a blessing: the man who, to avoid marriage and the ills women cause, chooses not to wed, arrives at grim old age lacking anyone to look after him. He does not lack livelihood while he lives, but when he dies, distant kinsmen share out his possessions. Then again, the man who does choose the portion of marriage and gets a good wife who is sound and sensible, even so spends his life in a contest between good and evil; while the man who gets the awful kind lives with unrelenting pain in his mind and heart – that is an ill without cure.

Thus there is no way of deceiving or evading the design of Zeus, since not even the son of Iapetos, sly Prometheus, escaped his heavy wrath, and for all his cleverness a strong fetter binds him.

(*Theogony* 535–616, trans. M. L. West, modified)

Hesiod relates here the 'duel of cunning' fought by Prometheus and Zeus at the moment when the nature of the relationship between men and the gods was being decided for good. On one side is Zeus conqueror of the Titans, who has distributed among the Olympians their portions of honour and privilege. On the other is Prometheus, son of the Titan Iapetos but not a personal enemy of Zeus. At issue is the distribution of the parts of a sacrificial victim as between the Olympians and mortal men.

Prometheus divides up an ox into two portions, one each for the two parties concerned. In an attempt to deceive Zeus, he covers the bare bones with fat, while the second portion consists of 'meat and entrails heavy with fat on the hide' (539–40). The first portion has an alluring appearance but beneath the fat it contains nothing that is edible. The second portion has a rebarbative look but conceals all the pieces that are good to eat. Of the two unequal portions Zeus deliberately chooses the trumpery one, since that is in reality the good one – good, that is, for the gods. For by sustaining themselves solely on the smoke rising from the bones burned on the altar, the Olympians are able to demonstrate their immortal nature, a nature completely detached from everything corruptible and in particular from the dead flesh of beasts which men, for their part, cannot do without. Zeus thereby deflects Prometheus' ruse against mankind, meditating vengeance the while.

In due course, therefore, Zeus denies to mortal men the fire that has hitherto been at their free disposal, hiding it from them and forbidding them to cook the meat that has been acquired through the share-out. But Prometheus liberates fire from its hiding-place and bestows it upon men, thereby endowing it with a twofold significance for them: on the one hand, fire unites men to the gods through the sacrificial flames of the altar; on the other hand, it separates men from the beasts with whom they share the condition of mortality, by permitting them to cook the beasts' flesh for food.

However, this gift of Prometheus to mankind arouses the anger of Zeus a second time, and his revenge now takes the form of an equally deceptive counter-gift. The myth's third episode tells the story of how the first woman was fashioned out of clay by Hephaistos and beautified by Athene. This is the woman who in the *Works and Days* is called Pandora, the 'gift of all the gods'; but she is a tainted gift, a 'beautiful evil', since beneath her beauty and seductiveness are concealed lying and deceitfulness.

The first act of the Hesiodic drama, the unequal division and distribution under which mankind received all the edible flesh of the victim, is presented in the text itself as an explanation of one part of the sacrificial ritual: 'hence it came about that on earth the race of men burns the white bones for the immortal gods on altars which exhale the perfume of incense' (*Theog.* 556–7). Yet the meaning of the myth as a whole is not exhausted by this aetiological function. Rather, its coherence is underlined at the narrative level by the way in which the episodes are linked to each other, and at the semantic level by the symbolic correspondences between them. In the final analysis, it is the very nature and function of sacrifice of the Promethean type that are illuminated by the Hesiodic myth.

In the same way that Prometheus schemed initially to deceive Zeus with an unequal distribution of the sacrificial ox, so Zeus in his turn deceived men by his gift to them of the first woman. Between these two episodes the theft of fire plays the mediating rôle. Prometheus' gift of fire to mankind appears at first to be a triumphant act of deception, but, because it provokes the anger and revenge of Zeus, it turns out in the end to fix immutably the nature of the human condition. Fire is thus revealed to be no less poisoned a gift than that of woman, in which men had at first been equally delighted. J.-P. Vernant has put it this way:

What is at issue in the conflict pitting the Titan's craftiness against the Olympian's faultless intelligence is, in the final analysis, the status of the human condition, the mode of existence characterizing humanity today. Sacrificial practice is presented as the first result and the most direct expression of the distance created between men and gods on the day that Prometheus embarked on the path of rebellion. The myth connects the ritual of sacrifice to primordial events that have made men what they are, mortal creatures living on earth in the midst of countless ills, eating grain from the fields they have worked, and accompanied by a wife. In other words, men have become a race of beings completely separated from those to whom at the outset they were very close, inasmuch as they sat at the same tables to share the same meals – the Blessed Immortals, who reside in heaven and feed on ambrosia, and towards whom now rises the smoke of sacrificial offerings ... just as this former proximity was expressed mythically by the image of a community of guests banqueting together, so the present separation is reflected in the contrast between two alimentary modes. The opposition of dietary régimes found at the very heart of the ritual seeks, however, to establish a kind of contact and communication between the two separated races, the tendency of which is to throw, as far as may be possible, a bridge from earth to heaven.

> (Vernant 'At man's table', in Detienne and Vernant 1989 [71]: 24, trans. P. Wissing, modified)

(ii) When is the killing of animals permissible?

Various myths of different kinds bear on the general question of the violent killing of animals, and illustrate the types of answers that were offered to the problem. Certain traditions, to which the vegetarian and Pythagorean currents of thought subscribed, conceived of an aboriginal stage of humanity in which bloody sacrifice was unknown and offerings were solely vegetable in character. It was within this framework of ideas that aetiological myths purporting to account for the first bloody animal sacrifice were located.

Consider, for example, the myth of Sopatros as told, after Theophrastos, by the third-century CE Neoplatonist Porphyry:

> For neither must the gods' altars be polluted by murder of animals nor should men touch such food, any more than they would beings identical to themselves. On the contrary, the practice still maintained at Athens [sc. in the Dipolieia festival] ought to be treated as a categorical moral imperative throughout one's life.
>
> In ancient time, as we said, men sacrificed the fruits of their harvest to the gods, but not animals; nor did they use them for their own nourishment. Now the story goes that in the course of a public sacrifice at Athens a certain Sopatros, who farmed in Attica though he was not an Athenian by birth, had laid on the offering-table quite conspicuously the sacrificial cake and other offerings for the gods, when one of the oxen that had just returned from the fields came up and devoured part of the sacrifice and trampled on the rest. Sopatros was enraged at this disturbance, and seeing that someone was honing an axe not far off grabbed it and slaughtered the ox. But after the ox had died, Sopatros' anger abated and he was seized with remorse at what he had done. So he gave the ox due burial, cursed himself with voluntary exile as an impious criminal, and went into exile on Crete.
>
> But now droughts gripped Attica, causing a terrible dearth for the Athenians who sent an official delegation to consult the Pythia at Delphi. Apollo's reply was that the exile living on Crete would put an end to their troubles and that, if they punished the murderer and set the

dead ox back on its feet in the process of the very same sacrificial ritual during which it had lost its life, it would go better for them – provided they then ate the ox without restraint or scruple. So they searched for and found Sopatros, who had been the cause of the whole affair, but Sopatros was of the opinion that he would only be cleansed of his curse and pollution if all the Athenians participated publicly in the sacrificial ritual. So he told those who had come to find him that an ox would have to be ritually slaughtered by the city of Athens as a whole. The envoys, however, were in a quandary as to who should act as the slaughterer, whereupon Sopatros offered to serve if they would make him an Athenian citizen and then participate with him in the official slaughter. To this they agreed, and on their return they instituted the arrangements which they still follow to this day.

They chose some maidens as water-bearers, to carry the water used for honing the axe and the knife. When the implements had been sharpened, one man handed over the axe, a second stunned the ox, while a third cut its throat. Yet others then flayed the beast, which was eaten by all the participants. After these operations the skin of the animal was stitched up and stuffed with straw, so that it could be set upright looking exactly as it had when it was alive. It was then harnessed to a plough as if about to go to work. They then held a murder-trial, in which all who had taken part in the ritual slaughter were required to defend themselves. The virgin water-bearers accused those who had sharpened the implements, the sharpeners indicted the man who had handed over the axe, the latter did the same to the man who had cut the ox's throat, while he in turn accused the knife which, lacking a voice to defend itself with, was found guilty of murder.

From that day to this, in the course of the Dipolieia festival held on the Athenian Akropolis, the aforementioned persons follow the identical rituals in the sacrifice of the ox. After placing on the bronze offering-table a sacrificial cake and some crushed grains they lead the designated oxen around it, and whichever one eats the offerings is the one that is slaughtered. The performers of sacrifice are always drawn from the same families, as follows: the descendants of the man who originally slaughtered the ox are all called Boutupoi ('Ox-strikers'), those who are descended from the man who led the ox around the table are called Kentriadai ('Descendants of the Goad-man'), and, finally, the descendants of the man who cut its throat are named Daitroi after the feast (*dais*) that followed the distribution of the meat. Once the hide has been stuffed and the trial concluded, the knife is drowned in the sea.

So we see that in ancient times it was not considered religiously acceptable (*hosion*) to kill the animals that labour jointly with us to

provide our livelihood. Likewise today must we take every precaution
not to commit such a crime.   (Porphyry, *On Abstinence* II.28–31)

   Here we have the foundation-myth of the Athenian Bouphonia
('Ox-murder') ritual. It seems at first sight to be confirming the
purity of the original, non-animal sacrifices and justifying the
necessity of returning to that pristine situation. But its true
significance was to show how the city of Athens was organized
around the alimentary sacrifice that enabled the members of the
community to demonstrate their mutual solidarity, by consuming
communally the portions of the ox dedicated to Zeus Polieus ('Of
the City'). At the same time the myth enabled the Athenians to
evade, through recourse to legal process (*via* the tribunal which
pronounced judgement on the murder), the guilt that would
otherwise have been attached to the act of killing. If we are to
identify and interpret correctly this dissonance between the
explicit discourse of the myth ('So we see that in ancient times
...') and its significance as a myth of civic legitimation that placed
the relationship between the soil and human labour at the heart
of the city's existence, we must situate it within a complex of
myths concerning the meanings of sacrifice and of labour in
which other plough-oxen are the objects of sacrifice.

   There are several such sacrificial myths involving Herakles.
Thus pseudo-Apollodoros (*Library* II.5.11–16) and Philostratos
(third century CE) among others describe in their different ways
how a sacrifice in honour of Herakles was instituted at Lindos on
the island of Rhodes. Here is the version of Philostratos, included
in his description of an imaginary picture-gallery:

A rough fellow, this, and, by Zeus, in a rough land; for this island is
Rhodes, of which the Lindians inhabit the roughest part, land good for
producing dried grapes and figs, but not kind to the ploughman and
impossible to drive a wagon over. The man has to be visualized as
crabbed, a farmer of 'premature old age' [Homer *Od.* xv.357]. This is
Theiodamas of Lindos, in case you have heard of him. What a bold
spirit! He is angry with Herakles, is Theiodamas, because while he was
ploughing Herakles stopped by and slaughtered one of his two oxen and
devoured it – quite in his usual manner. No doubt you have read about
Herakles in Pindar, how he arrived at Koronos' house and ate a whole
ox, not excluding the bones. Well, dropping in to visit Theiodamas
round about ox-releasing time, he prepared a fire (dung makes good

fuel) and roasted the ox, testing the flesh to see if it was tender yet, and practically accusing the fire of slowness.

The painting's details are so precise that even the nature of the terrain is clearly rendered; and where just a small patch of soil has been presented to the plough, it looks to me as if it is not at all unworkable. Herakles has his mind fixed on the ox and pays no attention to Theiodamas' cursing beyond giving a slight smile, but the farmer attacks him with stones. He is dressed in the Dorian manner, his hair is filthy, his forehead grimy; his thighs and arms would not disgrace a Spartan athlete. Such is the exploit of Herakles.

This Theiodamas is worshipped by the Lindians: so they sacrifice a plough-ox to Herakles, and begin the ritual with the same sort of curses as, I imagine, the peasant was uttering then. But Herakles rejoices at this and in return for their imprecations bestows benefits on the Lindians.

(Philostratos, *The Imaginary Picture-Gallery* II.24)

Two characteristic attributes of Herakles are on display in these accounts: his violence (he seizes the ox against the wishes of the labourer) and his legendary appetite (he devours the entire beast by himself). At the same time Herakles is presented as a perpetual wanderer in contrast to the labourer who is firmly attached to the piece of land he is working. Moreover, the sacrifice performed by Herakles is grossly untypical of civic sacrifice, inasmuch as it culminates in a solitary feast that takes cognizance neither of the customary sharing-out of the meat nor of the traditional stages of cooking – so famished is our hero that he grills the beast right out in the open and eats the lot himself. What can the meaning of this scandalous conduct be? Since it leads to the institution of a sacrifice in his honour, it is as if Herakles, by exploiting his status as an outsider and sacrificing a working ox, has authorized and even encouraged the men of Lindos to do likewise. The burden of the myth would seem to be that by means of his sacrifice Herakles had indicated to the Lindians that the sacrificial ox was one and the same as the plough-ox, that the activities of sacrificing and of working the land were connected in the same way as the production of cereals was linked to the procurement of edible flesh.

(iii) Myths of deviant sacrifice

Again, it is with reference to the central problem of sacrifice and the killing of animals that the *refusal* of bloody sacrifice by the Orphics is to be understood. This refusal was grounded in their myths of the death of Dionysos. Once upon a time, the Titans attracted the attention of the young Dionysos by showing him some toys. They then seized him and put him to death, treating him as if he were a sacrificial victim. They cut off his limbs and boiled them in a cauldron, then they spitted and roasted the entrails, before finally devouring them. Zeus punished the Titans by striking them with lightning, and from their ashes the human race was born. To Apollo was delegated the task of recovering Dionysos' heart, which the Titans had forborne to sacrifice.

Now, although the Titans' treatment of Dionysos did resemble normal sacrifice, it crucially inverted the order of the 'sacrificial cooking' (chapter 4). Normally, the *splankhna* were grilled first, before the other parts of the meat were boiled. This twofold process of normal cooking corresponded to an interpretation of sacrifice in terms of two successive stages in the cultural history of humanity: from the raw to the cooked, but, within the sphere of the cooked, from the roasted (a superficial and primitive mode) to the boiled, which required superior culinary art. The Titans' inversion of the roasting and the boiling destroyed this hierarchy of cultural values and thereby underlined the negative aspect of their cooking and sacrifice. By means of their crime the entire sacrificial procedure was stigmatized as criminal murder; and by thus condemning their distant ancestors, the Orphics anathematized the whole complex of human behaviour whereby living creatures were killed for the sake of their food.

The Orphics claimed to lead a life of purity, unsullied by the blood of animal sacrifices. In this, Orphism distinguished itself root and branch from Dionysiac orgiastic worship, and the Orphics consecrated the distance between the two in mythical terms by appropriating the tradition that Orpheus was torn to pieces by manic Thracian women. Accounts of the latter's motivation differed – they were taking revenge for the contempt Orpheus had shown either to them or to Dionysos; and there were also variant accounts of the women's identity – either they were technically Maenads or just women in a state of delirium. But the core of meaning common to all the versions was that by rending and scattering Orpheus' body the women had made Orpheus a victim of Dionysiac savagery.

The most typical expression of Dionysiac devotion was orgiastic madness (*mania*), characterized by manifestations of delirium (*ekstasis*) and possession (*enthousiasmos*) among the faithful. Devotees thus earned the alternative titles of Bacchants (Bakkhos being a by-name of Dionysos) and Maenads (literally 'Mad-women'), privileged followers of the god. Euripides' last tragedy, *Bacchae*, transposed these behavioural traits onto a mythic plane in order to portray the most extreme expressions of Dionysiac trance. Possessed by the deity, his female adepts abandoned their homes for the mountains. There they roamed by torchlight in a state of ecstasy and threw themselves without restraint into hunting for game, which they tore to pieces with their bare hands (*diasparagmos*) and devoured raw (*ōmophagia*) (see also chapter 13).

Here, then, are all the marks of a perversion and inversion of normal sacrifice and its functions: wild nature opposed to the cultured space of the city, the hunting of wild beasts as opposed to the killing of domestic animals, transgression of the rituals of slaughter and distribution, absence of the fire and cooking that would have transformed the raw meat into cultivated food. To indulge in Dionysiac sacrifice, that is to say, was a way of turning oneself into a savage and thereby rejecting civic sacrifice and the values it expressed. By overstepping the boundary separating men from the beasts Dionysiac orgiastic worship provided an alternative means of exploring the human condition, beyond the limits set by the Promethean model of sacrifice.

CONCLUSION

Our reading of these different myths – from the story of Prometheus right up to Dionysiac omophagy, by way of Pythagorean speculations on the death of the ox – points towards a cultural complex organized around alimentary practices, culinary procedures, and bloody animal-sacrifice. What this reading lays bare is a Greek discourse, both explicit and implicit, about 'the human condition as defined in its relation to beasts and in its relation to gods', a discourse premissed upon a 'sacrificial and nutritional model dominated by the relations between three terms – gods above, animals below, and men in between' (Detienne 1979 [202]: 93, 17).

CHAPTER 13

A polytheistic religion

DIVINE POWERS: GODS, *DAIMONES*, HEROES

The Classical Greeks did not define themselves as 'polytheists'. The nearest ancient equivalent to our 'polytheism', namely *polutheos doxa* (literally, 'belief in many gods'), was coined by Philo of Alexandria, a philosopher of the first century CE whose ancestral religion, Judaism, was monotheistic. But polytheists the Classical Greeks certainly were, since a polytheistic religion is characterized by the plurality of the divine powers that it recognizes and of the cults that it observes; indeed, for the Greeks everything, according to the formula attributed to Thales (sixth century BCE), was 'full of gods'. This diversity of gods, however, was not necessarily incompatible with the idea of a unity of the divine. As the Greeks saw it, the divine simply manifested itself in multiply diverse aspects.

The Greeks worshipped more than one type of divine power, of which there were three principal categories: gods, *daimones* and heroes. Within each category they distinguished several sub-categories. Each divinity, moreover, might be invoked under titles or epithets that emphasized different aspects of its power; Athene, for example, is known to have been honoured under as many as fifty or so such epithets, including Apatouria, Boulaia, Khalkioikos, Erganē, Parthenos and Polias. Polytheism as a system may thus be thought of as resembling a nest of Russian dolls. We shall now consider each of its aspects in turn.

GODS (*THEOI*)

The Greeks called their gods *athanatoi*, 'immortals'. Another name for them was *makares*, 'the blessed ones'. Although born on a particular day, they did not die. They nourished themselves on ambrosia, nectar and smoke – the incense-laden smoke that rose from the altars of men who offered sacrifices to them (chapters 4, 12). Through their veins there coursed, not blood, but an ethereal juice called *ikhōr*, as graphically described in the *Iliad* in the scene where Diomedes recognizes Aphrodite on the battlefield before the walls of Troy and wounds her:

> He hit her at the extremity of her delicate arm; his weapon penetrated the skin through the divine garment, and above the wrist of the goddess her immortal blood gushed out, *ichōr* such as flows in the veins of the blessed immortals. For the gods, who eat no bread nor drink dusky wine, are bloodless and called immortal therefore.
>
> (Homer *Iliad* v.337–45)

The gods, however, despite their anthropomorphic appearance, were not persons so much as powers, ordered and classified according to the system of Greek religious thought. The different types of supernatural power had their own dynamic, their own peculiar modes and spheres of operation and their inherent limitations. Each divinity had its own name, attributes and adventures, but they all owed their existence solely to the bonds that linked them in a systematic way to the totality of the divine universe. The notion of individualized divinity was not, however, thought incompatible with the existence of divine powers which were collective, indivisible and indissociable. The Graces, for example, were a group of three divinities often invoked under their collective title, although they could also appear separately under their own individual names. Likewise, the Muses and the Nymphs were worshipped collectively in a variety of local forms.

The gods whose identities were most sharply individuated could in their turn assume a whole range of guises specified by their particular cultic epithets, depending on the place where the cult was celebrated and the function that was being fulfilled. Thus at Athens the list of the communally worshipped instantiations of Zeus included Zeus *Hupatos* ('Most High'), who was worshipped with bloodless sacrifices, Zeus *Sōtēr* ('Saviour'), honoured at the Diisoteria festival in the month of Skirophorion (June–July), Zeus *Polieus* ('Of the City'), celebrated at the Dipolieia held in the same month, and Zeus *Meilikhios* ('Gentle'), worshipped at the Diasia festival in Anthesteriōn (beginning of October). Within an Athenian house one would find Zeus *Philios* ('Friendly', 'Loving'), lord of the feast, Zeus *Sōtēr*, who received the third offertory libation poured during the banquet, Zeus *Ktēsios*, guardian of property, Zeus *Herkeios*, protector of the enclosure, Zeus *Kataibatēs*, averter of lightning, and so on *ad* (almost) *infinitum*.

DAIMONES

Alongside the gods, the Greeks recognized the existence of mysterious forms of divine powers, both beneficent and maleficent, with the capacity to intervene in human affairs. Homer used *daimōn* in this sense, although he also employed it vaguely to designate divinity. Sometimes, *daimones* were regarded as forming a category of divine beings intermediate between gods and men, but Plato several times conjoined gods, *daimones*, heroes and the dead, on the one hand, in order to oppose them categorically to mankind, on the other. According to one tradition, it was Thales who first established the tripartite division between gods and *daimones* and heroes.

From the time of the comic dramatist Menander (late fourth/early third century) onwards, *daimones* came to be seen as 'guardians of mortal men', a sort of protective spirit or personal 'genius'. In the realm of philosophical speculation, the word and the notion of *daimones* received extensive development in connection with the Stoic idea of a personal, interior *daimōn*. In cult, however, the word occurred but rarely, whereas a different type of divine power, the hero, was omnipresent.

HEROES

The hero was a deceased person, whether identifiable by name or anonymous. His life and death, alike glorious and devoted to the service of the community, were associated with an era in the distant past. A hero might be recognized by the type of cult that was offered to him, which differed from that accorded to the unexceptional dead in respect of its longevity, the frequency and importance of the rituals of worship, and finally the nature of the worshipping community. The centre of the cult was the hero's tomb, the *hērōon*, or, failing a recognized burial-site, the place where the remains of the corpse were supposed to lie.

The majority of heroes were tied to a specific locality and unknown outside the valley or village where they were worshipped. Every Attic deme, for example, had its hero – or rather, heroes. On the other hand, a select few heroes, like Herakles, were international figures, recognized throughout the Greek world. It used to be maintained that heroes were paid 'chthonic' cult as opposed to the 'Olympian' cult paid to the gods, but in fact the rituals did not always differ in this respect. Sometimes, indeed, gods and heroes were worshipped in the same festivals. The respective magnificence of their worship was a function of the greater or smaller fame of the heroes and the importance of the community celebrating them. Thus the festival of the hero Theseus at Athens, the Theseia, was in every respect comparable to the festivals in honour of the goddess Athene.

Moreover, what was expected from heroes was of the same order as that which was expected from the gods; their sphere of intervention in human affairs was comparably vast and diverse. They delivered oracles, they effected cures, they provided protection, and they dealt out retribution. They were not mere intermediaries between the human and divine worlds, but rather completely independent divinities in their own right, who often had cultic personnel devoted to their service, operating from within flourishing sanctuaries. Indeed, they even had their own mythological apparatus attached to them, consisting of variously elaborated cycles of epic adventures. The stories told of Herakles, Theseus, Kadmos, Jason and Perseus, for instance, were endless; to retell them in any detail would turn this book into a catalogue. Common themes do run through the cycles, but local traditions and variants are also detectable. Heroic myth was no more of a monolith than the mythology of the gods. On the contrary, it was so adaptable and flexible that it could even be worked up into a romance like the third-century *Argonautica* by Apollonius of Rhodes.

So great are the multiplicity and diversity of heroes that there has been a long-standing scholarly concern to 'introduce some order' into their copious abundance. Such classificatory efforts are interesting for the way they reflect the developing historiography of religion. At times the emphasis has been placed on the alleged 'nature' of the heroes, whether they are conceived as faded gods, vegetation spirits, epic heroes, heroes of human history, or whatever. At other times what has been emphasized is their overt social function, in war, for example, or athletic competition, or initiation, or kinship relations, and so on. Recent research, however, has preferred to situate the heroic cults firmly in their historical context, stressing the link between the cults' first appearance and the transformation of the Greek city during the eighth century.

Between about 750 and 700, tombs that had been constructed in the Mycenaean era (*c.* 1600–1100) were given a new function as focuses of cult, and the deceased were endowed with heroic identities that might bear no relation to their status in historical actuality. The distribution of these cults marked the cities' appropriation of a territory, the brute physical possession of the soil being thus graced with an aura of religious legitimation through the cult of a hero. This tight nexus between heroic cult and the development of the civic community is particularly clear in the case of cults of founder-heroes. But within any one city a plurality of heroes attested to the stages of its evolutionary history, from that of primitive humanity to the emergence of civilization, and then from civilization to the birth of the city. Studying a city's system of cults and heroic myths can therefore help us to understand the way in which the Greeks conceptualized their own past history.

Every city, it goes without saying, did so in its own way. Athens, for instance, fabricated for itself a legendary tissue of origin myths around the characters of Erikhthonios and Theseus. Erikhthonios was a primordial being born of Earth but conceived as a result of Hephaistos' lust for Athene. This autochthonous figure went on to become the first king of Athens and eventually to receive a cult under the title of Poseidon-

Erekhtheus. Theseus, for his part, was the son of Aigeus (or, alternatively, Poseidon) and Aithra, daughter of the king of Troizen. After numerous exploits, such as the following, related by Pausanias, he was at last recognized by Aigeus and succeeded him on the Athenian throne:

> One of the legends about Theseus told at Troizen is that Herakles went to visit Pittheus there and at dinner took off his lion-skin; some little boys came in to watch him, and one was Theseus, aged about seven. When they saw the lion's hide, all the other boys ran away, but Theseus approached it without too much terror, grabbed an axe from the servants and at once made a fierce attack on it, thinking it was a real lion. This is the first story about him at Troizen; the next is that Aigeus put boots and a sword under a rock to be proofs of identity for the boy, and sailed away to Athens. When Theseus was sixteen he pushed the rock over and went away wearing what Aigeus had deposited. This story is represented pictorially on the Akropolis, all done in bronze except for the rock. (Pausanias 1.27.8, trans. P. Levi, modified)

As king, Theseus was supposed to have effected the *sunoikismos* or 'housing-together' of the inhabitants of all Attica and founded the city of Athens properly speaking. The continuation of the above passage from Pausanias provides a Theseic aetiology for a dedication on the Athenian Akropolis by one of the easternmost Attic demes, that of Marathon:

> Another of the deeds of Theseus is represented in an offering: this is the story. There was a bull creating havoc all over Crete, especially around the river Tethris. Wild beasts were apparently more terrifying to human beings in those days, like the lions of Nemea and Parnassos, the serpents in many parts of Greece and the boars of Kalydon, Erymanthos and Krommyon in Korinthia; they used to say some of them grew out of the ground and some were holy and belonged to gods, and others were let loose to punish the human race. The Cretans claim this bull was sent to their country by Poseidon, because Minos was lord of the Greek sea and yet failed to pay Poseidon special respect. They say this bull was carried over from Crete to the Peloponnese and killing it was one of the Twelve Labours of Herakles.
>
> When it was released onto the plain of Argos, it dashed away through the Isthmus of Corinth and up through Attica to the deme of Marathon, killing whomever it met, including Minos' son Androgeōs. Minos was convinced the Athenians must be responsible for Androgeōs' death. He

came over with a fleet and attacked them, and did so much damage that they agreed to take seven girls and seven boys to Crete, for the fabulous Minotaur that lived in the Labyrinth at Knossos. Afterwards the story goes that Theseus drove the bull of Marathon to the Akropolis and sacrificed it to the goddess. The dedication commemorating this deed is by the deme of Marathon. (1.27.9, trans. P. Levi, modified)

Theseus then fought – among other opponents – the Amazons, made a descent into Hades, and finally died on the island of Skyros.

Thus these two heroes, each in his individual way, mark significant stages in the origins of Athens. Through Erikhthonios the Athenians identified themselves as 'autochthonous', that is to say, born from the very soil and therefore inhabiting the territory of Attica from the dawn of their history; this was a myth that played a rôle of considerable importance in Athenian political ideology of the Classical period. In Theseus the Athenians invented a civilizing hero of the stamp of Herakles (a principally Peloponnesian culture-hero) who provided support for their hegemonial ambitions in that same period. But the history of his cult at Athens was one of ups and downs; now honoured, now forgotten, it was not until the end of the fifth century that Theseus achieved definitive incarnation as the model of a founder-king of a moderate democracy.

Other cities besides Athens had enormous cycles of heroic legend. For example, Thebes's myth of origins was centred on the deeds of Kadmos. This embraced his quest for Europe, his victory over the dragon, the birth of the Spartoi ('Sown Men') from his sowing of the dragon's teeth, his foundation of Thebes, his marriage to Harmonia, their descendants, the first legendary kings of the city and their succession-struggles, leading up to the story of Oedipus and his descendants.

One final example: Argos. Here it was Phoroneus, the first man to reign on earth, who mythically established a primeval form of communal life, invented fire, carried out the first animal sacrifice and forged armour and weapons. A prolonged drought supervened, broken finally by the immigrant Danaos and his daughters, for one of whom, Amymonē, Poseidon caused a spring to gush forth with his trident as a sweetener for his proposal of marriage. Then and only then could Argos become a true city.

WAYS OF APPROACHING THE PANTHEON

The most striking trait of polytheism is the existence of pantheons, collectivities of divinities who yet retained their own individual names, identities and functions. The plural form, pantheons, has to be insisted on. For the Greeks did indeed invent and conceptualize several possible combinations, and hierarchies, of divinities, not only in their different cities and at different epochs, but also in accordance with the differently structured conceptions of the world peculiar to particular groups; the Orphics, for example, had their own particular brand of pantheon. So the following list of the twelve 'Olympians' represents solely a classificatory convenience, not a canon of gods to whom cult must without exception or exemption be paid: Zeus, Poseidon, Demeter, Hera, Ares, Aphrodite, Artemis, Apollo, Athene, Hermes, Dionysos and Hephaistos. These twelve appear, for instance, in the divine assembly on the Parthenon frieze. But the list could be varied, often so as to include Hestia and Hades in place of Ares and Dionysos. Perhaps we might say that the number twelve remained stable, whereas the identity of the component deities did not.

Merely to list the names, though, is only a beginning: the question is how these gods should be studied. The standard response to this problem of method has been to catalogue them. Philologists have assembled, sifted and pored over all the relevant texts, while archaeologists have uncovered their sanctuaries and cult-places. Their combined labours have enabled scholars to write the 'history' and the 'geography' of each god by collating the scanty details of the respective rituals, myths and cult-places. But such an approach is flawed. For, as J.-P. Vernant has put it (1991[42]: 271), it reduces the pantheon to 'a mere conglomeration of gods, an assemblage of unusual personages of diverse origin, the products, in random circumstances, of fusion, assimilation and segmentation. They seem to find themselves in association rather by virtue of accidents of history than by the inherent requirements of an organized system . . . ' We might, for example, criticize in this light the numerous books that A. B. Cook devoted to Zeus: although they tell the reader everything there is to know about Zeus's epithets and cult-places, they convey no understanding of this divinity's place within the Greek pantheon as a whole, with the result that the pantheon's *raison d'être* remains an enigma.

Instead, therefore, we should embrace the very different approach to the study of the pantheon sketched out in the works of Georges Dumézil (especially 1966[218]). The essential point of this is to concentrate on the *structures* of the pantheon rather than on the divinities taken in isolation:

It is imperative that we keep in mind a rule of method that we forget only at the peril of multiple confusions. In characterizing a divinity the definition of its mode of operation is more informative than a list either of the sites of its activity or of the occasions on which its services are demanded. An important divinity is inevitably invoked by all and for all, sometimes in quite unexpected contexts, far removed from its principal province, and yet it still does operate there. However, merely establishing the eccentricity of this particular intervention leads one into the errors of lumping that one indiscriminately with other, central, interventions, and claiming that the divinity, since it is capable of escaping from any constricting definition, is 'omnivalent' or 'indeterminate'. But if, on the contrary, one pays attention, not to the *where*, but to the *how* of the divinity's operation, one almost always ascertains that even in its most aberrant interventions it preserves a constancy of manner and method. The true objective of the study, therefore, is to determine the manner and the method of operation.   (Dumézil 1966[218]: 179–80)

Thus we should no longer study, for example, Hestia and Hermes or Athene and Poseidon in isolation from each other, but should rather seek to establish in precisely what respects the functions, modes of intervention, myths and rituals of these two pairs of gods are similar to or opposed to each other, what are the frontiers of their respective fields of operation, what are their reciprocal relationships, and what logic governs their being invoked. We should proceed in the same way with Apollo and Dionysos, with all the divinities who preside over human marriage (below), and so on.

If this approach is adopted, the specific characteristics of each god stand out much more clearly, so that we can see just how far the pantheon – rather than being an incoherent jumble of gods, a maze where only specialists can find their way – is a vital intellectual construct, possessing its own logic, and functioning within and for the benefit of the society that gave it birth. To quote Vernant again:

We have to identify in the pantheon the manifold structures and to detect all the forms of grouping in which the gods are habitually associated or in opposition. The pantheon is a complicated system of relationships in which each god is part of a variegated network of associations with other gods; it surely has the function of a classificatory system, applicable to the whole of reality – to nature and to human society as much as to the supernatural world. It is, however, a system in which the main structures do not exactly coincide and which has to be followed along its several lines like a table with a number of columns and many entries. It is these structures of the pantheon that are the subject of research, not the deities in isolation. Their variety offers a wide prospect of possible comparison, especially as each of them is located and functions on several levels. The Hermes-Hestia couple, for instance, represents not only the complementary nature of two divine powers, the immovable goddess of the hearth and the mobile god of transitions, exchanges and movements; this theological structure is also an intellectual one. It is a conception of space as a centre and an enclosure, and of movement as the possibility of passing from any one point to another, to which this couple in their contrasts and their essential fellowship give definition. Furthermore, the divine couple and the mental category are not lost in the stratosphere of ideas. They have their place in the workings of institutions. They organize and regulate matrimonial practices, the rites of descent, and the opposition between masculine and feminine tasks. They distinguish between two kinds of economic goods, those lying stored with Hestia in the enclosed space of the dwelling and those that roam the open sweep of the country with Hermes. Each facet of any analysis in which religious structures, categories of thought and social practices overlap closely is apt to initiate a process of comparison.

(Vernant 1991[42]: 277–8, translation corrected)

In short, the Greeks' polytheistic system was a rigorously logical ensemble, designed for the purpose of classifying divine capacities and powers, and fitted very tightly into the cities' *modus operandi*. We shall not therefore draw up a mere catalogue of the gods nor, on the other hand, shall we address ourselves to the collectivity of the divine figures as they might be treated today. Instead, we shall select a few examples as mutually supportive approaches to the study of the pantheon: first, the divinities that preside over marriage and over technology, since they demonstrate the complementary nature of divine powers; secondly, Apollo and, in the background, his 'brothers' Hermes and Dionysos, since study of these three underlines the complementary logic governing the invention of each separate divine figure; and, finally, the pantheon of one particular city, Mantineia, as presented by Pausanias, since this well illustrates both the diversity of local practices and the richness of the field of study constituted by the polytheisms of the Greeks.

DIVINITIES OF MARRIAGE

Marriage ritual, as we saw in chapter 7, prescribed the offering of sacrifices to Zeus Teleios, Hera Teleia, Aphrodite, Peitho and Artemis. But depending on the city in question, any of the following might also be prayed to for aid: the Nymphs, Demeter, the Graces, Hermes, the Fates (*Moirai*) and Athene. However, merely to say that each of these was 'a marriage divinity' would hardly help to explain why it was thought necessary to invoke more than one. The truth is that these divinities were in no way interchangeable.

Hera, daughter of Rhea and sister-wife of Zeus, bore in this context the epithet *Teleia*, meaning 'achieving', 'perfect' or 'accomplished'. By this the Greeks indicated their normative view that for a woman marriage was the goal of her life's journey, the token of maturity achieved. The Athenians preferred to celebrate weddings in Gamelion (January–February), the month of their calendar in which they celebrated the *Theogamia* festival commemorating the union of Hera with Zeus. Hera's rôle in marriage was to guarantee the contractual element, the formal affiancement which made of a woman a lawfully wedded wife. In this capacity the goddess was of paramount importance, since the survival of a Greek city as a civic corporation was secured by the reproduction of legitimate children who alone were entitled to citizen rights. Typically Hera was represented as an austere goddess, but there are stories that present her as a seductress, when she beguiles Zeus into making love with her (*Iliad* xiv), or as a totally autonomous power engendering children without benefit of male semen. The figure of Hera is complex – like that of the lawfully wedded Greek wife.

Artemis owed her place within marriage ritual to her function as divine protectress of the savage world, of all those beings – including young humans, both boys and girls – who have not yet entered the domain of civilization. The Archaic *Homeric Hymn to Artemis* begins by paying tribute to her status as huntress in the wild:

> I sing the noisy Artemis of the golden arrows, the venerated virgin, the Archeress who with her darts strikes down the stags, full sister of Apollo of the golden lance, her who, through the shadowy mountains and the wind-battered peaks, bends her bow of pure gold, devoted to the joy of the hunt, and lets fly groan-provoking arrows.
>
> (*Homeric Hymn to Artemis* 1–6)

Sacrifices offered to Artemis marked the moment when a Greek left behind his or her childhood, although it is the associated offerings made by the girls – of their hair, toys and dolls – that are the more strikingly memorable. The boys too, though, had to quit the domain of Artemis, not only by becoming citizen-soldiers but also by marrying. Certain rituals, like the one performed in Artemis' sanctuary on the island of Samos, emphasized the duty incumbent upon both sexes to propitiate Artemis before marriage. But it was no less dangerous (as Admetos would have been the first to admit) to forget to thank Artemis on taking one's leave of her world than it was to refuse to leave it in the first place (like Hippolytos). In the latter case, offence would be caused to Aphrodite, another marriage divinity.

Aphrodite's speciality was to 'awaken sweet desire in the hearts of the gods and to make pliant to her laws the race of mortal men, the birds of Zeus, all the beasts that the earth and sea nourish ... [Excepting only Artemis, Athene and Hestia] nothing can ever escape Aphrodite, whether blessed immortal or mortal man' (*Homeric Hymn to Aphrodite* 2–5, 34–5). It was thanks to Aphrodite that desire and pleasure were present in marriage, blessings that Atalante no less than Hippolytos sought, with complete lack of success, to escape. The gifts bestowed by Aphrodite within marriage itself made possible a fecund union, but uncontrolled indulgence in sexual gratification was thought to imperil the regulatory function of the marital bond within the city's reproductive economy. The domain where Aphrodite held absolute sway lay outside marriage, in the world of prostitutes – hence her limited rôle within the marriage ritual.

Peitho, goddess of Persuasion, was Aphrodite's companion, and in her art resembled Hermes. For Hermes, god of spatial boundaries and movements across them, prepared the path leading the young bride from the house of her father to that of her husband. It was he too who watched over the safe accomplishment of this passage. Within marriage Hermes employed his powers of persuasion, prompting in the newlywed bride (*numphē*) honeyed words with which to beguile her husband.

Demeter was the goddess of cultivated soil, making her contribution from the time of sowing to that of harvest. When a young girl entered upon marriage, she entered also into the domain of the cultivated life, symbolized for the Greeks by the growing of cereal crops. This was the sphere of Demeter, who also was responsible for making children grow. Marriage ritual, as we saw (chapter 7), was full of allusions to the preparation and cooking of cereals. The bride herself was allegorized as a field which, when tilled and seeded by the husband, would produce a crop of legitimate children. Married women continued to worship Demeter, especially through the Thesmophoria festival, which was reserved solely for them to celebrate and was designed chiefly to secure the fertility of the wombs of citizen wives.

Athene's connection with marriage was an indirect one; it was she who taught the young girl to work wool and to weave, that being the wife's principal contribution to the economy of the *oikos*. In the city of Troizen, however, under the epithet Apatouria, Athene was apparently linked with the passage from nubile maidenhood to the status of wife, and to achieve that end she deployed all her cunning intelligence (*mētis*) at this delicate and crucial moment for the city's future.

To conclude this brief overview of the divinities who operated within the orbit of marriage, we may recall the story of the creation of Pandora as told in Hesiod's *Works and Days* 60–82 (chapter 12). Pandora was the first woman, confected by the gods at the wish of Zeus and created in the image of a goddess. According to Hesiod's description, she was represented as a young girl on the eve of her nuptials.

DIVINITIES OF TECHNOLOGY

If one selects a single social function, say that of technical production, as the guiding thread of an investigation of the Greek pantheon, one encounters a wide range of divinities, from heroes to Olympian gods, each concerned with a different aspect of it.

We may start with Thetis. In Hesiod's *Theogony* she was a primordial sea-goddess, but the Spartan poet Alkman in his theogony (composed *c.* 600) turned her into the divine foundress of metallurgy. Then there were the Telkhines, first attested rather later. These primordial beings, born from the sea and concealing beneath their black eyebrows a dazzling gaze, were the instigators both of great blessings and of great ills. They were said, for example, to have fashioned the first statues of the gods with the aid of their practical skills. But their irrepressible malevolence prompted them to desiccate plant-life with magic potions and render the land infertile by flooding it with the infernal waters of the River Styx, and that prompted Zeus to blitz them with his thunderbolt.

The Kabeiroi, offspring of the union of Hephaistos and Kabeiro, daughter of the Old Man of the Sea, Proteus, lacked any such malevolence. They were skilled in the uses of fire, and the Greeks associated them with the crab, since its pincers resembled a blacksmith's tongs. The ten Daktyloi of Mt Ida on Crete, five men and five women, discovered iron and worked it with skill, creating implements both of war and of agriculture.

The Telkhines, Kabeiroi and Daktyloi are collective groups, with little internal differentiation. But some characters associated with craft skill had a more individualized history, among them the Titan Prometheus, and Daidalos. Prometheus, son of Iapetos and brother of Epimetheus, is certainly the best known of these heroes. We have already considered his rôle in the institution of animal sacrifice (chapter 12). Although he did not invent fire (that was the achievement of Hermes), it was he who placed it at mankind's disposal by stealing it from the gods, with the consequences that we have seen described in Hesiod's *Theogony*. Prometheus also figured, most notably in the Aeschylean play *Prometheus Bound*, as the inventor of all the arts and crafts (*tekhnai*) – not only woodwork, ploughing and writing, but also medicine and divination.

Daidalos son of Metion ('the man of *mētis*') was a hero. Athenian by origin, his life of adventure led him as far afield as Crete and Sicily. He was the inventor both of a great number of objects and devices (statues, a labyrinth, a dam) and of the equipment and components necessary for constructing them (from the plumb-line to glue). The figure cut by this ambiguous personage, by turns a benefactor and a murderer, clearly illustrates the correspondingly Janus-like image the Greeks had of craftsmen and their *tekhnē* in general: on one side of the coin a benefactor of mankind, on the other a social menace.

A number of gods, finally, had some connection with the technological function; we shall consider here the two principal such divinities, Hephaistos and Athene. Hephaistos with his crippled legs and crooked gait was apt to provoke the Olympian gods to unkind laughter. He had been conceived parthenogenetically by Hera 'without union of love, in anger against her spouse', and scarcely had he been born than his mother hurled him from heaven into the sea. A figure of fun devoid of honour and grace, he nevertheless possessed the cunning intelligence (*mētis*) that many gods lacked and a great store of technical knowledge, in particular a mastery of the forge and the arts of metalworking. He worked with noble metals like gold, silver and copper, creating from them wondrous jewellery, statues that one would swear were breathing, and splendid arms and armour. He fashioned the double axe with which he struck the blow that brought about Athene's birth from the head of Zeus. His skill gave him the power to forge unbreakable fetters, like those which he used to bind Hera to her throne, or to trap his adulterous wife Aphrodite in bed with Ares. He himself lusted after Athene, with whom he had much in common, but the semen he intended for her fertilized the earth beneath instead, and from it was born Erikhthonios, the first Athenian (see above).

In myth Hephaistos was frequently associated with Athene, as we have just seen. So too in cult. At Athens, to give but one example, the two divinities shared the temples of the Erekhtheion on the Akropolis and the Hephaisteion in the Kerameikos district below, and they were the joint honorands of the Khalkeia or smiths' festival. Among Athene's innumerable functions, those connected with craft technology all had one common denominator: their reliance on *mētis*, a quality that was, naturally enough, characteristic of the goddess whose mother – before Zeus intervened – was Metis herself. *Mētis*, in the guise here of technical skill, inspired Athene's patronage of woodworkers (carpenters, chariot-makers, shipwrights), her guidance of helmsmen and her assistance to potters and weavers. But the productive activities she presided over, which involved weaving, arranging or constructing, required a technical know-how different in kind from that possessed by Hephaistos, so that, although both divinities were closely associated with artisans and their technical activity, their intervention called for very different qualities.

It is this difference in the way the divinities intervened in what at first sight appear to be identical fields that explains the multiplicity of divinities involved with both technological production and marriage. At the same time, by minute study of the particularity of each divine power within a precisely defined sphere it is possible to detect the features that are common to their different areas of intervention. Thus Athene, for example, whether incarnated as Athene Promakhos, Athene Polias, or Athene Erganē, preserved her common identity as a goddess 'well endowed with cunning intelligence' (*polumētis*).

APOLLO: THE LYRE AND THE BOW

To illustrate, on the one hand, the complexity of the divine figures and, on the other, the way the pantheon functioned as a whole, we shall begin with a divine couple that is at once mutually antithetical and complementary: Apollo and Dionysos, both sons of Zeus. Between the two we shall find a third brother, Hermes, insinuating himself: a god of speech like Apollo, though in a different way, and like Dionysos a god who assisted in the crossing of boundaries, but again in a different way.

What coherence is there to be found among the diverse Apollos whose cults and epithets correspond to each other from city to city, but without repeating themselves precisely? Taking some of the best known examples, we may cite first the Lakonian Apollo of Amyklai (located just south of Sparta but integrated with the

capital politically). Here he was associated with the hero Hya-
kinthos in the major annual festival named for the latter, the
Hyakinthia; this was the occasion for a *panēguris* (see chapter 10),
involving the dedication of a brand new robe (*peplos*) for Apollo's
cult-statue, that brought together all the people of the area. The
Apollo of the Athenian Thargelia and Pyanopsia festivals presided over complex cult-acts involving the offering of vegetable
foods and rituals of purification (chapter 10). The Apollo of Delos
was worshipped under a twofold aspect; principally, he received
hecatombs on the 'horned' altar, so called, according to a tradition preserved by Callimachus (*Hymn to Delos* 58–64), because it
was originally constructed from the horns of goats slain by
Artemis on the heights of Mt Kynthos; secondarily, in his guise of
Apollo Genetor he also received bloodless offerings on a neigh-
bouring altar that was never touched by fire. Finally, and most
famously, there was the Apollo of Delphi, Apollo Pythios, whose
utterances were transmitted through his mouthpiece, the Pythia.
Besides the well-known quadrennial Pythian Games (chapter 11),
the strange festival of the Septerion was also held in his honour
every ninth year, to celebrate his victory over the snake Python
and his purification from the taint of that murder.

Myths provide us with a key to interpretation, since they
furnish elements of the structure that bound together the different
divine functions evoked by this or that cult into a coherent
ensemble. The *Homeric Hymn to Delian Apollo* is a prime
source. It was composed in two sections at different periods in the
Archaic age, the former recalling the birth and development of the
god on Delos, the second (the so-called 'Pythian Section')
recounting Apollo's arrival at Delphi and the establishment of
his cult there. Yet the terms in which the *Hymn* is couched seem
to go beyond the immediate geographical settings of Delos and
Delphi to characterize the god's principal modes of operation, as
in this description of Apollo's birth (gods were exempted from the
rule prohibiting births on the island):

And as soon as labour-easing Eileithyia had set foot on Delos, the pangs
gripped Leto and she longed to give birth. So she threw her arms round a
palm-tree and sank her knees in the soft grass, and the earth beneath her
smiled. Then the child leaped forth into the light of day, and all the
goddesses ululated.

Then, great Phoibos, the goddesses bathed you purely and cleanly in clear water, swathed you in a white robe, of fine texture and newly-woven, and fastened a golden band around you. Nor did his mother suckle Apollo of the golden dart, but Themis with her immortal hands prepared for him the flower of nectar and delicious ambrosia; and Leto rejoiced, since she had borne a sturdy son and an archer.

But as soon as you had consumed that divine nourishment, Phoibos, you could no longer be confined by golden cords nor did these bonds hold you any more, but all their ends were loosed. At once Phoibos Apollo addressed the immortal goddesses:

'May the dear lyre and the curved bow be mine; and I shall reveal too to men through my oracles the infallible designs of Zeus.'

So spoke Phoibos, the long-haired and far-shooting, and began to walk upon the broad-pathed earth; and all the goddesses were amazed at him. Then Delos was entirely covered with gold as she beheld the offspring of Zeus and Leto, overjoyed that the god had chosen her for his dwelling-place and preferred her to other islands as well as to the mainland. (*Homeric Hymn to Delian Apollo* 115–38)

'May the dear lyre and the curved bow be mine; and I shall reveal too to men through my oracles the infallible designs of Zeus.' Thus did Apollo express himself on his eventual arrival in the world, and in this formula Georges Dumézil has recognized two of the three 'functions' that as he sees it (p. 146) organize all Indo-European ideology: the sacred function of communication between gods and men, symbolized by the lyre, and the function of military violence represented by the bow. The third function, that of wealth-bringing agricultural production, is arguably represented symbolically by the gold that (so Callimachus sang) covered Delos at the time of the god's birth:

The child sprang forth, and the Delian nymphs, descended from an ancient river, intoned far and wide the sacred song of Eileithyia. At once the brazen aether re-echoed the piercing cry, and Hera begrudged it not at all, for Zeus had effaced her anger.

In that hour, o Delos, all your foundations became of gold; with gold your rounded lake flowed all day long, and golden was the foliage put forth by the olive-tree that witnessed the god's birth, and with gold too flowed the deep flood of Inopos in its swirling course.

And you yourself raised the infant from the golden soil and laid him in your lap, and spoke thus: 'O great goddess, goddess of many altars and many cities, who bring forth all things, and you, fertile lands, continents, and islands which surround me, here am I, Delos, hard to cultivate. Yet from me shall Apollo be called Delian, and no other land shall be so cherished by any other god, not Kerkhnis so loved by Poseidon lord of Lekhaion, not Kyllene's hill by Hermes, not Crete by Zeus, as I by Apollo. No more the wild roving island shall I be.'

(Callimachus *Hymn to Delos* 255–75)

That primordial gilding was to be replaced in time by the wealth of offerings that pilgrims brought to Delos, as to Delphi, to compensate for the natural resources these holy sites lacked owing to the poverty of their soil. However, the unifying principle of the structure that linked the various cults of Apollo, not just those of Delos and Delphi, was Apollo's articulate voice (Dumézil 1982[225]). This manifested itself on all three levels, as prayer and oracle, as battle-cry, and as everyday economic intercourse among men.

The lyre and the bow, then, are the symbols of this god's two essential modes of operation, which seem to give order and shape to all his other activities and thereby allow us to offer a coherent reading of them. But they are also consistent with the intrinsic ambivalence of the god that has been detected behind Apollo's ambiguous epithet Phoibos, which meant simultaneously 'the brilliant one' and 'he who instils fear (*phobos*)'. That ambivalence would account for the fact that the god who killed mortals with his arrows (as in *Iliad* v.40–55) or encouraged righteous vengeance (for example, Orestes' revenge on Clytemnestra and the killing of the sacrilegious Pyrrhos) could also be the divine source of purification – for the Orphics, indeed, Apollo became the very incarnation of purity, who had therefore to be worshipped solely with vegetable offerings.

At Didyma and Klaros in Asia Minor, and even more so at Delphi (his uniquely special sanctuary), Apollo was above all the god of divination, mediating the word of his father Zeus through the mouths of his priestesses. This oracular function was associated with the rôle of the lyre, the most potent instrument of the sacred art of music and song. In both divination and music-making, Apollo served to make possible the communication through which harmony might be established between the worlds of gods and men, and it was thanks to his divine intercession too that the reign of harmony might be extended to relationships within the world of men. As a Panhellenic god, Apollo's Pythian festival brought together Greeks from all four corners of the Greek world. The image of Delphi as the centre of the universe was popularized by a tradition that can be traced as far back as Pindar. But in the course of time, and with the encouragement of philosophers, the sanctuary came to be seen more particularly as the heart of a moral code whose central emphasis was placed on due measure in all things ('Nothing to excess').

But while Apollo was the god of the lyre, he was also the god of the bow, a threatening weapon of war. It is in this redoubtable guise that he is presented at the opening of the *Iliad* as coming to exact vengeance for the Greeks' maltreatment of his Trojan priest Khryses and striking them down quite mercilessly in answer to his pleas. He also appears thus armed before the assembly of the gods on Olympos to demand his due requital, and the poet of the *Homeric Hymn to Delian Apollo* (1–4) speaks of 'Archer Apollo whose tread made the other gods tremble in the dwelling of Zeus. All rose from their seats at his approach, when he strung his famous bow.' This explains why men attributed to Apollo the plagues (*loimoi*) that decimated herds of animals and human cities, and why it was to him also that they addressed themselves for relief from them. For their sufferings must have been caused by some pollution, and Apollo was also the master of purification.

His bow, moreover, also made him a tutelary divinity, bearing the epithets *alexikakos* or *apotropaios* – that is, 'he who wards off or turns away evil' through his arrows, as when, for instance, he killed the serpent Python who was devastating the land around Delphi before the god was himself established in residence there. At Athens a statue of Apollo Alexikakos was set up to commemorate his aid in bringing to an end the Great Plague that struck in 430. At Elis in the Peloponnese he bore the near-synonymous epithet of Akesios, the 'healer'. When acting as a god of medicine (he was also the father of Asklepios), Apollo's ministrations took the form of eliminating rather than treating diseases, whether of humans, animals or crops. As healer, Apollo was publicly acknowledged at the doors of houses and the gateways of cities by means of the *eiresione*, a branch covered with offerings for him.

It was the lyre and the bow, too, that equipped Apollo for his function as 'founder-leader' (*arkhēgētēs*), the patron of colony-foundation. Moreover, the lyre, which as the instrument of harmony presided over the wise legislative programmes that received Delphi's imprimatur, formed with the tautly-strung bow a sort of double metaphor emphasizing the close conjunction of these two powers in Apollo (cf. J. Carlier in Bonnefoy 1991[2] s.v. 'Apollo'). For, just as the tension of the lyre-strings conjured up the image of the bow, enabling Pindar to speak of the lyre as 'the long-range bow of the Muses' (*Olympians* ix.5–12), so Homer (*Odyssey* xxi.405ff.) could compare the bow (Odysseus') to a lyre. This helps to explain how in his capacity as a god of controlled tension Apollo could cover the spectrum from immaculate purity at one extreme to terror and death at the other.

However, to define Apollo in terms of his functions is at the same time to situate him in relationship to the other divine forces whose spheres of operation overlapped with his. In delimiting his field of action, in other words, we find those of other divinities being put in their proper place. The Greek pantheon, to repeat, did not consist of a mere juxtaposition of divinities but of a structured ensemble within which each god was defined by his or her relationships with the rest.

In terms of the divine hierarchy, Apollo appears to have been Zeus's favourite son. We have seen him being received formally by Zeus in the assembly of the gods, and broadcasting his father's voice through his sanctuaries on earth. But an even better way of determining his precise station in the pantheon is to consider his position in relation to the status of two of his brothers, Hermes and Dionysos.

Hermes' rank illuminates clearly the specificity of that of the other two. In the *Homeric Hymn to Hermes* the manner of the god's birth is recounted, followed by his attempted theft and concealment of the cattle belonging to his brother Apollo. When he was summoned to appear before Zeus, Hermes at first mendaciously denied all knowledge of the crime. His next gambit was to exploit his theft as a means of obtaining a quite distinct divine status and a place among the 'Immortals'. Like Apollo, Hermes was a son of Zeus, and, like him again, a god of communication through speech; indeed, he was the inventor of the lyre. Yet he nevertheless occupied a completely different place within the pantheon. For the lyre did not make him a god of music. The art (*tekhnē*) which had gone into its invention served rather to produce an object for him to exchange, one of several that Hermes created for a variety of purposes. In this case it was by offering Apollo the lyre as compensation for the cattle he had stolen from him that Hermes both effected a reconciliation with his brother and secured for himself the position on Olympos that he coveted.

Similarly, speech did not have the same function in his mouth as it did in Apollo's. For him it was not a medium of revelation or truth, but a means of persuasion, a stratagem, by which he was able to win over even Zeus and thereby plead his case successfully before him. Hermes, in short, if we set him side by side with Apollo, represented the infiltration of guileful discourse, or rather perjury, among the gods, alongside the Apolline discourse of truth. These two faces of communication were thus separately represented by the two brothers: Hermes the mediator and the man of wiles, Apollo the utterer of truth that sped unerringly towards its mark like the flight of an arrow.

With his other brother Dionysos, whom Zeus cherished equally, Apollo's ties were of a quite different nature. Indeed, a strong tradition placed them in direct opposition to each other, counterposing a nocturnal Dionysos (with his entourage of Maenads, chapter 12) to a luminous Apollo, master of music and purity. Other strands of evidence, however, argue for a more complex interrelationship between them, based on mutuality and complicity. There was, above all, the conjoint sovereignty of Apollo and Dionysos over the Delphic sanctuary (chapter 11). Then there was the division of cultic labour agreed between them during the winter season: while Apollo went on sabbatical leave among the Hyperboreans, the winter months were devoted to Dionysiac worship, with the dithyramb, Dionysos' special hymn, reigning in triumph. But once Apollo had returned from the north, Delphi resounded once more with his triumphal song, the paian. Dionysos' presence at Delphi was, moreover, stamped on the very soil of the sanctuary, since this was where he had his tomb, right in the heart of Apollo's temple next to the tripod on which the Pythia sat to prophesy. We know too from Pausanias (x.19.4) that both Apollo and Dionysos were depicted on the Temple of Apollo in its fourth-century reconstruction, Apollo and the Muses at one corner of the pediment, Dionysos and the Thyiades (female followers assimilated to Maenads) at the other.

DIONYSOS: GOD OF WILD POSSESSION (*ENTHOUSIASMOS*)

Dionysos was the 'twice-born'. His mother Semele had rashly desired to gaze on her lover Zeus in all his glory and was struck down by a thunderbolt. But his father rescued the embryo and sewed it into his own thigh, from which Dionysos was granted a second, divine birth. He was raised by Semele's sister Ino, who, in order to save him from the persecution of Hera which, according to some traditions, was driving him insane, disguised him as a girl. With his enemies in hot pursuit (notably Lykourgos king of Thrace, who drove him into the sea where he was rescued by Thetis), Dionysos fled through Greece and the Orient. But in the end the hunted god returned, and his arrival or rather return often formed the focus of local cults that represented him as the god from abroad.

Such myths are the source of a powerful tradition of interpretation, nineteenth-century in origin, which sees Dionysos as a non-Greek god, from either Thrace or the Orient, who imposed himself in Greece by main force. That, however, is to read in a crudely literal way myths whose concern was rather with the god's essential function. For the main function of Dionysos was to reveal to every individual what he or she had of the stranger within them, an interior alterity which the god's cults taught his devotees to discover by the circuitous route of the mask and the trance.

In contradistinction to Hermes, the god of transitions and divine cicerone who facilitated passage between contraries, Dionysos effaced boundaries, and by assuming and incarnating contrary characteristics in himself he threw all neatly defined categories into confusion. Thus his following of satyrs muddled up the categories of man and beast, while he himself confounded those of male and female by his feminine appearance and dress (he wore the *peplos* rather than the *khitōn*). During the Anthesteria festival, an occasion when the dead mingled with the living, he was the only god whose temple was allowed to remain open, and he presided over the disguises and masquerades that accompanied this period of commingled unease and gaiety. During the October Oskhophoria festival the young boys who processed carrying bunches of grapes were disguised as girls. Likewise, male revellers participating in the *kōmoi* at the Great Dionysia wore female clothing. These festivals, moreover, all involved public gatherings and processions in which all the inhabitants of the city were mixed up together, including slaves and children (especially at the Khoës). Crucially, however, this Dionysiac jumbling of boundaries was conducted within the framework of the city and was indeed regulated by it.

Myth, as we have seen (chapter 12), laid the emphasis on the unleashing of Dionysiac madness. In the streets of the city, by contrast, the god's formal procession assumed a more orderly aspect, and Dionysiac orgies were reduced to institutionalized form. Epigraphic texts document the official existence of maenadic cult-groups (*thiasoi*) and show that initiation into Dionysiac mysteries was accomplished within a recognized civic framework. Such *thiasoi* proliferated in the course of the Hellenistic period, welcoming among their membership many of the people who ordinarily were somewhat neglected by the civic religion, above all women. For example, a cultic regulation from Miletos of the first half of the third century BCE (*LSAM*[59]: no. 48) lays down the procedure for the celebration of Dionysiac Mysteries and prescribes the rôle of the priestess. The old ritual of omophagy is recalled symbolically by the piece of raw flesh that the priestess has to place in a basket, the original wild chase through the mountains has been tamed into a formal procession, and the trance is made subject to precise rules.

Athenian vase-paintings of the fifth century present two different images of Dionysiac celebration within the city. On the one hand, there is the masculine *kōmos*, performed under the influence of wine and to the accompaniment of music (played on the *aulos* and *barbitōn* – a kind of stringed instrument) and dancing. On the other, there are the cavortings of the Maenads, Dionysos' particular devotees, who are shown crowned with ivy, brandishing the *thursos* and the *kantharos* (a goblet with high-swung handles typical of Dionysiac worship), and processing, now in a serious and orderly fashion, now abandoned utterly to delirium and trance.

In Boiotia (during the Agrionia festival at Khaironeia), at Sparta (where two female cult-societies, the Leukippides and the Dionysiades, participated in the Dionysia festival), at Alea in Arkadia, at Elis and elsewhere, the cults of Dionysos were distinguished by chases, flagellations, ecstatic dancing, sacrifices and *orgia* (secret ceremonies) in which women were the principal participants. It was the women, too, who occupied centre stage during the Theoinia and Iobakkheia celebrations at the Anthesteria festival at Athens. Chief among them was the Basilinna, wife of the Basileus or 'King' Arkhon. She and her entourage of fourteen priestesses performed the secret rites that included a sacred marriage (*hieros gamos*) with Dionysos himself, a public function of the utmost importance.

Within this civic context of Dionysiac worship the use of trance should be viewed as ritualized social behaviour aimed at bringing about a change of state and status in the worshipper, enabling him or her to become 'other' and thereby assume a form of alterity defined by precise civic norms and values. The two dimensions of this experience, the collective and the personal, cannot be separated out: the trance was collective, in that it unfolded as a group phenomenon within the membership of the cult-society, and yet at the same time it affected individually each member of the group, who found himself or herself brought face to face with the god. It is wrong therefore to interpret the phenomenon (with Rohde 1925[254]) as a state of internal crisis within which each individual was impermeably insulated, or to see Dionysiac worship as a stage on the road to the discovery of an immortal inner life and as an essentially mystical experience.

The Lydian women who accompany Dionysos on his return to Thebes at the opening of Euripides' *Bacchae* and form his *thiasos* graphically illustrate this condition of 'madness':

DIONYSOS

I, Dionysos, am back in this land of Thebes.
I was born here, of Semele, daughter of Kadmos,
blasted from her womb by a bolt of blazing thunder.

I am here, a god in the shape of a man,
walking by the banks of Ismenos, the waters of Dirke.
Look out there, near the houses! That home in ruins,
still smoking, smouldering still with unquenchable flame,
is my mother's monument, her thunder-dug grave,
undying evidence of spiteful Hera's rage.
I praise Kadmos, who turned his daughter's grave into consecrated
    ground,
a living temple that I shrouded with clustering vine.
    I left behind the gold-abounding lands of Lydia
and Phrygia, Persia's sun-beaten plains and Baktria's giant walls,
crossing the winter-scorched earth of the Medes
and the length of happy Arabia, in short,
all Asia down to its shimmering seashores
where Greeks and barbarians freely mingle
in teeming, shapely-towered cities.
In Greece this is the first of its cities I visit.
I danced my way throughout the East,
spreading my rituals far and wide – a god
made manifest to men.
    Of all Greek cities, Thebes is the one I chose
to rouse into a new awareness,
dressing Greek bodies in fawnskins,
planting the thyrsus in Greek hands,
my ivied spear. My mother's sisters –
were there ever more unsisterly sisters? –
gossiped that this Dionysos was no child of Zeus,
that Semele had slept with some man and
then – on Kadmos' cunning advice –
attributed her sinful conception to Zeus.
No wonder Zeus struck her dead, they would prattle,
taking a lover and brazenly lying!
    Well! These sisters, all three,
I've stung into a frenzy and steered them
from their homes into the mountains,
where I left them raving. Complete of course
with orgiastic trappings. What is more,
all the women of Thebes, but all,
I've sent stampeding out of doors. They're up there now,
milling with Kadmos' daughters under the fresh-smelling pines
or high upon the rocks. This city must learn,
even against its will, how much it costs

to scorn to be initiated in my Bacchic mysteries.
So shall I vindicate my virgin mother
and reveal myself to mortals as a god,
the son of Zeus.
    Now Kadmos has conferred the powers of his throne
and its honours on the son of another daughter, Pentheus.
This god-fighting upstart snubs me; banishes my name
from public libations and private prayer.
He'll soon find out, and every Theban with him,
whose birthright is divine and whose is not.
Once that score is settled, I'll move on
to reveal myself in other lands. But should this city,
in blind anger, take up arms to drive my Bacchae from the hills,
I'll give them war, leading my women's army.
I have disguised myself as a mortal,
adopting the ways and features of a man.
    You, women of Tmolos, Lydia's towering mountain,
my band of initiates, you,
whom I unplucked from your primitive lands
to be my travel-companions and my assistants,
raise up your native Phrygian drums
that pulse to rhythms that are Mother Rhea's and mine.
Surround the royal home of Pentheus with your beat
and turn the city out to see. Meanwhile,
I'll make my way to those Kithairon slopes
that seethe with Theban Bacchae
and join their dance.

CHORUS

            Out of the heart of Asia
            down from the sacred heights of Tmolos
            have I come running. For the god Bromios
            fatigue is sweet to the limbs,
            and effortless effort the trek,
            greeting the Bacchanals' god with shouts of joy.

            Who is there in the street? Who?
            Who is lurking in the house? Stand still,
            stand back and purify your lips,
            while I chant a prayer immemorial,
            in customary praise of Dionysos.

            Oh, happy is he who, blessed by his knowledge
            of the gods' rites, discovers purity.

Who opens his heart to togetherness.
Who joins in the mountain-dancing
and sacred cleansing rituals. He,
who sanctifies the orgies of Kybele,
the mother of fertility,
waving the thyrsus high,
crowning his head with ivy,
in honour of Dionysos.
Go, Bacchae, go, go, go. Bring
Bromios the godly son of a god – our Dionysos –
down from the Phrygian hills
out into the spacious streets of Greece, Bromios.

Him, whom his mother carried
to premature and painful birth
when in a crash of thunder
she was death-struck by a fiery bolt.
But quicker than death,
Zeus son of Kronos swept him up and plunged him
into a makeshift womb –
secure from Hera's eyes –
in the thick of his thigh,
fastened with clasps of gold.
As time ripened into fate,
he delivered a bull-horned god
and crowned him with a crown of serpents.
Thus was invented the custom
for thyrsus-carrying Maenads
to twine snakes in their hair.

Oh Thebes, Semele's nurse,
crest your walls with ivy.
Burst into greenness, burst
into a blaze of bryony,
take up the Bacchanalian beat
with branches of oak and of pine,
cover your flesh with fawnskin
fringed with silver-white fleece
and lifting the fennel-wand
touch god
in a fit of sanctified frenzy.
Then all at once, the whole land will dance!
Bromios will lead the dancing throngs to the mountain,

the mountain, which is home to that mob of women,
who rebelled against shuttle and loom
answering the urge of Dionysos.

Oh holy heights of Crete
cradling the caves of the Kouretes
where Zeus was born.
There, the triple-crested Korybantes
traced in vibrant drumskin
the circle of my joy.
They married its percussive strength
to the wailing sweetness of Phrygian flutes,
then put it into Rhea's hands
to draw the earth-beat out
and make it throb in Bacchic song.
In time, the frenzied Satyrs
from the mother-goddess stole the drum
and struck up dances for the feasts,
held every second year,
to honour and give joy to Dionysos.

How sweet to the body, when
breaking loose from the mountain revels
one collapses to the ground in a fawnskin
after hunting the goat.
How sweet the kill –
the fresh-smelling blood –
the sacramental relishing
of raw flesh ...
To the mountains of Phrygia, Lydia,
how the mind races back!
And Bromios is our chorus-leader, *evoi*!

Your ground flows with milk,
flows with wine, flows with nectar from bees.
Like smoke from a Syrian incense,
Bakkhos arises with his torch of pine.
He runs, he dances in a whirl of flame,
he rouses the faithful
crazing their limbs with his roar,
while he races the wind,
his soft hair streaming behind.
And his call resounds like thunder:
'Go, my Bacchae, go!

Let Tmolos with its golden streams
reverberate with songs of Dionysos,
and the vibrant crash of drums.
Sing out in joy
with loud Phrygian cries,
while the holy sweet-throated flute
climbs the holy scale and the scaling Maenads climb
up the mountain, the mountain.'
It is then that a girl like me
knows happiness. When she is free,
like a filly playfully prancing
around its mother,
in fields without fences.

(Euripides, *Bacchae* 1–167, trans. M. Cacoyannis, modified)

The madness of these celebrants is controlled and socialized madness (*mania*), as opposed to the uncontrolled frenzy (*lussa*) which later in the play grips those who refuse to recognize the god – Agaue and her women of Thebes, and (see above quotation) Pentheus. The same opposition, between ritualized madness and murderously bestial raving, can also be found in other myths of Dionysos and his epiphanies.

There is, for example, the story of the Minyades, royal princesses of Orkhomenos in Boiotia where Dionysos was raised. They refused Dionysos' appeal, and preferred to remain in the palace weaving, whereas the other women abandoned their usual tasks and spread out over the surrounding countryside up into the mountains, assuming the guise of Maenads (wearing fawnskins, crowned with ivy, and carrying *thursoi*, tambourines and *auloi*). Back in the palace, tendrils of ivy and vine miraculously brought their weaving to a halt, and the princesses, belatedly converted and gripped now by a murderous frenzy, tore one of their own children to pieces and devoured him. But when they wanted to join forces with the other Maenads, the latter drove the Minyades away in horror. Madness and death, in other words, are well within the purview of Dionysos, but only as the price that has to be paid by anyone who has either failed to look the god squarely in the face in order to discover himself or herself through the mask's empty gaze, or deliberately ignored or repudiated him.

The figure of Dionysos was represented in a variety of cultic media. Among these the mask, as depicted on the so-called Lenaia series of Attic vase-paintings, was particularly significant. Here the mask is shown supported either on a stake fixed in the ground or on a sort of truncated column; it is accompanied by an article of draped clothing in the style of the female *peplos* adorned by a fawnskin and fastened by a belt – in other words, Maenads' dress. Dionysos, who is both absent and present in the empty garment, thus offers to those who can recognize him an image both of the Other and of that which makes other.

The means whereby Dionysos gave expression to his power over the vine are yet another instance of the dangerous attraction he exerted for people who did not know how to put his peculiar gifts to beneficial use. God of luxuriant vegetation and moistness in general, he was also the god who introduced the grapevine to Attica. But before the inhabitants of the region had learned how to use wine properly, employing ritual to turn the beverage into an instrument of sociability, a series of disasters occurred. Ikaros joined with some shepherds in drinking the neat wine that Dionysos had given them, but in their drunken stupor the shepherds killed him; his daughter Erigone hanged herself in despair, and the daughters of Attica went mad in consequence.

So in a sense Dionysos stands for the profitable use of madness. Just as Apollo could at the same time both inflict ill and cure it, so Dionysos was the god who both maddened and knew how to cure madness. Dionysiac rituals, which covered the spectrum of transgressive forms of behaviour from omophagy, through the controlled imbibing of wine, to falling into a trance, offered to each individual the chance to experience, in a context that was simultaneously collective and individual, 'the Other' within himself or herself. This was an experiential apprenticeship that could take a person to the limits of madness, unless it were regulated by this 'double god' (as Euripides calls him), at once man and woman.

It becomes comprehensible, then, that the theatre was another of Dionysos' spheres of influence, since in that setting a member of the audience could be or see himself as 'other' for the duration of a dramatic performance. It was also by means of the theatre that Dionysos was able to establish himself at the very heart of the city under the gaze of all. So far from being content to be recognized only by marginal sects, Dionysos claimed his rightful place as a god on a par with the other divinities of the civic community.

Let us return, finally, to Delphi. In his encounter there with Apollo, Dionysos, the god of enthusiastic possession, found himself side by side with the god of articulate speech, Apollo the 'sonorous', in the sanctuary where the Greeks located the very navel of the earth. It was as if the two modes of communication with the sacred that they represented, the one based on the transmission of clear speech, the other on a bewitching look, had found in Delphi just the place to put down their roots.

THE PANTHEON IN OPERATION: THE CITY OF MANTINEIA (fig. 11)

Every Greek city (and there were more than a thousand in all) honoured a number of gods and heroes with sanctuaries and cults, establishing a hierarchy among them and telling locally adapted versions of their myths. As the pantheon varied from city to city, so the mythology varied accordingly. Nor was the establishment of a city's particular combination of sanctuaries and cults something that was set in stone from its foundation to the end of antiquity. A city's pantheon had its history, in other words, sometimes difficult to reconstruct and even more so to interpret. In the hope of making a contribution towards a better understanding of the diversity and complexity of Greek poly-theism, we have thought it useful to select a single city's pan-theon as a case-study. Our choice of Mantineia is of course somewhat arbitrary. However, in respect of its size, its by no means first-rank historical importance, and the documentation available, Mantineia does seem to us to be representative of a larger number of cities than the exceptionally complex case of Athens.

Mantineia is located in the Peloponnese, in the northeast of the region of Arkadia and on the border with the Argolis. Its civic territory, measuring some thirteen kilometres from north to south and between four and seven kilometres from east to west, was bounded by those of Alea, Orkhomenos, Megalopolis

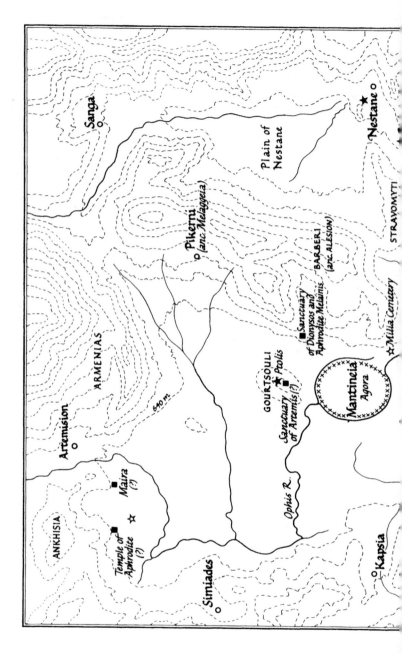

11   Mantineia and its territory

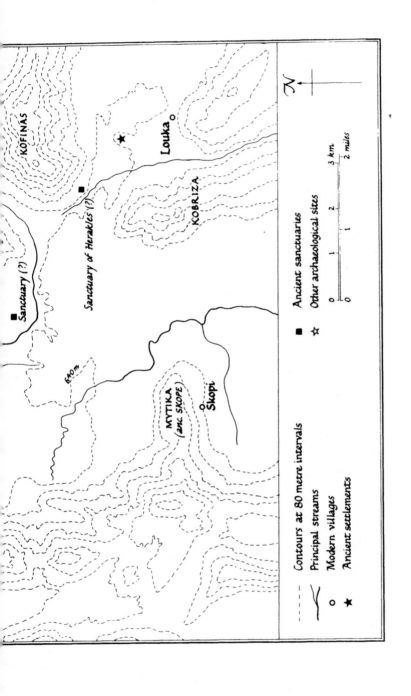

KOFINAS

Sanctuary (?)

640 m

Sanctuary of Herakles (?)

MYTIKA
(anc. SKOPE)

Skopi

Louka

KOBRIZA

N

■ Ancient sanctuaries

☆ Other archaeological sites

0   1   2   3 km
0   1   2 miles

------ Contours at 80 metre intervals

〰 Principal streams

○ Modern villages

★ Ancient settlements

(founded 368), Tegea and Argos. Pausanias' *periēgēsis* ('guide-book') lists the sanctuaries and cult-places, whether still operational or ruined, that a contemporary traveller of the late second century CE might visit; this is our principal source of information on the religious geography of the city's territory, the Mantinike:

[In the city]

The Mantineians have a double temple divided pretty well in the middle by a wall. One part of the temple has a statue of Asklepios by Alkamenes, and the other part is a sanctuary of Leto and her children; their statues were made by Praxiteles two generations after Alkamenes, with the Muses and Marsyas piping carved on the pedestal. [...] The Mantineians have other sanctuaries of Zeus the Saviour and of the god called Bountiful [Epidotes] as he gives generously to human beings. There is also a sanctuary of the Dioskouroi and elsewhere a sanctuary of Demeter and Korē, where they keep a fire burning and take great care never to let it go out. And I saw a temple of Hera by the theatre, with statues by Praxiteles of Hera enthroned with Athene and Hera's daughter Hebe. Beside Hera's altar is the grave of Kallisto's son Arkas. [...] They call this place where Arkas' grave is The Altars of Helios. Not far from the theatre there are some famous monuments of the dead: the one called Hestia Koine ['Public Hearth'], which is circular, is where they said Antinoe daughter of Kepheus was buried. [...] Behind the theatre there were the remains, with a statue, of a temple of Aphrodite Summakhia ['Allied Aphrodite']; the inscription on the base said it was dedicated by Nikippe the daughter of Paseas. The Mantineians built this sanctuary as a memorial for future ages of the sea-battle at Actium where they served with the Romans [i.e., with Octavian against Antony]. They worship Athene Alea too, and they have a sanctuary and a statue of her. They have accepted Antinoös as a god: his shrine is the newest in Mantineia. The emperor Hadrian had a particular passion for him. [...] In the Mantineian agora there are a bronze portrait of a woman whom the Arkadians call Diomeneia daughter of Arkas and a hero-shrine to Podares who they say died in the battle against Epameinondas and his Thebans.

[In the country (khōra)]

The mountain above the stadium is Alesion, which they say is named after the wandering (*alē*) of Rhea; there is a sacred wood of Demeter on this mountain. By the very edges of the mountain is the sanctuary of Poseidon Hippios, which is not far from the Mantineian stadium.

I am writing the story of this sanctuary by hearsay and out of other people's books. The modern sanctuary was built by Hadrian, who put inspectors over the workmen to see that no one looked inside the ancient sanctuary or shifted a stone of its ruins: he ordered them to build the new temple all round it. They say this sanctuary of Poseidon was originally built by Agamedes and Trophonios by working and joining logs of oak, and they kept people out without building any barrier round the entrance, just by stretching a woollen thread across it, perhaps in the belief that, since the people of those days respected religion, a thread would be enough to frighten them away, or perhaps there may have been some kind of strength in the thread.

> (Pausanias VIII.9–10, extracts, trans. P. Levi, modified)

The other sanctuaries in the *khōra* earned only a brief mention from Pausanias, viz.:

in the north of the plain a sanctuary of Artemis and the tomb of Penelope (VIII.12.5), a spring called the fountain of the Melias-tai – 'These Meliastai perform the mysteries of Dionysos, and a hall of Dionysos and a sanctuary of Black Aphrodite stand by the spring' (VIII.6.5), and the spring Alalkomeneia (named for an epithet of Athene) (VIII.12.7);

in the south of the plain 'a stade or so from Epameinondas' grave stands a sanctuary of Zeus Kharmon' (VIII.12.1), the graves of Pelias' daughters (VIII.11.1), and the grave-mound of Arei-thoös, at the place called Phoizon (VIII.11.4);

on the periphery 'beyond the ruins of Nestane is a sacred sanctu-ary of Demeter to whom the Mantineians hold a festival every year' (VIII.8.1). Finally, along the road to Orkhomenos lay 'Mt Ankhisia with the monument of Ankhises at the foot of the mountain . . . By Ankhises' grave stand the ruins of a sanctuary of Aphrodite' (VIII.12.8–9).

At the outset it is worth noting the large number of different cult-places, the fact that certain divinities had several cults, and the disparate dates at which cults were established. Figure 11 indicates the finds of archaeological data and some probable identifications of sanctuaries.

The first of our questions, which need not be answered in

Pausanias' topographical order, is, what comprised Mantineia's pantheon? The city's patron and guardian deity was Poseidon Hippios ('the Horseman'), represented on the city's coinage with trident or dolphin; his priest gave his name to the official year (such-and-such happened 'in the priesthood of so-and-so'). His sanctuary, located at the city's gates, was an *abaton*, a 'no-go area' barred (literally) to all but the priest; anyone else entering it was liable to be punished with death for the violation. The festival in honour of Poseidon, the Posoidaia (as it was called in Arkadian dialect), included athletic competitions.

Poseidon Hippios, however, was not only the city's patron; he was also master both of underground water and of horses, two vital functions in a city where drainage was a constant problem and horse-raising was a major economic activity of the wealthy. His cult can be traced back to the origins of the city in the eighth or seventh century, although in myth the foundation of the sanctuary was attributed to two Boiotian heroes, Agamedes and Trophonios. The sanctuary remained active into the Roman imperial era; Hadrian (CE 117–38), as we saw, chose to restore it to the condition attested by Pausanias.

Zeus was worshipped at Mantineia under five epithets, or rather in virtue of five different functions at five different cult-places: Zeus Keraunos ('Thunderbolt', an identification of the god with the natural phenomenon), Zeus Soter ('Saviour', so named because he was identified as a protector and guarantor of the city when it was rebuilt in 371 after its dismembering by the Spartans in 385), Zeus Kharmon ('he who rejoices' or, more exactly perhaps, 'he who takes pleasure in war'), Zeus Euboulos ('Good Counsellor'), and Zeus Epidotes ('Bountiful', like Euboulos a guardian of the city's prosperity).

Demeter was honoured in the countryside with both a sanctuary and a sacred wood, and in the town centre with a sanctuary she shared with Korē, in which there burned a perpetual flame. Korē's cult gave rise to the Koragia festival which included a procession, a sacrifice, a banquet, followed by celebration of mysteries, a tour of the goddess's statue through the town and its return to the sanctuary. Apparently the Korē worshipped at Mantineia was originally an independent divinity whose cult was later attached to that of Demeter on the model of the Panhellenic cult of Demeter and Korē.

Athene appeared under two epithets, Alea and Alalkomeneïs ('Protectress', 'Repeller of Danger'). Alea (which could mean either 'Asylum' or 'Heat') was an independent deity known elsewhere in Arkadia, and honoured in the Archaic era as a goddess promoting fecundity in humans and the fertility of animals and crops. Over time her cult was gradually assimilated to that of Athene. Dionysos' sanctuary was near the spring of the Meliastai, and we know of the existence (but nothing more) of *orgia*, secret rites, among his rituals.

Aphrodite featured in three guises. As Melainis ('the Black One') she represented a subterranean power. Secondly, there was her sanctuary at the foot of Mt Ankhisia; the latter was associated with the legend, peddled by the Romans, of Venus' union with Ankhises (father of Aeneas). Finally, under the epithet of Summakhia ('of Alliance'), a cult of Aphrodite again commemorated a recent event, in this case Mantineia's alliance with Octavian (later Augustus) against Antony at the Battle of Actium in 31 BCE.

Antinoös owed his divine (not heroic) cult to the initiative of Hadrian, his former lover. The young man was represented as Dionysos, and the ritual included mysteries. Every fourth year the Antinoeia games were held, on the model of the Olympics. Among Mantineia's hero-cults a lively one was that of Podares, who had died fighting Epameinondas at the second Battle of Mantineia in 362; his *hērōon* was situated honorifically in the agora.

Of the other divinities cited by Pausanias – Artemis, Apollo, Leto, Asklepios, Hera and Hebe, and the Anakes (Dioskouroi) – we know neither their special attributes at Mantineia nor the forms of their worship. We can only assume that their characteristics were the same as those recognized elsewhere in the Greek world. Nevertheless, what is most striking in the study of the pantheon of a city like Mantineia is, first, its marked local originality and, secondly, the influence of the city's history on its composition.

As for the former, one finds at Mantineia feminine figures of goddesses such as Athene Alea and Korē that were quite different from the 'canonical' images of Athene and Korē but strongly resembled their namesakes in other Arkadian cities. As for the influence of the city's past, that manifested itself, on the one hand, in the constant modification of the divine figures, and on the other in the adoption of new gods and the creation of fresh cults. Thus Archaic figures like Alea and Korē were amalgamated or juxtaposed with Panhellenic divinities, such as Athene or Korē's mother Demeter; and among the new gods and cults there were, for example, Aphrodite Summakhia, adopted after Actium, and Antinöos, created in the era of Hadrian. In short, the pantheon as it was exemplified at Mantineia was neither stereotyped nor static. It constitutes a classic demonstration of a polytheistic religion's capacity to adapt and evolve.

CHAPTER 14

Forms of imaginative projection

DIFFERENT WAYS OF REPRESENTING THE DIVINE

The Greeks did not recognize one and only one mode of representing the divine, the familiar anthropomorphic statue. Different forms of representation coexisted peacefully in any given epoch. In this chapter we attempt to answer two questions: what were these different forms? And what can they teach us about Greek conceptions of the divine?

First, though, some remarks of a general nature are in order. The special characteristic of all religious representation is to endow the divinity being figured with a presence without obscuring the fact that it is not actually there. The cultic image must at the same time be thoroughly material – it can be touched, moved, manipulated – and yet leave no doubt that it stands for something which is not actually present. In the ancient Greek world, however, images were not conceived in the same terms as they are today. Notions of likeness and imitation of an external model, which are basic to our definition of an image, were not fundamental for the Greeks. At least until the beginning of the fifth century BCE, none of the plastic forms in which the divine was expressed could be subsumed into the category of either likeness or imitation. These Archaic Greek representations gave form to that which had none, but they were not mimetic.

The Greeks employed a large number of different words for representations of the divine: *xoanon*, *bretas*, *andrias*, *palladion*, *agalma*, *kolossos*, *eikōn* and *eidōlon*, among others. This variety corresponds to the multiplicity of expressions of the divine in figural form. The *bretas* and *xoanon*, for example, were virtually aniconic, making no attempt at likeness. They were thought of as having dropped out of the sky, like the *xoanon* of Athene Polias eventually housed in the Erekhtheion on the Athenian Akropolis (Appendix II). Such figures were put to a variety of cultic uses. Sometimes they were carried in procession, in other cases they were ritually bathed; or they could be dressed in clothes fashioned with the most elaborate care, such as the *peplos* woven by the Arrhephoroi and Ergastinai for the statue of Athene Polias at Athens. For the most part, though, they remained shut up within their temples. Once, perhaps, they had been the property of individual families, but when the civic community of the *polis* was instituted they became public assets and were therefore housed in public temples.

A herm was a rectangular pillar bearing on its base a representation of the male phallus and at its apex a sculpted head supposed to represent Hermes (see fig. 18). They are first attested at Athens in the late sixth century, when Hipparkhos, brother of the tyrant Hippias, had fifty of them erected on the roads running from Athens into the surrounding country, each one bearing an improving maxim. Herms were set up practically everywhere – in the countryside, at the entrance to sanctuaries, at crossways, alongside roads, outside private houses. Their function was to structure space, marking the indissociability of the human and the divine ascendancy over the city's territory. As we have seen (chapter 2), these herms were objects of worship, and to damage them, for example by mutilating the genitals, was a heinous sacrilege.

Kouroi is the name given by archaeologists and art-historians to life-size stone statues of standing youths sculpted in the Archaic period, between *c.* 600 and 480, and usually depicted in the nude. Some of these sculptures were funerary in function, being placed as markers over the tomb of a dead man or youth; others were votive, dedicated to a god in a sanctuary. They were in no way likenesses of either the deceased or the dedicator, or of the recipient deity. Modelled in the form of a human body, they represented rather attributes and values of the divine. For example, a *kouros* offered by an athlete symbolized the gifts bestowed by the gods on a victor at the games: vitality, youth, speed, strength, virility and beauty. *Mutatis mutandis*, the same was true of their feminine equivalents, the draped statues labelled generically *korai*.

The preceding example makes it possible for us to gain a better understanding of the anthropomorphic statue, that is, the statue of a god in human form. The fact that the Greeks sculpted such statues of their gods does not imply a belief that the gods resembled men or had bodies that were in every respect human; what the Greeks did believe was that the beauty, youth or perfection of a real human body evoked qualities of the divine. Greek anthropomorphism is part of the wider issue of 'the body of the divine', which J.-P. Vernant has presented as follows: 'To pose the problem of the body of the gods is thus not to ask how the Greeks could have equipped their gods with human bodies. It is rather an investigation of how this symbolic system functions, how the corporeal code permits one to think of the relations between man and god ...' (Vernant 1991 [42]: 31).

One method very frequently adopted by the Greeks to express the divine was the mask. The mask was a full-face representation, still very rare as an iconographic type in the Archaic period, which implicated the spectator in a relationship of fascination. Certain divinities, such as Dionysos, were represented by masks in their rituals of worship. In numerous vase-paintings the mask of Dionysos can be seen propped against a pillar, itself dressed up in clothes, while cult is performed around it. Worshippers too were sometimes masked, for example in the cult of Orthia (later assimilated to Artemis) at Sparta, where adolescent youths performed a masked dance before entering the adult world. These masks depicted terrifying figures and so symbolized the savage, non-civic world the youths were abandoning on becoming adult citizens; in Dionysiac rituals satyr-masks were used. Thus, wearing a mask was a means of ceasing to be oneself and, for the duration of the ritual, incarnating the power of the divine.

In sum, the objects that were utilized to figure the divine in Classical Greece were many and various, and the Greeks employed several different modes of representation at one and the same period. For example, an Athenian of the fifth century might pay cult to the herms in the civic Agora, participate in rituals around the mask of Dionysos, accompany Athene's *xoanon* in the Panathenaic procession, and venerate the chryselephantine statue of Athene Parthenos permanently housed in the Parthenon. This is just one of many examples that could be adduced to prove that the different forms in which the divine was figured do not correspond to successive stages in the evolution of Greek religious thought. It is false to claim that there was a development from aniconic representation to naturalism. For in Homer the gods were already completely anthropomorphized, whereas in the Classical era, some three centuries later, pillars and stones could perform a very potent symbolic function and constitute the living heart of rituals.

ANTHROPOMORPHIC REPRESENTATIONS OF THE GODS

So much for the general problems raised by the Greeks' figuration of the divine. Turning to the particular, what was it that enabled a Greek to individuate a deity visually? The answer is that a god could be identified with certainty from an assemblage of attributes and postures, although, as with the pantheon as a whole, there existed a host of local representational variations. The accompanying line-drawings (by courtesy of François Lissarrague) illustrate the way in which some of the divinities were represented in Attic vase-painting.

As a general rule Zeus was instantly recognizable by the thunderbolt he brandished (fig. 12), Poseidon by his trident (fig. 14), Dionysos by the *thursos* (fig. 15), Athene by her aegis (goatskin worn as a kind of breastplate; fig. 12), Apollo by his lyre (fig. 16), Artemis by her bow, quiver and arrows, Demeter by her ear of wheat, Hephaistos by his axe (fig. 13), and so forth. But although the representations of a given god obeyed certain formulaic conventions, there was still scope for modifications and manipulations that had their own individual rationale. To illustrate the process we shall consider here the representation of Dionysos in vase-painting.

He appeared initially with a human body clothed in a long pleated robe. Lord of wine (which he had the capacity to drink neat), he was represented holding his characteristic attributes of

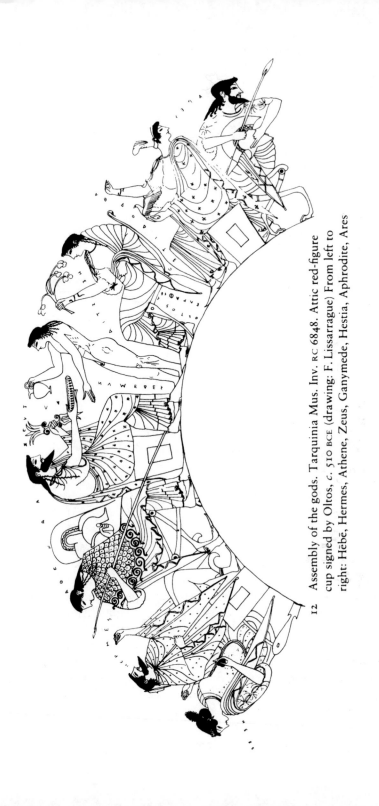

12 Assembly of the gods. Tarquinia Mus. Inv. RC 6848. Attic red-figure
cup signed by Oltos, c. 510 BCE (drawing: F. Lissarrague) From left to
right: Hēbē, Hermes, Athene, Zeus, Ganymede, Hestia, Aphrodite, Ares

13   Hephaistos. Berlin (Pergamon) Mus. Inv. 2273. Attic red-figure cup
by the Ambrosios Painter, *c.* 500 BCF (drawing: F. Lissarrague)

either a *kantharos* or a drinking-horn. Tendrils of grapevine or
ivy (as in fig. 15) envelop and crown him, and his companions
carry a *thursos* (stick with a cluster of ivy at the end). His familiar
creatures are the lion, panther and snake (notorious for their
savagery) and the donkey and he-goat (emblems of lubricity).
Though sometimes depicted alone, he is often shown surrounded
by satyrs and Maenads. He may also be represented by a pillar,
either clad in a long robe and surmounted by a mask (see above),
or just supporting a mask of the god depicted either full-face or
in profile; around the pillar rituals of worship are shown being
performed.

14 Poseidon. Stater (two-drachma silver coin) of Poseidonia,
c. 530–510 BCE (drawing: F. Lissarrague)

Lastly, the face of Dionysos can also appear on its own,
perhaps set between the two 'eyes' that occur frequently as a
motif on drinking cups and amphoras. To quote F. Frontisi-
Ducroux (in Bérard *et al.* 1989 [248]: 156, slightly modified):
'when it is the face of Dionysos with its haunting expression that
is inscribed between the two eyes, there is no longer any question
of self-control or taking precautions. One must succumb to the
ascendancy of the god. In the mask that gazes from the side of an
amphora, as in the mask the banqueter brings up to his own face,
the wine itself is visualized, even as it is about to be drunk, in the
glow of the divine liquid – the god himself. The confrontation
between the drinker and Dionysos, across the raised cup, creates

15 Dionysos. Munich Inv. 2344. Attic red-figure amphora by the
Kleophrades Painter (detail), *c.* 500 BCE (drawing:
F. Lissarrague)

an almost initiatory connection, a mirror-game in which the god
flashes a reflection of his divinity towards the man.' This final
example, illustrating both the figuration of the divine on a drinking cup and its day-to-day handling by the drinker, is a clear
index of the extent to which images of the gods invaded the world
of men, and a measure of the gulf, in their respective perceptions
of the divine, between the polytheistic Greeks and the practitioners of a monotheistic religion like Christianity.

16   Apollo. Rome (Vatican Museums) Attic red-figure hydria,
    c. 490–480 BCE (drawing: F. Lissarrague)

GROUP IMAGES OF THE GODS

Divinities were represented either in isolation (as we have seen in
the case of Dionysos, fig. 15) or in groups (fig. 12). There is a
purposive rationale behind the manner in which the groups are
composed; the presence of certain divinities, the absence of
others, the indication of hierarchy among the gods, and the

context of their assembly – all have a specific meaning. Groups of gods were set in the pediments of temples, often with a particular reference to some famous episode in the mythology of the chief deity being honoured in that place. On the Parthenon at Athens, for example, the birth of Athene was represented on one pediment, the dispute between Athene and Poseidon for the tutelage of Attica on the other, while around Athene were depicted the other gods and mythical characters who played a rôle in these dramas. But assemblies of the gods (like that convened for Athene's birth) were less commonly represented in sculpture than in vase-painting (fig. 12).

In Attic vase-painting, gods are most often depicted in groups for one specific motive, clustered around a particular action (for examples see Rumpf 1928 [14].) The most striking occasions for this type of tableau were the wedding of Peleus and Thetis, the birth of Athene and the formal introduction of Herakles among the gods of Mt Olympos. The attitudes of the gods, marked by their gestures, are carefully constructed within the frame of the image. The scene might revolve about an axis with, for example, Zeus seated on his throne, or Apollo playing his lyre to entertain the gods. Alternatively, it might depict the assembly of the gods in a continuous circle, as in the file of chariots bringing the gods to the wedding of Thetis, for instance.

It is not our purpose to offer any explanation of these scenes here. We have cited these examples, rather, to illustrate the diversity, the complexity and the richness of the Greek representational repertoire for figuring the divine. But we would urge upon our readers the need to interpret these images in somewhat the same way that they would written texts: that is to say, they must be grouped in series, analysed into their constituent parts and then relocated within the context that gave them their original meaning, the totality of the Greeks' symbolic representations.

REPRESENTATION OF RITUALS

Greek images were not confined to the representation of gods and heroes; they also served to depict the most diverse religious rituals. They did not, however, aim to show every last detail, but instead selected just those elements they wanted to depict. In

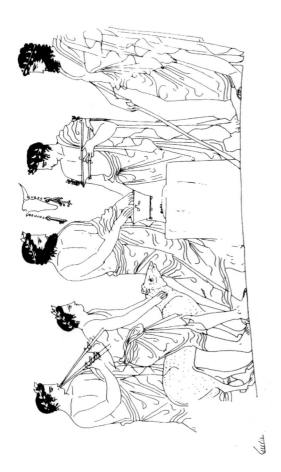

17 Sacrificial Scene. Boston (MFA) Inv. 95.25. Attic red-figure krater, *c.* 440 BCE (drawing: F. Lissarrague) 'On either side of a cuboid altar two officiants are standing. The one on the right holds in his left hand a *kanoun*, the sacrificial basket that contains the barley-grains, and the *makhaira* (knife for cutting the victim's throat); in his right hand he extends over the altar a *khernips*, a bowl in which the officiant on the left is about to plunge his hands. Held symmetrically by the same person, these two instruments have a common purpose: they contain respectively the water and the grains which will be thrown over the victim to obtain its consent to the sacrifice. The animal is kept in a state of calm, to the left of the altar, by an assistant behind whom there follows a flautist. On the right of the image, completing its symmetry, stands the priest, under whose eyes the ceremony as a whole unfolds, without any trace of violence.' (Commentary by J.-L. Durand and F. Lissarrague, 'Heros cru ou hôte cuit: histoire quasi cannibale d'Héraklès', in F. Lissarrague and F. Thélamon (eds.) *Image et céramique grecque* (Rouen, 1983): 154)

18 Sacrificial Scene. Naples. Attic red-figure krater, *c.* 470 BCE (drawing:
    F. Lissarrague) 'The scene organizes according to the same
    symmetrical model, focussed on the altar, the moment in the
    sacrificial ritual when the meat is being prepared for consumption. At
    the centre of the image stands the altar, over whose fire the spitted
    splankhna are being roasted; it bears traces of blood, the only
    recognizable sign of the previous slaughter of the victim. To the left a
    bearded man pours a libation from a goblet over the meat which the
    young man on the right is roasting on spits (*oberloi*) held over the
    flames. At the far right, a spit of the same type is posed vertically,
    handguard facing downwards near to the ground. In the background
    on the right there is a herm in frontal view. On the left another
    young man is carrying on his shoulders the tricorn sacrificial basket
    containing the barley-grains. The image makes crystal clear the
    connection between the spits and the consumption of the meat.'
    (Commentary by Durand and Lissarrague, *ibid.*: see caption to
    fig. 17)

other words, like the images of the gods, they offered their own individual interpretation of the rituals they represented. The elements that were chosen for special emphasis derived their meaning from the code of gestures and conduct by which Greek culture was constituted. Representations of animal sacrifice, already a well-studied subject (see Bibliography to this chapter), can give us an insight into the processes whereby a ritual was represented.

To begin with, the men and the animals make their way in file towards the altar. The men wear crowns and perform most of the rituals standing up (fig. 17). The preliminary libation before the sacrifice is often depicted, but the act of slaughtering only rarely. Even so, the altar is shown with bloodstains to indicate the important stage in the ritual drama when the victim's throat is cut and the blood is made to gush out onto the altar. Then come the butchering, and the separation of the gods' portions from those allocated to humans. The entrails are grilled. The cuts of meat are boiled in a cauldron and/or roasted over the fire on enormous spits (fig. 18). The inclusion within the image of one or more of the requisite ritual objects – altar, water-basin, vessel to catch the animal's blood, three-handled basket containing barley-groats and the sacrificial knife, carving table – suffices to indicate that it is a sacrifice which is being depicted.

It is rare for an image to represent more than one stage of the ritual; the hydria in the Villa Giulia Museum in Rome, showing an entire sacrificial programme, is quite exceptional. Usually it is thought adequate to represent one or other of the principal moments in order to evoke the totality of the sacrificial ritual. Whereas the written texts firmly emphasize the concluding stage of the ritual, the communal consumption of the cooked meat, visual images do not represent this in direct connection with the preceding scenes of slaughter and butchery. On the other hand, there are countless visual representations of banqueting on its own.

One final way of reading the images of sacrifice is to look for the numerous deviations from the norm. Scenes of Herakles sacrificing are particularly informative. They omit the regulated distribution, and they place the main emphasis on the violence of the sacrificial act. In short, they present the hero as if he were virtually a ... cannibal.

Visual representations of rituals, to sum up, are a precious aid to our understanding of cultic rituals and their symbolism, provided, that is, that we do not regard the images as mere visual illustrations which add nothing to the written evidence. Rather, we should see the images as documents in their own right, with their own peculiar logic, and as such offering fresh data for the study of Greek religion.

CONCLUSIONS

One important fact has emerged from our very cursory survey of the questions raised by the study of the Greeks' figuration of the divine: this is the large degree to which all their systems of representation – pantheons, myths, visual images – were mutually supportive. If there was a logic at work behind the constitution of the pantheon and the elaboration of myths, this was no less true of the creation of the visual images of the divine that populated the Greek city. Moreover, these systems of representation cannot be separated from the rituals which gave expression to the underlying systemic structures. It is clearly impossible, for example, to study a statue in isolated abstraction from the ritual use to which it was put. To conclude, the two aspects of Greek religion that we have described successively in this book – the cultic practices (Part II) and the systems for representing the divine (Part III) – have to be conceptualized and interpreted as a unified totality.

PART IV

Envoi

CHAPTER 15

Concluding reflections

A QUESTION OF *PSUKHĒ*

Throughout this book we have tried to show that the religion of the Greeks was 'other', desperately foreign; that it had its own peculiar categories and frames of reference; and that it has to be defined in relation to the values of the Greek city, within the context of which its structures had overriding significance. We have observed, too, that the beliefs of the Greeks, like those of each and every culture-group, were a function of the psychological categories which organized their perception of the world.

We have stressed that, in the process of analysing the Greeks' religious concepts, misinterpretation may arise through confusing their categories with our own. For example, there has been a tendency to privilege those aspects of Greek religion which appear to betoken a piety that is allegedly 'superior' because closer to the values of Christianity. This has led to the practices of sects like the Pythagoreans and Orphics being interpreted as if they heralded a new conception of the divine. In the same inappropriate spirit, mystery-cults and initiations have often been misconstrued according to the model of soteriological religions and misrepresented, therefore, as preparations for an afterlife implying beliefs which in reality have nothing to do with the civic religion of the Greek city. To us, in our effort to understand the Greeks' religion, it has seemed more interesting to relate all these practices to other contemporary ones, to which they formed a response, and with which they comprised a coherent whole.

The career of the notion of *psukhē*, typically translated as 'soul', illustrates well the hazards of over-hasty, Christianizing conflation. What we would prefer to say – without intending merely to provoke – is that the Greeks had no soul, at least not before Plato. For the Greeks of the Archaic and Classical periods the *psukhē* was typically a sort of 'double' or mirror-image of the deceased, the spectral shade that flitted between the worlds of the quick and the dead when a corpse had not received the prescribed burial rites. It was a power from the world beyond the grave, the world of the dead, which could become embodied visibly in, for instance, the rough-hewn idols known as *kolossoi* – there are various pieces of evidence to show that these could act as substitutes for the deceased.

This category of the mirror-image or 'double' is bound up with a mental universe organized quite differently from ours, within which the *psukhē* was a reality perceived as being simultaneously external and intangible. When the notion made its first appearance, between the sixth and fifth centuries BCE, among the Pythagorean sects and then in wider philosophical circles, it was linked to the concept of *daimōn*. For Plato, as later for the Stoics, this latter term designated an element foreign to a person's mortal nature, partaking rather of the divine. In association with this newfangled conception of the *daimōn* the *psukhē* was transformed by Plato from being the phantom and double of the deceased into 'a power that exists at the very heart of the living man ... both an objective reality and a subjective inner experience ...' (Vernant 1983 [255]: 334).

This move marks the birth of the psychological idea of 'the person', so far as Greek civilization is concerned (Vernant 1991 [256]). From the conception of the *psukhē* as the phantasmal double of the body the step was taken of conceiving of the body inversely as the phantasmal double of the soul. That in turn opened the floodgates to a new wave of reinterpretation which tended to privilege a 'philosophic religion' above the religious ideas held in common by the ordinary inhabitants of the Classical Greek city.

CONTINUITY AND CHANGE

However, civic religion did not simply disappear with the Greek cities' loss of political independence. The establishment of the Hellenistic kingdoms in the late fourth century BCE in no way signalled the demise of the religious system that had become institutionalized during the preceding epoch. On the contrary, the persistent vigour of the official cults, in which the kings participated alongside the cities, is well attested. The gods still received offerings of statues and temples, as the dedications that have been rediscovered demonstrate. Sanctuaries continued to be maintained or renovated, new festivals were inaugurated, and the sacred treasure-houses were further enriched with public dedications. Similarly, private offerings and dedications afford plentiful evidence of continuing individual piety.

Certainly, there was a long-established tradition within the cities themselves of the intelligentsia's criticizing the gods' anthropomorphic natures and their all too human failings. But these speculations remained confined to philosophical circles and, so long as they were not felt to breach the cities' laws, remained largely external to the sphere of everyday practice and had no effect on conventional beliefs. However, the cities were now exposed to a new world of ideas, and this did bring in its train some modifications to religious behaviour. One sign of this was the multiplication of oriental cults, which came to satisfy the aspirations of individuals no longer fulfilled by the traditional cult-practices alone. But still the traditional religious system as a whole continued to function normally and was to enjoy a prolonged lease of life. Delphi, for example, remained an oracular centre right up to the end of the fourth century CE, and Olympia continued to welcome athletes and pilgrims until an Imperial edict of Theodosius the Great abolished the Games in CE 393.

Over the centuries, however, the spirit of these devotions did alter, and the collective dimension of Greek religion with its function of providing reassurance to the civic community as a whole did gradually wither. As the repetition of ancient rituals became rigidly formulaic and meaningless, and recourse to magic and soothsayers blossomed, so at the same time the old spirit was superseded by that of personal communication with the godhead.

Yet these trends also provoked a conservative reaction among those who harked back to the past for their points of reference and models of behaviour, apologists who in their homilies defined a piety that was faithful to their reconstituted image of the men of yore.

At the close of this tradition, while Christianity was achieving ascendancy, some men still bore witness to the coherence of the ancient religious model both by their behaviour and in their writings. For them this model was an integral part of a value-system that was inseparable from the world which gave them their sense of identity, a world now under threat. Of such a stamp were men like Plutarch (first-second century CE), priest of Apollo at Delphi; Pausanias (second century CE), indefatigable tourist of the cult-places of the past and initiate of the Mysteries of Demeter; and Porphyry (third century CE), author of a defence of the traditional civic religion entitled *Against the Christians*. The preoccupations of these intellectuals were, moreover, mirrored in the inscriptions carved on stone, the writings entrusted to papyrus, the *ex-voto* dedications and the narrative myths which all attested to a popular piety that remained vital as long as city life survived the vicissitudes of what had by then become the Roman Empire.

APPENDIX I

The Classical Greek temple

In chapter 6 we located the temple historically, geographically and functionally within the civic space of a city's public sanctuary. Here we add some technical details regarding its architectural details and illustrate them with a range of plans.

THE DIFFERENT PARTS

The basic plan (fig. 19) was rectangular and comprised two parts, one of which, the *sēkos*, was closed off, the other, the peristyle or exterior colonnade, open. The closed off part consisted of at least one room, the *naos* or in Latin *cella*, which housed the god's cult-statue. Often this room was entered from a *pronaos* or vestibule. A rear chamber (*opisthodomos*) completed the basic plan. In certain temples there was also an *aduton* (literally 'a place to which access was barred'), a sort of holy-of-holies which communicated with the *cella*.

The disposition and number of columns determined the type of temple (figs. 19–20). A temple entirely surrounded by columns is said to be 'peripteral', and if the columns are ranged in two rows, 'dipteral'. When there was only a single colonnade and that was placed on the façade, it is called 'prostyle' (fig. 20b). The number of columns on the façade is expressed in technical jargon as 'hexastyle' (six), 'octostyle' (eight), and so on. The length of temples varied considerably. The earliest, truly monumental ones measured a hundred feet (according to the local value for the foot), and hence were called 'hundred-footers' (*hekatompeda*). So for brevity's sake one might refer to a temple in technical parlance as 'peripteral, hexastyle, hecatompedon' – readers should not be alarmed by this architectural jargon, although they will have to decode it!

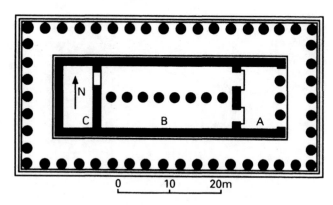

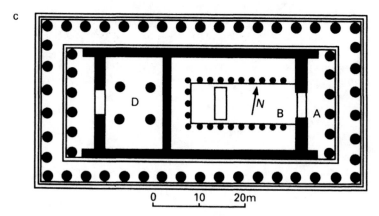

19   Plans of Temples: a Temple of Hera, Poseidonia (so-called 'Basilica'). b Temple of Hephaistos and Athene Hephaistaia, Athens (so-called 'Theseion'). c Parthenon, Athenian Akropolis. A = *pronaos*, B = *naos*, C = *aduton*, D = *opisthodomos*

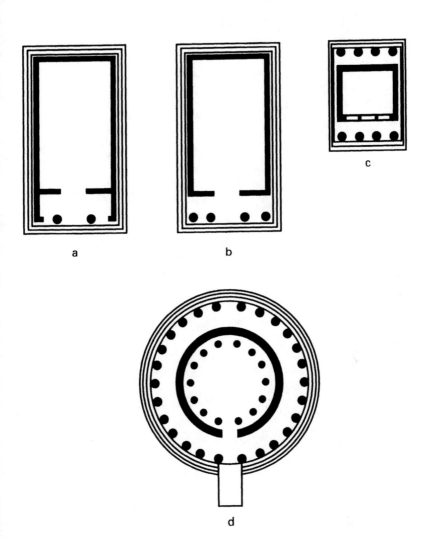

20   Types of Temples: a *In antis*. b Prostyle. c Amphiprostyle.
d *Tholos*

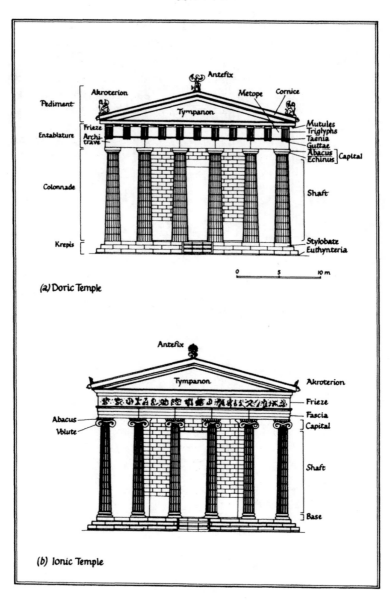

21   Temple façades: a Doric. b Ionic

ELEVATION (fig. 21)

The temple rested on a platform (*krēpis*) with three levels. The uppermost level is known as the 'stylobate', because it supported the colonnade. In section the temple displays column (shaft and capital), architrave, frieze of metopes alternating with triglyphs, pediment and roof. The Ionic type (fig. 21b) differs in having a base to the column, a fascia in place of the architrave and a continuous frieze. The parts susceptible of sculptural adornment were the metopes and pediments; sometimes, as on the Parthenon, there was the extra feature of a frieze running around the top of the *sēkos* between the colonnade and the main body of the *naos*.

THE ORDERS (fig. 22)

The three Classical orders – Doric, Ionic and Corinthian – are distinguished fundamentally by their respective types of capital. But a basically Doric temple could be varied with features drawn from Ionic (the continuous frieze of the Parthenon, for example) or Corinthian (the *naos* of the late-fifth-century temple of Apollo Epikourios at Bassai in Arkadia contained a Corinthian capital).

DECORATION

The pediments, metopes and frieze were sculpted, as we have seen, but akroteria and antefixes placed on the temple's roof and the triglyphs that interrupted the metopes were no less integral features of the overall decoration. The stonework of the walls, moreover, was stuccoed, and the sculptural reliefs were painted in bright colours and sometimes also provided with highly polished metal accessories (e.g. a warrior's spear or a horse's reins). The original effect was therefore utterly unlike the bleached whiteness of the basic stone which is all that is visible today.

THOLOI (fig. 20d)

Most temples were rectangular in plan, but a very few were circular and belong to the category known as *tholoi* (literally, 'round buildings', or 'beehives'). Those in sanctuaries of Asklepios at Epidauros and of the Great Gods at Samothrake are famous examples. However, not all *tholoi* were cultic in function: the Tholos in the Athenian Agora, for instance, served as the dining-room of the Council of

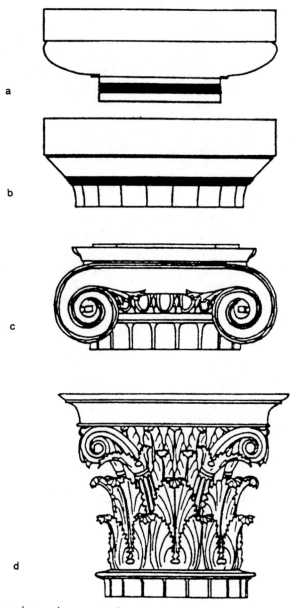

22   The orders: column capitals. a Doric: Archaic period. b Doric:
      Hellenistic period. c Ionic. d Corinthian

500's standing committee. Nor was the circular form of temple tied, as was long claimed, to a particular type of ritual, namely funerary cult. In general, archaeologists are now prepared to recognize the diverse functions that can be fulfilled by buildings of the same plan rather than constructing grandiose theories of allegedly universal validity.

The monuments of the Athenian Akropolis (fig. 23)

THE PERIKLEAN BUILDING PROGRAMME

After about 450 the Athenians stopped fighting the Persians, and from 445 they were for over a decade at peace also with their major Greek rival, Sparta. It was during this quite exceptional pacific interlude that the great Akropolis building programme was launched. Its chief political architect was Perikles, who also served on the board of building commissioners (*epistatai*). The rebuilt Akropolis conveyed different messages to different groups of worshippers and other visitors. Here is how it struck one cultural pilgrim in the second century CE:

The Akropolis has a single entrance; it offers no other because the whole rock is abrupt and strongly-walled. The Propylaia has a roof of white marble, which down to my day is still without peer for the size and beauty of the stone. I cannot say for certain whether the equestrian statues represent the children of Xenophon, or were simply made for decorative effect. To the right of the Propylaia is the temple of Nikē Apteros ('Wingless Victory'). From here you can see the sea clearly, and they say this is where Aigeus plunged to his death . . . To the left of the Propylaia is a building containing paintings . . . At the actual entrance to the Akropolis are statues of Hermes Propylaios and the Graces, said to be by Socrates son of Sophroniskos . . . [Pausanias now describes everything he passes on his way up to the Parthenon, including numerous statues whose legendary associations he relates.]

As you approach the temple called the Parthenon, everything on the pediment has to do with the birth of Athene; the rear pediment shows Poseidon and Athene quarrelling for control of the country. The cult-statue is made of ivory and gold. It has a sphinx on the middle of the helmet . . . and griffins are worked in on either side of it . . . As for

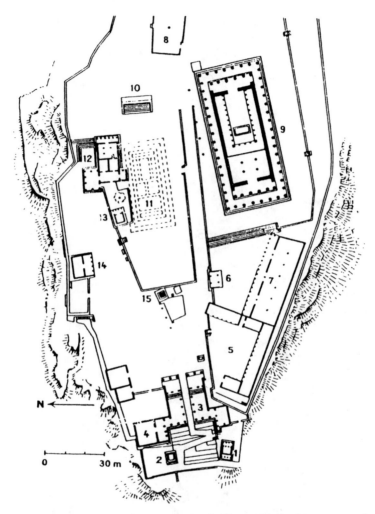

23   The Athenian Akropolis. 1 Temple of Athene Nikē. 2 Monument of
Agrippa. 3 Propylaia. 4 Pinakothēkē. 5 Precinct of Artemis Brauronia. 6
Precinct of Athene Erganē. 7 Khalkothēkē. 8 Precinct of Zeus Polieus. 9
Parthenon. 10 Altar of Athene. 11 Old Temple of Athene. 12 Erekhtheion.
13 Pandroseion. 14 House of the Arrhephoroi. 15 Statue of Athene
Promakhos

the statue of Athene, it is represented standing upright, wearing an ankle-length tunic with a head of Medousa carved in ivory on her breast. Athene is holding a Victory about 1.60 metres high in one hand and in the other a spear. At her feet is a shield, and there is a snake near the spear symbolizing Erikhthonios. On the plinth of the statue is carved the birth of Pandora.

(Pausanias 1.22.4–24.7, excerpts, trans. P. Levi, modified)

PARTHENON

What we, like Pausanias, call 'the Parthenon' for short (strictly that was just one segment of the temple as a whole) was dedicated to Athene Parthenos ('Virgin') and constructed according to the design of Kallikrates and Iktinos between 447/6 and 433/2. The chryselephantine cult-statue in the *cella*, completed by 438/7, was by Pheidias (see below). In plan the Parthenon was an exceptional monument both for its dimensions and for the care lavished on its architecture (cf. Appendix I). It was also exceptional for the richness of its ornamentation, especially sculptural.

Metopes ran all round the exterior façade of the temple, ninety-two of them altogether. On the east elevation was represented the Battle of the Gods and the Giants, on the west a combat between the Greeks and an oriental people generally interpreted from their clothing as Persians, on the south the Lapiths against the Centaurs, and on the north the sack of Troy.

The famous Parthenon frieze, one metre high and 160 metres long, ran around the top of the external walls of the *sēkos* or *cella*. The single subject depicted was a version of the Panathenaic procession, making it the sole non-mythological scene known on a Greek temple. The sculptures are in parts well preserved, and this is a uniquely valuable document for the study of Classical Greek carving. But historians too get fired up in their passion to 'read' the frieze as the ideal projection of the self-image of Athens (or at any rate the Panathenaic festival).

The sculptures of the west pediment portrayed the struggle between Athene and Poseidon for the control of Attica, a peculiarly Athenian myth. Athene and Poseidon occupy the centre of the composition; Athene is offering the olive tree, while Poseidon causes a spring to gush forth at a stroke of his trident. Behind them is a pair of horses drawing chariots, with, on Athene's side, Hermes, and, on Poseidon's side, Iris, both messengers of the gods. The chariots are being led by two female figures, Amphitrite and perhaps Nikē. Then on the left side there is a series of superhuman figures including the autochthonous founder-hero Kekrops.

The sculptures of the east (front) pediment told the story of the birth of Athene, but all that survives are those at either extremity. On the left the chariot of Helios (the sun-god) emerges, while on the right the chariot of Selene (the moon-goddess) is seen disappearing. Other divine figures are also visible at the extremities, but of the central scene all is lost. In vase-paintings Athene is shown emerging fully armed from the cranium of her father Zeus.

THE STATUE OF ATHENE PARTHENOS

Nothing survives of Pheidias' masterwork, although we do have a fragmentary record of the commissioners' accounts, and the statue was frequently described in antiquity, as by Pausanias. To his abbreviated description above we may add that the shield was emblazoned on the outside with an Amazonomachy (battle against the Amazons), and on the inside decorated with a Gigantomachy (battle between Gods and Giants). On Athene's sandals was shown the fight between the Lapiths and the Centaurs. The total height of the statue including the plinth was twelve metres. The face, arms and feet were done in ivory, the clothes were covered in gold plaques that could be removed at need. The statue was completed in 438, as we learn from the building accounts, and erected in the *cella*.

OTHER MAJOR MONUMENTS

The monumental entrance-way known as the Propylaia was constructed between 437 and 432 according to the plans of Mnesikles; it was remarkable and unique for the lavish use of marble in a 'secular' structure, but the outbreak of the Peloponnesian War interrupted work and, partly for reasons of cost, it was never completed. The Erekhtheion was, despite its name, not only the house of Erekhtheus, legendary king of Athens; it also contained the cults of Athene Polias, represented by an ancient olive-wood image, and of Poseidon – hence its highly irregular plan and mixture of architectural and sculptural elements. Begun in 435, it too was interrupted by the Peloponnesian War, but unlike the Propylaia it was eventually completed, in 408/7. The surviving building accounts reveal the presence of slaves among the craftsmen. Finally, there is the temple of Athene Nikē. This new cult with its democratically selected priestess was apparently established in the 440s, but the temple was not begun before 421 nor completed until the last decade of the fifth century.

THE PLEASURE OF THE REMODELLED AKROPOLIS

Athens henceforth had a sanctuary that the whole of Greece could admire. Athene herself, too, if we may believe Plutarch, found the project agreeable:

The Propylaia of the Akropolis was completed [not so, in fact] in five years by the architect Mnesikles. A miracle that occurred during the construction shows that the goddess, far from being uninterested, herself took a hand in the work and aided its completion. The most energetic and ambitious of the construction-workers slipped and fell from the top of the gateway. He was in a pitiable state and given up for dead by the doctors. Perikles was in despair, when the goddess herself appeared to him in a dream and prescribed a treatment which he applied with quick and easy success. It was on this occasion, so the story goes, that Perikles caused to be set up the bronze statue of Athene Hygieia ('of Health') and placed it on the Akropolis near the altar which was already in position.   (Plutarch, *Life of Perikles* 13.12)

BIBLIOGRAPHY

[*Translator's note*: This Bibliography, which is inevitably selective and intended to be suggestive, falls into two halves: I contains works of a generalized character – encyclopaedias, handbooks, works of overall interpretation; II is keyed specifically to the chapters of the present book. The whole reproduces essentially the 'Bibliographie' of the French original, but besides listing English translations where appropriate it adds several English-language publications considered especially suitable for its intended readership. Numbers in square brackets preceding entries are designed to ease reference between text and Bibliography. Items prefixed with * also include helpful bibliographies.] NOTE TO 1997 IMPRESSION: The opportunity of a reprint has been taken to add some recent works. These are grouped at the end of the bibliography and are arranged in sections according to those used in the main bibliography

I. GENERAL

i Encyclopaedias, handbooks and sourcebooks

[1] *Atlas des religions* (1988), ('Encyclopaedia Universalis'). Paris

[2] *Y. BONNEFOY (ed.) (1991) *Mythologies*, 2 vols. (French original Paris 1981). Chicago and London. [Greek mythology in vol. 1, Part 4, pp. 325–511]

[3] J. CHARBONNEAUX, R. MARTIN and F. VILLARD (1971) *Archaic Greek Art, 600–480 BC* (French original, Paris 1968). London

[4] J. CHARBONNEAUX, R. MARTIN and F. VILLARD (1972) *Classical Greek Art, 480–330 BC* (French original, Paris, 1969). London

[5] R. CRAHAY (1966) *La Religion des Grecs*. Paris. [Sourcebook]

[6] C. V. DAREMBERG, E. SAGLIO and E. POTTIER (eds.) (1873–1919) *Dictionnaire des antiquités grecques et romaines*, 5 vols. in 10. Paris

[7] J. FERGUSON (1980) *Greek and Roman Religion: a source book*. Park Ridge, NJ

[8] F. C. GRANT (ed.) (1953) *Hellenistic Religions. The Age of Syncretism.* New York

[9] P. GRIMAL (1986, 1991) *The Dictionary of Classical Mythology,* abridged edn (French original, Paris 1951). Oxford, repr. Harmondsworth

[10] *LIMC: Lexicon Iconographicum Mythologiae Classicae* (Zurich and Munich 1981–)

[11] *RE:* A. F. VON PAULY, G. WISSOWA and W. KROLL (eds.) (1894–1972) *Realencyclopädie der classischen Altertumswissenschaft.* Stuttgart

[12] D.G. RICE and J. E. STAMBAUGH (1979) *Sources for the Study of Greek Religion* (Society of Biblical Literature). Missoula, Montana

[13] W. ROSCHER (ed.) (1882–1921) *Ausführliches Lexikon der griechischen und römischen Mythologie.* Leipzig (with Supplements, 1921–)

[14] A. RUMPF (1928) *Die Religion der Griechen* (Bilderatlas zur Religionsgeschichte 13–14). Leipzig. [208 photographs, line-drawings and plans]

ii General studies of Greek religion

[15] A. H. ARMSTRONG (ed.) (1986) *Classical Mediterranean Spirituality. Egyptian, Greek, Roman* ('World Spirituality' series). London

[16] U. BIANCHI (1962) *La religione greca,* in P. Tacchi-Venturi (ed.) *Storia delle religioni* vol. 2. Turin

[17] *W. BURKERT (1985) *Greek Religion. Archaic and Classical* (German original, Stuttgart 1977). Oxford. [A very comprehensive synthesis (list of general works 1910–1975 at 343n.1; bibl. 473–8)]

[18] I. CHIRASSI COLOMBO (1983) *La religione in Grecia.* Rome

[19] E. DES PLACES (1969) *La Religion grecque: dieux, cultes, rites et sentiment religieux dans la Grèce antique.* Paris. [Concentrates on analysing the evolution of religious feeling.]

[20] E. R. DODDS (1951) *The Greeks and the Irrational.* Berkeley, Los Angeles and London. [Not a history of religion, but a study of the way the Greeks themselves interpreted the irrational]

[21] *P. E. EASTERLING and J. V. MUIR (eds.) (1985) *Greek Religion and Society.* Cambridge. [A very accessible manual with chapters by leading British experts on Greek religion, e.g. J. P. A. Gould, 'On making sense of Greek religion' (1–33)]

[22] L. R. FARNELL (1896–1907) *Cults of the Greek States,* 5 vols. Oxford. [A reference work]

[23] A.-J. FESTUGIÈRE (1944) 'La Grèce' in M. Gorce and R. Mortier (eds.) *Histoire générale des religions* vol. 2: 27–147. Paris. [An approach to Greek religion which cannot be ignored]

[24] *L. GERNET and A. BOULANGER (1932, 1970) *Le Génie grec dans la religion* (repr. with an extremely useful complementary bibliography). Paris. [Classical and Hellenistic periods; old but still indispensable]

[25] L. GERNET (1968) *Anthropologie de la Grèce antique.* Paris. [Several chapters deal directly with religion. The English translation *Anthropology of Ancient Greece* (Baltimore 1981) is not recommended; among the reviews of the latter see esp. M. B. Arthur *MLN* (special number on comparative literature) 98.5 (Dec. 1983): 1374–80]

[26] P. LEVEQUE (1985) *Bêtes, dieux, et hommes.* Paris

[27] R. MARTIN and H. METZGER (1976) *La Religion grecque.* Paris. [Not a synthesis, but has chapters on various aspects of Greek religion]

[28] M. P. NILSSON (1925) *A History of Greek Religion*, with a preface by J. G. Frazer. Oxford

[29] M. P. NILSSON (1940) *Greek Popular Religion.* New York

[30] M. P. NILSSON (1948) *Greek Piety.* Oxford

[31] M. P. NILSSON (1967–74) *Geschichte der griechischen Religion*, 2 vols. 3rd edn Munich. [Classic study]

[32] *R. PARKER (1986) 'Greek religion', in J. Boardman *et al.* (eds.) *The Oxford History of the Classical World:* 254–74. Oxford. [Excellent brief survey]

[33] J. RUDHARDT (1958) *Notions fondamentales de la pensée religieuse et actes constitutifs du culte dans la Grèce ancienne.* Geneva. 2nd edn 1992. [A constant point of reference in the writing of the present book]

[34] L. SECHAN and P. LEVEQUE (1966, 1990) *Les grandes divinités de la Grèce.* Paris. [Taking the study of the different gods as its starting-point, this broaches the principal aspects of Greek religion with exemplary clarity]

[35] C. SEGAL (1982) 'Afterword: Jean-Pierre Vernant and the study of ancient Greece', *Arethusa* 15: 221–34. [V.'s exceptional contribution seen as influenced crucially by the historical psychology of Meyerson, the sociology of Gernet, the structural methodology of Dumézil and Lévi-Strauss and the philology of Benveniste, and as standing at the crossroads of history, philosophy, religion, literary criticism, sociology, anthropology and ethnography]

[36] G. SISSA and M. DETIENNE (1989) *La Vie quotidienne des dieux*

grecs. Paris [Not so much their everyday life, but the gods at work among men]

[37] C. SOURVINOU-INWOOD (1990) 'What is *polis* religion?' in O. Murray and S. Price (eds.) *The Greek City from Homer to Alexander*: 295–322. Oxford

[38] C. SOURVINOU-INWOOD (forthcoming) 'Further aspects of *polis* religion', *AION* 10 (1988): 259–74. [In solidarity with the approach of the present book S.–I, argues that 'the *polis* provided the fundamental, basic framework in which Greek religion operated']

[39] J.-P. VERNANT (1980) *Myth and Society in Ancient Greece* (French original, Paris 1974). Hassocks

[40] J.-P. VERNANT (1983) *Myth and Thought among the Greeks* (trans. of 2nd French edn., Paris 1975; but see now 3rd edn, 1985). London

[41] *J.-P. VERNANT (1989) 'Greek religion', in R. M. Seltzer (ed.) *Religions of Antiquity. Religion, history and culture: selections from 'The Encyclopedia of Religion'* (ed. M. Eliade, New York 1987): 163–92. New York. [Also available in French, with new introduction and enlarged bibliography, as *Mythe et religion en Grèce ancienne* (Paris 1990)]

[42] J.-P. VERNANT (1991) *Mortals and Immortals. Collected Essays,* ed. F. I. Zeitlin. Princeton. [Excellent editorial introduction: 3–24; individual essays cited under separate numbers in Part II of this bibliography]

II. BIBLIOGRAPHY TO COMPLEMENT THE CHAPTERS OF THIS BOOK

[As a rule, works listed in the 'General' section (I.ii) are not repeated here.]

1 The necessity of cultural estrangement

THE PLACE OF RELIGION IN THE CITIES

[43] J. RUDHARDT (1981) *Du mythe, de la religion grecque et de la compréhension d'autrui = Rev. europ. des sciences sociales/ Cahiers Vilfredo Pareto* vol. 19, no. 58. Geneva. [A collection of fourteen of Rudhardt's articles (1964–81), with 'Avant-Propos'. 284pp]

[44] J. RUDHARDT (1981) 'Sur la possibilité de comprendre une religion étrangère' (1964) repr. in Rudhardt 1981 [43]: 13–32

[45] J.-P. VERNANT (1979, 1991) 'Greek religion, ancient religions' (Collège de France Inaugural Lecture, 5 December 1975, repr. in Vernant 1979 [46], trans. with revisions and bibliographical notes in, and cited from, Vernant 1991 [42]: 269–89)

[46] J.-P. VERNANT (1979) *Religions, histoires, raisons*. Paris. [Collection of essays and lectures]

[47] P. VEYNE (1988) *Did the Greeks Believe in their Myths?* (French original, Paris 1983). Chicago

2 *Some fundamental notions*

THE IDEA OF THE SACRED

[48] E. BENVENISTE (1969) *Le Vocabulaire des institutions indo-européennes* vol. 2, *Le Sacré*. Paris

[49] W. R. CONNOR (1988) '"Sacred" and "secular". Ἱερὰ καὶ Ὅσια and the classical Athenian concept of the state', *Ancient Society* 19: 161–88

[50] F. WILLIGER (1922) *Hagios: Untersuchungen zur Terminologie des Heiligen in der hellenisch-hellenistischen Religion*. Giessen

THE IDEA OF PURITY

[51] M. DOUGLAS (1966, 1970) *Purity and Danger. An analysis of the concepts of pollution and taboo*. London, repr. Harmondsworth

[52] L. MOULINIER (1952) *Le Pur et l'impur dans la pensée et la sensibilité des Grecs jusqu' à la fin du IVe siècle avant J.-C.* Paris. Reviewed by Vernant 1980 [39]: 110–29

[53] *R. PARKER (1983, pb. 1990) *Miasma. Pollution and purification in early Greek religion*. Oxford

PIETY

[54] J. SCHEID (1985) *Religion et piété à Rome*. Paris. [Esp. ch. 1 (piety and impiety)]

3 *Sources of evidence*

[*Translator's note:* in principle, *any* ancient source – literary, epigraphical, archaeological – may be somehow relevant to the study of Greek religion; the following items should not be seen as especially privileged, except in the sense that their contribution is a particularly compendious or concentrated one.]

LITERARY SOURCES

[55] PS.-APOLLODOROS *Library* (Eng. trans. and comm. by J. G. Frazer, Loeb Classical Library edn, Cambridge, MA and London 1921)

[56] PAUSANIAS *Description of Greece* (6 vols. ed. J. G. Frazer, London 1898; Eng. trans. and comm., 2 vols., P. Levi, Harmondsworth 1971); cf. C. Habicht *Pausanias' Guide to Ancient Greece*. Berkeley, 1985

INSCRIPTIONS

[57] *IG: Inscriptiones Graecae*. Berlin, 1873–1981

[58] *LSCG, LSS*: F. SOKOLOWSKI (ed.) *Lois sacrées des cités grecques*. Paris, 1969, with *Supplément*, Paris, 1962

[59] *LSAM*: F. SOKOLOWSKI (ed.) *Lois sacrées d'Asie Mineure*. Paris, 1955

[60] *M/L*: R. MEIGGS and D. M. LEWIS (eds.) *A Selection of Greek Historical Inscriptions to the end of the fifth century BC*. Oxford, 1969, repr. with add. and corr., 1989

[61] *SEG: Supplementum Epigraphicum Graecum*. Leiden, 1923–72; 1976–

[62] *Syll³*: W. DITTENBERGER *Sylloge Inscriptionum Graecarum*, 3rd edn. 5 vols. Leipzig, 1915

[63] M. N. TOD (ed.) (1948) *A Selection of Greek Historical Inscriptions* vol. 2: *From 403 to 323 BC*. Oxford

TRANSLATED DOCUMENTS

[64] C. W. FORNARA (ed.) (1983) *Archaic Times to the End of the Peloponnesian War*, 2nd edn Cambridge

[65] P. HARDING (ed.) (1985) *From the End of the Peloponnesian War to the Battle of Ipsus*. Cambridge

[66] M. M. AUSTIN (ed.) (1981) *The Hellenistic World from Alexander to the Roman Conquest*. Cambridge

ARCHAEOLOGY

[67] I. M. MORRIS (1987) *Burial and Greek Society. The rise of the Greek state*. Cambridge

Bibliography

[68] A. M. SNODGRASS (1987) *An Archaeology of Greece. The present state and future scope of a discipline*. Berkeley, Los Angeles and London

CONTEMPORARY APPROACHES

See [43–7]

4 Rituals

SACRIFICE

[69] G. BERTHIAUME (1982) *Les Rôles du mageiros. Étude sur la boucherie, la cuisine et le sacrifice dans la Grèce ancienne.* Leiden

[70] W. BURKERT (1983) *Homo Necans. The anthropology of ancient Greek sacrificial ritual and myth* (German original, Berlin 1971). Berkeley. [For a very different view, tracing sacrificial practices to deep and distant, Stone Age roots]

[71] *M. DETIENNE and J.-P. VERNANT (eds.) (1989) *The cuisine of Sacrifice among the Greeks* (French original, Paris 1979). Chicago [bibliography by J. Svenbro: 204–17]

[72] J.-L. DURAND (1986) *Sacrifice et labour en Grèce ancienne: essai d'anthropologie religieuse.* Paris and Rome

[73] E. DURKHEIM (1912) *Elementary Forms of the Religious Life* (French original, Paris 1910). London

[74] R. GIRARD (1977) *Violence and the Sacred* (French original, Paris 1972). Baltimore

[75] R. GIRARD (1987) *Things Hidden since the Foundation of the World* (French original, Paris 1978). London

[76] C. GROTTANELLI and N. PARISE (eds.) (1988) *Sacrificio e società nel mondo antico.* Rome

[77] H. HUBERT and M. MAUSS (1964) *Sacrifice: its Nature and Function* (French original 1898, repr. in M. Mauss *Oeuvres* vol. 1: *Les fonctions sociales du sacré* (Paris 1968): 193–307). London

[78] O. MURRAY (ed.) (1990) *Sympotica. A symposium on the symposion.* Oxford

[79] W. ROBERTSON SMITH (1894) *Lectures on the Religion of the Semites.* Edinburgh

[80] J. RUDHARDT and O. REVERDIN (eds.) (1981) *Le Sacrifice dans l'Antiquité* (Entretiens Hardt 27). Vandœuvres-Geneva. [Compare and contrast the contributions of:]

[81] J.-P. VERNANT (1991) 'Théorie générale du sacrifice et mise à mort

dans la *thusia* grecque' (1–21, trans. as, and cited from, 'A general theory of sacrifice and the slaying of the victims in the Greek *thusia*', in Vernant 1991 [42]: 290–302) and

[82] G. S. KIRK (1981) 'Some methodological pitfalls in the study of ancient Greek sacrifice (in particular)', *ibid*: 41–80

PRAYER

[83] H. S. VERSNEL (1981) 'Religious mentality in ancient prayer', in Versnel (ed.) *Faith, Hope and Worship. Aspects of religious mentality in the Ancient World*: 1–64. Leiden

5 Religious personnel

[84] M. BEARD and J. A. NORTH (eds.) (1990) *Pagan Priests*. London. [Esp. ch. 3, 'Priests and power in classical Athens': 73–91 (by R. Garland)]

[85] R. GARLAND (1984) 'Religious authority in Archaic and Classical Athens', *ABSA* 79: 75–123

[86] J. MARTHA (1882) *Les Sacerdoces athéniens*. Paris

6 Places of cult

CULT-PLACES

[87] E. MELAS (ed.) (1973) *Temples and Sanctuaries of Ancient Greece. A companion guide* (German original, Cologne 1970). London and New York. [Essays on individual sites by leading Greek archaeologists]

[88] R. OSBORNE (1987) *Classical Landscape with Figures. The ancient Greek city and its countryside*: 165–92. London

[89] G. ROUX (ed.) (1984) *Temples et sanctuaires*. Lyons

THE DEVELOPMENT OF SANCTUARIES AT THE BIRTH OF THE GREEK CITY

[90] F. DE POLIGNAC (1984) *La Naissance de la cité grecque. Cultes, espaces et société, VIIIe–VIIe siècles avant J.-C.* Paris

[91] A. M. SNODGRASS (1977) *Archaeology and the Rise of the Greek State*. Cambridge (Inaugural Lecture)

Bibliography

VOTIVE OFFERINGS

[92] A. H. JACKSON (1991) 'Hoplites and the gods: the dedication of captured arms and armour' in V. D. Hanson (ed.) *Hoplites. The Classical Greek Battle Experience*: 228–49. London and New York

[93] T. LINDERS and G. NORDQUIST (eds.) (1987) *Gifts to the Gods. Proceedings of the Uppsala Symposium 1985*. Uppsala. [Papers on votive offerings from around the prehistoric and historical Mediterranean]

[94] F. T. VAN STRATEN (1981) 'Gifts for the Gods', in Versnel 1981 [83]: 65–151

7 Rites of passage

'POPULAR' RELIGION

[95] J. D. MIKALSON (1983) *Athenian Popular Religion*. Chapel Hill and London

[96] M. P. NILSSON (1940) *Greek Popular Religion*. New York

RITES OF PASSAGE

[97] A. VAN GENNEP (1960) *The Rites of Passage* (French original, Paris 1909). London

FROM CHILDHOOD TO ADULTHOOD

[98] A. BRELICH (1969) *Paides e Parthenoi*. Rome

[99] L. BRUIT ZAIDMAN (1991) 'Les filles de Pandore. Femmes et rituels dans les cités', in G. Duby and M. Perrot (eds.) *Histoire des Femmes*, vol. 1 *L'Antiquité*, under the direction of P. Schmitt Pantel: 363–403. Paris; now Eng. trans. Cambridge, MA and London 1992

[100] P. BRULE (1987) *La Fille d'Athènes*. Paris

[101] C. CALAME (1977) *Les Choeurs de jeunes filles en Grèce archaïque*, 2 vols. Rome

[102] S. G. COLE (1984) 'The social function of rituals of maturation: the *koureion* and the *arkteia*', ZPE 55: 233–44

[103] R. GARLAND (1990) *The Greek Way of Life*. London

[104] H. JEANMAIRE (1939, 1978) *Couroi et Courètes. Essai sur l'éducation spartiate et les rites de l'adolescence dans l'Antiquité hellénique*. Lille and Paris, repr. New York

[105] J. S. LA FONTAINE (1985) *Initiation. Ritual drama and secret knowledge across the world.* Harmondsworth

[106] *R. SALLARES (1991) *The Ecology of the Ancient Greek World:* 160–92. London and New York [Applies 'age class system' model of proto-historic Greek society to explain the extreme classical Greek emphasis on transition to adulthood]

[107] *C. SOURVINOU-INWOOD (1988) *Studies in Girls' Transitions. Aspects of the* arkteia *and age representations in Attic iconography.* Athens

[108] P. VIDAL-NAQUET (1986) *The Black Hunter. Forms of thought and forms of society in the Greek world* (French original, corr. impr. Paris 1983). Baltimore

DEATH

[109] R. GARLAND (1985) *The Greek Way of Death.* London and Ithaca

[110] S. C. HUMPHREYS (1983) *The Family, Women and Death. Comparative studies.* London and Boston

[111] G. GNOLI and J.-P. VERNANT (eds.) (1982) *La Mort, les morts dans les sociétés anciennes.* Cambridge and Paris

[112] D. C. KURTZ and J. BOARDMAN (1971) *Greek Burial Customs.* London and New York

[113] J. POUILLOUX (1954) *Recherches sur l'histoire et les cultes de Thasos,* vol. 1. Paris

[114] G. ROUGEMONT (ed.) (1977) *Corpus des Inscriptions de Delphes. Lois sacrées et règlements religieux,* vol. 1. Paris

[115] C. SOURVINOU-INWOOD (1987) 'Images grecques de la mort: représentations, imaginaire, histoire', *AION* 9: 145–58

[116] J.-P. VERNANT (1985, 1991) *La Mort dans les yeux.* Paris (trans. in part in Vernant 1991 [42]: 111–38)

[117] J.-P. VERNANT (1989) *L'Individu, la mort, l'amour. Soi-même et l'Autre en Grèce ancienne.* Paris

[118] J.-P. VERNANT 1991 [42]: Parts I–II

8 Settings of religious life

RELIGIOUS ASSOCIATIONS: GENERAL

[119] P. FOUCART (1873) *Des Associations religieuses chez les Grecs.* Paris

[120] N. F. JONES (1987) *Public Organization in Ancient Greece. A documentary study.* Philadelphia

ATTIC DEMES

[121] G. DAUX (1963) 'La grande démarchie: un nouveau calendrier sacrificiel d'Attique', *BCH* 87: 603–34
[122] G. DAUX (1983) 'Le calendrier de Thorikos au Musée J.-P. Getty', *AC* 52: 150–74
[123] J. D. MIKALSON (1977) 'Religion in the Attic demes', *AJP* 98: 424–35
[124] R. PARKER (1987) 'Festivals of the Attic demes', in LINDERS and NORDQUIST 1987 [93]: 137–47
[125] D. WHITEHEAD (1986) *The Demes of Attica 508/7 to c. 250 BC*: 176–222. Princeton

TRIBES

[126] E. KEARNS (1985) 'Change and continuity in religious structures after Cleisthenes', in P. A. Cartledge and D. Harvey (eds.) *CRUX. Essays in Greek history presented to G. E. M. de Ste. Croix on his 75th birthday*: 189–207. Exeter and London
[127] D. ROUSSEL (1976) *Tribu et cité: études sur les groupes sociaux dans les cités grecques aux époques archaïque et classique*. Paris

9 Religion and political life

GENERAL

[128] M. P. NILSSON (1951, 1986) *Cults, Myths, Oracles and Politics in Ancient Greece*. Lund, repr. Göteborg

FOUNDATION OF CITIES

[129] W. LESCHHORN (1984) *'Gründer der Stadt'. Studien zu einem politisch-religiösen Phänomen der griechischen Geschichte*. Stuttgart
[130] I. MALKIN (1987) *Religion and Colonization in Ancient Greece*. Leiden

WAR

[131] A. BRELICH (1961) *Guerri, agoni e culti nella Grecia arcaica*. Bonn
[132] M. H. JAMESON (1991) 'Sacrifice before battle', in Hanson 1991 [92]: 197–227

[133] R. LONIS (1979) *Guerre et religion en Grèce à l'époque classique*. Paris

[134] W. K. PRITCHETT (1979) *The Greek State at War*, vol. 3: *Religion*. Berkeley

ATHENIAN AGORA

[135] J. M. CAMP (1980) *Gods and Heroes in the Athenian Agora* ('Agora Picturebook' no. 19). Athens

[136] J. M. CAMP (1986) *The Athenian Agora. Excavations in the heart of Classical Athens*. London and New York

10 *The festival system: the Athenian case*

GREEK FESTIVALS (EXCEPT ATHENS)

[137] M. P. NILSSON (1906, 1957) *Griechische Feste von religiöser Bedeutung, mit Ausschluss der attischen*. Leipzig, repr. Stuttgart

THE ATHENIAN FESTIVAL CYCLE

[138] A. BRUMFIELD (1981) *The Attic Festivals of Demeter and their relation to the agricultural year*. New York

[139] L. DEUBNER (1932) *Attische Feste*. Berlin

[140] J. D. MIKALSON (1975) *The Sacred and Civil Calendar of the Athenian Year*. Princeton

[141] H. W. PARKE (1977) *Festivals of the Athenians*. London and New York

[142] E. SIMON (1983) *Festivals of Attica. An archaeological commentary*. Madison

ATHENIAN THEATRE

[143] H. C. BALDRY (1971) *The Greek Tragic Theatre*. London

[144] J.-C. CARRIERE (1979) *Le Carnaval et la Politique, une introduction à la comédie grecque*. Paris

[145] P. A. CARTLEDGE (1990) *Aristophanes and his Theatre of the Absurd*. Bristol

[146] W. R. CONNOR (1990) 'City Dionysia and Athenian democracy', in J. R. Fears (ed.) *Aspects of Athenian Democracy* (*Classica et Mediaevalia Diss.* XI): 7–32. Copenhagen

[147] s. GOLDHILL (1986, corr. impr. 1988) *Reading Greek Tragedy.* Cambridge

[148] F. H. SANDBACH (1977) *The Comic Theatre of Greece and Rome.* London

[149] J.-P. VERNANT and P. VIDAL-NAQUET (1988) *Myth and Tragedy in Ancient Greece* (French original, 2 vols., Paris 1972–1986). Cambridge, MA (in 1 vol.)

[150] *B. ZIMMERMANN (1991) *Greek Tragedy. An introduction* (German original, Munich and Zurich, 1986). Baltimore and London

11 *The Panhellenic cults*

PANHELLENIC CULTS

[151] M. DELCOURT (1947) *Les Grands Sanctuaires de la Grèce antique.* Paris

[152] C. A. MORGAN (1990) *Athletes and Oracles. The transformation of Olympia and Delphi in the eighth century BC.* Cambridge

[153] R. V. SCHODER, SJ (1974) *Ancient Greece from the Air.* London. [Archaeological sites photographed from an aeroplane; besides the photographs, the author provides a plan, description and bibliography for each site. Very useful]

OLYMPIA AND THE OLYMPIC GAMES

[154] W. DÖRPFELD (1935) *Alt-Olympia.* Berlin

[155] L. DREES (1968) *Olympia: Gods, artists, athletes.* London

[156] M. I. FINLEY and H. W. PLEKET (1976) *The Olympic Games: the First Thousand Years.* London

[157] H.-V. HERRMANN (1972) *Olympia: Heiligtum und Wettkampfstätte.* Munich

DELPHI AND DIVINATION

[158] M. DELCOURT (1955, 1981) *L'Oracle de Delphes.* Paris

[159] H. W. PARKE and D. E. W. WORMELL (1956) *The Delphic Oracle,* 2 vols. Oxford

[160] R. PARKER (1985) 'Greek states and Greek oracles', in P. A. Cartledge and F. D. Harvey 1985 [126]: 298–326

G. ROUGEMONT 1977 [114]

[161] G. ROUX (1976) *Delphes, son oracle et ses dieux.* Paris

[162] G. SISSA (1989) *Greek Virginity* (French original, Paris 1987): 9–14 *et passim.* Cambridge, MA and London. [On the Pythia]

[163] J.-P. VERNANT (ed.) (1974, 1991) *Divination et rationalité.* Paris. [Vernant's introduction is translated as 'Speech and mute signs' in Vernant 1991 [42]: 303–17]

EPIDAUROS

[164] A. BURFORD (1969) *The Greek Temple-builders at Epidauros: a social and economic study of building in the Asklepian sanctuary, during the fourth and early third centuries BC.* Liverpool

[165] E. J. and L. EDELSTEIN (1945) *Asclepius. A collection and interpretation of the testimonies,* 2 vols. Baltimore

[166] G. ROUX (1961) *L'Architecture de l'Argolide aux IVe et IIIe siècles.* Paris

[167] A. TAFFIN (1960) 'Comment on rêvait dans les temples d'Esculape', *Bull. Ass. G. Budé:* 325–66

ELEUSIS

[168] W. BURKERT (1987) *Ancient Mystery cults.* Cambridge, MA

[169] K. CLINTON (1974) *The Sacred Officials of the Eleusinian Mysteries.* Philadelphia

[170] A. DELATTE (1954) 'Le Cycéon, breuvage rituel des mystères d'Eleusis', *BAB* 40: 690–752

[171] P. FOUCART (1914) *Les Mystères d'Eleusis.* Paris

[172] J. GOODWIN (1981) *Mystery Religions in the Ancient World.* London and New York

[173] G. E. MYLONAS (1961) *Eleusis and the Eleusinian Mysteries.* Princeton

[174] M. OLENDER (1990) 'Aspects of Baubo: ancient texts and contexts' (French original, 1985) in D. M. Halperin, J. J. Winkler and F. I. Zeitlin (eds.) *Before Sexuality. The construction of erotic experience in the ancient Greek world:* 83–114. Princeton

[175] D. SABBATUCCI (1965) *Saggio sul misticismo greco.* Rome

12 *Myths and mythology*

INTERPRETATIONS OF MYTH (A SMALL SELECTION)

[176] R. ACKERMAN (1973) 'Writing about writing about myth', *JHI* 34: 147–55. Review-article on KIRK 1970 [187] and FELDMAN and RICHARDSON 1972 [185]

[177] *J. BREMMER (ed.) (1987) *Interpretations of Greek Mythology.* London and Sydney

[178] W. BURKERT (1979) *Structure and History in Greek Mythology and Ritual.* Berkeley. [Highly individual approach, seeking parallels with animal behaviour to explain alleged psychodynamics of ritual]

[179] W. BURKERT (1980) 'Griechische Mythologie und die Geistesgeschichte der Moderne', in O. Reverdin (ed.) *Les études classiques aux XIXe et XXe siècles: leur place dans l'histoire des idées* (Entretiens Hardt 26): 159–99. Vandœuvres-Geneva

[180] M. DETIENNE (1981) *L'Invention de la mythologie.* Paris [The Eng. trans. *The Creation of Mythology* (Chicago 1986) is not recommended. Radical claim that the category 'myth' is an 'invention' perpetrated by the would-be scholarly discipline of 'mythology' beginning with Fontenelle in the eighteenth century]

[181] M. DETIENNE (1989) *L'Ecriture d'Orphée.* Paris

[182] G. DUMEZIL (1968–71–73) *Mythe et Epopée,* 3 vols. Paris. Esp. vol. 1: L'Idéologie des trois fonctions dans l'épopée des peuples indo-européens

[183] *L. EDMUNDS (ed.) (1990) *Approaches to Greek Myth.* Baltimore

[184] *P. ELLINGER (1984) 'Vingt ans de recherches sur les mythes', *REA* 86:7–29. [A very comprehensive overview of research on myths, with a detailed reference bibliography (131 items)]

[185] B. FELDMAN and R. D. RICHARDSON (1972) *The Rise of Modern Mythology, 1680–1860.* Bloomington

[186] *R. L. GORDON (ed.) (1981) *Myth, Religion and Society. Structuralist essays by M. Detienne, L. Gernet, J.-P. Vernant and P. Vidal-Naquet.* Cambridge and Paris

[187] G. S. KIRK (1970) *Myth: its meaning and functions in ancient and other cultures.* Berkeley and Cambridge

[188] G. S. KIRK (1974) *The Nature of Greek Myths.* Harmondsworth

[189] E. R. LEACH (ed.) (1967) *The Structural Study of Myth and Totemism.* London

[190] P. LEVEQUE (1972) 'Formes et structures méditerranéennes dans la

genèse de la religion grecque', *Praelectiones Patavinae* 1972: 145–79

[191] C. LEVI-STRAUSS (1972–77) *Structural Anthropology*, 2 vols. (French originals, Paris 1958–1973). London

[192] C. LEVI-STRAUSS (1968–77) *Mythologiques*, 4 vols. (French originals, Paris 1964–71). London (translated under individual titles)

[193] *C. R. PHILLIPS III (1991) 'Misconceptualizing Classical mythology', in M. A. Flower and M. Toher (eds.) *Georgica. Greek Studies in honour of George Cawkwell* (BICS Supp. 58): 143–51

[194] W. B. TYRRELL and F. S. BROWN (1991) *Athenian Myths and Institutions: words in action.* New York

J.-P. VERNANT 1980 [39] and 1983 [40]

J.-P. VERNANT and P. VIDAL-NAQUET 1990 [149]

[195] F. VIAN (1952) *La Guerre des Géants: le mythe avant l'époque hellénistique.* Paris

THEOGONIES, COSMOGONIES

[196] A. BALLABRIGA (1986) *Le Soleil et le Tartare: l'image mythique du monde en Grèce archaïque.* Paris

[197] F. M. CORNFORD (1952) *Principium Sapientiae. The Origins of Greek philosophical thought.* Oxford

[198] G. S. KIRK, J. E. RAVEN and M. SCHOFIELD (1983) *The Presocratic Philosophers.* 2nd edn. Cambridge. Esp. ch. 1: 'The forerunners of philosophical cosmogony': 7–74. [Text, trans. and comm.]

[199] C. RAMNOUX (1959) *La Nuit et les enfants de la Nuit.* Paris

[200] J.-P. VERNANT (1982) *The Origins of Greek Thought* (French original, Paris 1962). Ithaca and London

[201] M. L. WEST (ed.) (1966) *Hesiod, Theogony.* Oxford

ORPHIC COSMOGONY

[202] M. DETIENNE (1979) *Dionysos Slain* (French original, Paris 1977). Baltimore. Esp. ch. 4 ('The Orphic Dionysos and roasted boiled meat': 68–94, 109–17)

[203] W. K. C. GUTHRIE (1952) *Orpheus and Greek Religion. A study of the Orphic movement.* 2nd edn. London

[204] I. M. LINFORTH (1941) *The Arts of Orpheus.* Berkeley

D. SABBATUCCI 1965 [175]

[205] M. L. WEST (1983) *The Orphic Poems.* Oxford

13 A polytheistic religion

DIVINE POWERS

[206] W. K. C. GUTHRIE (1950) *The Greeks and their Gods.* London

[207] C. R. LONG (1987) *The Twelve Gods of Greece and Rome.* Leiden. [Regionally organized study of representations of the Twelve as a group]

[208] N. LORAUX (1991) 'Qu'est-ce qu'une déesse?', in G. Duby and M. Perrot (eds.) *Histoire des Femmes*, vol. 1 *L'Antiquité*, under the direction of P. Schmitt Pantel: 31–62. Paris; now Eng. trans. Cambridge, MA and London 1992

[209] W. F. OTTO (1954) *The Homeric Gods. The spiritual significance of Greek religion* (German original, Bonn 1929). Boston

HEROES AND HEROINES

[210] A. BRELICH (1958) *Gli eroi greci: un problema storico-religioso.* Rome

[211] C. CALAME (1990) *Thésée et l'imaginaire athénien.* Lausanne

[212] L. R. FARNELL (1921) *Greek Hero Cults and Ideas of Immortality.* Oxford. [Outdated theoretical framework, but valuable collection of evidence]

[213] E. KEARNS (1989) *The Heroes of Attica* (*BICS* Supp. 57). London

[214] N. LORAUX (1981) *Les Enfants d'Athéna, idées athéniennes sur la citoyenneté et la division des sexes.* Esp. 52–6. Paris. [Autochthonous heroes of Attica]

[215] A. D. NOCK (1944, 1972) 'The cult of heroes' (*HThR* 37: 141–74), repr. in Z. Stewart (ed.) *Essays on Religion and the Ancient World*, vol. 2: 575–602. Oxford

[216] C. ROBERT (1920–6) *Die griechische Heldensage*, 5 vols. Berlin

[217] F. VIAN (1963) *Les Origines de Thèbes, Cadmos et les Spartes.* Paris

APPROACHES TO THE PANTHEON

[218] G. DUMEZIL (1966) *La Religion romaine archaïque.* Paris

[219] M. DETIENNE and J.-P. VERNANT (1978, 1991) *Cunning Intelligence in Greek Culture and Society* (French original, Paris 1974). Hassocks, pb. repr. Cambridge, MA

MARRIAGE

[220] M. DETIENNE (1977) *The Gardens of Adonis: spices in Greek mythology* (French original, Paris 1972, repr. 1989). Hassocks

[221] *J.-P. DARMON and M. DETIENNE (1991) 'The powers of marriage in Greece', in BONNEFOY 1991 [2]: 395–403

TECHNOLOGY

[222] L. BRISSON and F. FRONTISI-DUCROUX (1991) 'Gods and Artisans: Hephaestus, Athena, Daedalus', in BONNEFOY 1991 [2]: 384–90. [Hephaestus (L.B.); Athene and Daedalus (F.F.-D.)]

[223] M. DELCOURT (1957, 1982) *Héphaïstos ou la légende du magicien.* Paris

[224] F. FRONTISI-DUCROUX (1975) *Dédale, mythologie de l'artisan en Grèce ancienne.* Paris

APOLLO

[225] G. DUMEZIL (1982) *Apollon sonore et autres essais.* Paris

[226] E. SIMON *et al. LIMC* [10]: II.1 (1984): 183–464

HERMES

[227] L. KAHN (1978) *Hermès passe.* Paris

[228] R. G. OSBORNE (1985) 'The erection and mutilation of the Hermai', *PCPhS* n.s. 31: 47–73

DIONYSOS

[229] J. N. BREMMER (1984) 'Greek maenadism reconsidered', *ZPE* 55: 267–86

[230] M. DARAKI (1985) *Dionysos.* Paris

[231] M. DETIENNE (1989) *Dionysos at Large* (French original, Paris 1985). Cambridge, MA and London

[232] A. HENRICHS (1984) 'Loss of self, suffering, violence: the modern view of Dionysus from Nietzsche to Girard', *HSCP* 88: 205–40

[233] H. JEANMAIRE (1970) *Dionysos, histoire du culte de Bacchus.* 2nd edn. Paris

[234] P. MCGINTY (1978) *Interpretation and Dionysos. Method in the study of a God.* Cambridge, MA

[235] W. F. OTTO (1965) *Dionysus: myth und cult* (German original, Frankfurt-am-Main 1933). Bloomington and London

Bibliography

THE PANTHEON IN OPERATION: MANTINEIA

[236] M. JOST (1985) *Sanctuaires et cultes d'Arcadie*. Paris

OTHER LOCAL PANTHEONS

[237] P. BRUNEAU (1970) *Recherches sur les cultes de Délos à l'époque hellénistique et à l'époque impériale*. Paris

[238] F. GRAF (1985) *Nordionische Kulte. Religionsgeschichtliche und epigraphische Untersuchungen zu den Kulten von Chios, Erythrai, Klazomenai und Phokaia*. Rome. [Useful review in English by J. Bremmer, *Mnemosyne*, series 4, 43 (1989): 260–3]

[239] R. PARKER (1989) 'Spartan religion', in A. Powell (ed.) *Classical Sparta: techniques behind her success*: 142–72. London

[240] J. POUILLOUX (1954–8) *Recherches sur l'histoire et les cultes de Thasos*, 2 vols. (vol. 2 with C. Dunand). Paris

[241] A. SCHACHTER (1981–6) *Cults of Boeotia*, 2 vols. and index vol. London. (Vol. 3 forthcoming.)

14 Forms of imaginative projection

FORMS OF IMAGINATIVE PROJECTION: GENERAL PROBLEMS

[242] R. L. GORDON (1979) 'The real and the imaginary: production and religion in the Graeco-Roman world', *Art History* 2: 5–34

[243] J.-P. VERNANT (1983) 'The representation of the Invisible and the psychological category of the Double: the Colossos' (French original 1962), in Vernant 1983 [40]: 305–20

[244] J.-P. VERNANT (1990) *Figures, idoles, masques*. Paris

[245] J.-P. VERNANT (1991) 'The birth of images' (French original 1975), in Vernant 1991 [42]: 164–85

[246] J.-P. VERNANT (1991) 'From the "presentification" of the invisible to the imitation of appearance' (French original 1983), in Vernant 1991 [42]: 151–63

FORMS OF IMAGINATIVE PROJECTION: PARTICULAR STUDIES

[247] B. ALROTH (1989) *Greek Gods and Figurines. Aspects of the anthropomorphic dedications*. Uppsala

[248] C. BERARD *et al.* (1989) *A City of Images. Iconography and society in Ancient Greece* (French original, Lausanne 1984). Princeton

[249] C. BERARD, C. BRON and A. POMARI (eds.) (1987) *Images et société en Grèce ancienne. L'iconographie comme méthode d'analyse.* Lausanne

[250] T. H. CARPENTER (1991) *Art and Myth in Ancient Greece.* London and New York

J.-L. DURAND 1986 [72]. [Discusses representation of rituals in images]

[251] F. LISSARRAGUE (1990) *The Aesthetics of the Greek Banquet. Images of wine and ritual* (French original, Paris 1987). Princeton

[252] F. LISSARRAGUE and F. THELAMON (eds.) (1983) *Image et céramique grecque.* Rouen. Includes P. Schmitt-Pantel and F. Thélamon 'Image et histoire. Illustration ou document' (9–20).

C. SOURVINOU-INWOOD 1987 [107]

[253] C. SOURVINOU-INWOOD (1990) 'Myths in images: Theseus and Medea as a case study', in EDMUNDS 1990 [183]: 393–445

15 Concluding reflections

THE CAREER OF *PSUKHĒ*

[254] E. ROHDE (1925) *Psyche* (German original, 8th edn., Berlin, 1909). London. [Great learning, outdated in theory]

[255] J.-P. VERNANT (1983) 'Some aspects of personal identity in Greek religion' (French original, 1960) in Vernant 1983 [40]: 323–40

[256] J.-P. VERNANT (1991) 'Psuche: simulacrum of the body or image of the divine?', in Vernant 1991 [42]: 186–92

HELLENISTIC PERIOD

F. C. GRANT 1953 [81]

[257] L. H. MARTIN (1987) *Hellenistic Religions: an introduction.* Oxford

[258] Z. STEWART (1977) 'La religione', in R. Bianchi Bandinelli (ed.) *La società ellenistica*: 503–616. Milan. [Good synthesis]

ROMAN IMPERIAL PERIOD: PAGAN AND CHRISTIAN HELLENISM

[259] A. H. ARMSTRONG (1990) *Hellenic and Christian Studies.* Leiden

[260] G. W. BOWERSOCK (1990) *Hellenism in Late Antiquity.* Cambridge. Esp. ch. 2 ('The idolatry of holiness') and ch. 4 ('Dionysus and his world').

Bibliography

[261] R. LANE FOX (1986, 1988) *Pagans and Christians*. New York, pb. repr. Harmondsworth

[262] S. R. F. PRICE (1984) *Rituals and Power: the Roman imperial cult in Asia Minor*. Cambridge. [Important for method]

Appendix I The Classical Greek temple

[263] H. BERVE and G. GRUBEN (1963) *Greek Temples, Theatres and Shrines* (German original, Munich 1961). London

[264] P. E. CORBETT (1970) 'Greek temples and Greek worshippers: the literary and archaeological evidence', *BICS* 17: 149–58

Appendix II The monuments of the Athenian Akropolis

[265] C. J. HERINGTON (1955) *Athena Parthenos and Athena Polias*. Manchester

[266] G. T. W. HOOKER (ed.) (1963) *Parthenos and Parthenon (G&R* Supp. 10). Oxford

[267] R. J. HOPPER (1970) *The Acropolis*. London

[268] L. SCHNEIDER and C. HÖCKER (1990) *Die Akropolis von Athen. Antikes Heiligtum und Modernes Reiseziel*. Cologne

[269] J. TRAVLOS (1971) *Pictorial Dictionary of Ancient Athens*. London and New York

ADDENDA

§I.i A. MOTTE, V. PIRENNE-DELFORGE & P. WATHELET (eds.) (1992) *Guide bibliographique de la religion grecque* (Kernos Suppl. 2). Liège

§I.ii *J. BREMMER (1994) *Greek Religion (G&R* New Surveys in the Classics 21). Oxford

W. BURKERT (1995) 'Greek *poleis* and civic cults: some further thoughts', in M.H. Hansen & K.A. Raaflaub (eds.) *Studies in the Ancient Greek Polis*: 201–10. Stuttgart

R. HÄGG, N. MARINATOS & G. C. NORDQUIST (eds.) (1988) *Early Greek Cult Practice*. Stockholm

R. OSBORNE & S. HORNBLOWER (eds.) (1994) *Rituals, Finance, Politics. Democratic accounts presented to David Lewis*. Oxford

S. PRICE (forthcoming, 1998) *The Religions of Greece*. Cambridge

§2 A. MOTTE (1988) 'L'expression du sacré dans la religion grecque', in J. Ries (ed.) *L'expression du sacré dans les grandes religions*: 117ff. Louvain-la-Neuve

§3 R. HÄGG (ed.) (1993) *Ancient Greek Cult Practice from the Epigraphical Evidence*. Stockholm

§4 R. ETIENNE 'Autels et sacrifices', in A. SCHACHTER (ed.) [see §6]: ch. VII

M. H. JAMESON, D. R. JORDAN & R. D. KOTANSKY (1993) *A Lex Sacra from Selinous*. Durham, North Carolina

R. OSBORNE (1993) 'Women and sacrifice in Classical Greece', *CQ* 43: 392–405

V. J. ROSIVACH (1994) *The System of Public Sacrifice in Fourth-Century Athens*. Atlanta

F. VAN STRATEN (1995) *Hiera Kala. Images of animal sacrifice in Archaic and Classical Greece*. Leiden

D. AUBRIOT-SÉVIN (1992) *Prière et conceptions religieuses en Grèce ancienne jusqu'à la fin du Ve siècle av. J.-C.* Lyon

§5 U. KRON (1996) 'Priesthoods, dedications, and euergetism. What part did religion play in the political and social status of Greek women?' in HELLSTRÖM & ALROTH (eds.) (1996) [see §9]: 139–82

§6 J. M. HALL (1995) 'How "Argive" was the Argive Heraion? The political and cultic geography of the Argive plain, 900–400 B.C.', *AJA* 99: 577–613

F. DE POLIGNAC (1995) *Cults, Territory and the Origins of the Greek City-State*. Chicago

A. SCHACHTER (ed.) (1992) *Le sanctuaire grec*. Geneva N. MARINATOS & R. HÄGG (eds.) (1993) *Greek Sanctuaries: New approaches*. London and New York

S. E. ALCOCK & R. OSBORNE (eds.) (1994) *Placing the Gods: Sanctuaries and sacred space in Ancient Greece*. Oxford

T. LINDERS & B. ALROTH (eds.) (1992) *The Economics of Cult in the Ancient Greek World*. Uppsala

F. VAN STRATEN (1992) 'Votives and votaries in Greek sanctuaries', in SCHACHTER (ed.) (1992): ch. VI

§7 K. DOWDEN (1989) *Death and the Maiden. Girls' initiation rites in Greek mythology*. London & New York

R. HAMILTON (1992) *Choes and Anthesteria. Athenian iconography and ritual*. Ann Arbor

I. MORRIS (1992) *Death-ritual and Social Structure in Classical Antiquity*. Cambridge

§8 R. PARKER (1996) *Athenian Religion: a history*. Oxford

C. CALAME (1996) *Mythe et histoire dans L'Antiquité grecque. La création symbolique d'une colonie*. Lausanne

§9 R. GARLAND (1992) *Introducing New Gods. The politics of Athenian religion*. London

P. HELLSTRÖM & B. ALROTH (eds.) (1996) *Religion and Power in the Ancient Greek World*. Uppsala

M. H. JAMESON (1991) 'Sacrifice before battle', in V. D. Hanson (ed.) *Hoplites*, 197–227. London & New York

§10 J. NEILS et al. (1992) *Goddess and Polis. The Panathenaic Festival in Ancient Athens*. Princeton

N. LORAUX (1993) *The Children of Athena*. Princeton

J. D. MIKALSON (1992) *Honor Thy Gods. Popular religion in Greek tragedy*. Chapel Hill

R. PADEL (1992) *In and Out of the Mind. Greek images of the tragic self*. Princeton

R. PADEL (1995) *Whom Gods Destroy. Elements of Greek and tragic madness*. Princeton

H. YUNIS (1988) *A New Creed. Fundamental religious beliefs in the Athenian polis and Euripidean drama*. Göttingen

§11 J. BOUSQUET (ed.) 1989. *Corpus des Inscriptions de Delphes. Lois sacrées et règlements religieux*, vol. 2. *Les comptes du quatrième et du troisième siècle*. Paris

L. R. LI DONNICI (1995) *The Epidaurian Miracle Inscriptions. Text, translation and commentary*. Atlanta

H. FOLEY (1994) (ed.) *The Homeric Hymn to Demeter*. Princeton

§12 R. BUXTON (1994) *Imaginary Greece. The contexts of mythology*. Cambridge

C. CALAME (1996) *Mythe et histoire dans l'Antiquité grecque. La création symbolique d'une colonie*. Lausanne

F. GRAF (1993) *Greek Mythology*. Baltimore

P. BORGEAUD (ed.) (1991) *Orphisme et Orphée (en l'honneur de Jean Rudhardt)*. Geneva

§13 P. CARTLEDGE (1997) *The Greeks. A portrait of self and others*. rev. edn. Oxford

E. KEARNS (1992) 'Between God and Man: status and function of heroes and their sanctuaries', in SCHACHTER (ed.) 1992 [see §6]: ch. II.

J. LARSON (1995) *Greek Heroine-Cults*. Madison

D. LYONS (1997) *Gender and Immortality: Heroines in ancient Greek myth and cult*. Princeton

A. AVAGIANOU (1991) *Sacred Marriage in the Rituals of Greek Religion*. Berne etc.

J. H. OAKLEY & R. SINOS (1993) *The Wedding in Ancient Athens*. Madison

Bibliography

J. SOLOMON (1994) (ed.) *Apollo. Origins and Influences.* Tucson & London

T. H. CARPENTER & C. A. FARAONE (eds.) (1993) *Masks of Dionysus.* Ithaca

J. A. DABDAB TRABULSI (1990) *Dionysisme. Pouvoir et société en Grèce jusqu'à la fin de l'époque classique.* Paris

F. FRONTISI-DUCROUX (1991) *Le dieu-masque: une figure du Dionysos à Athènes.* Paris

F. FRONTISI-DUCROUX (1995) *Du masque au visage. Aspects de l'identité en Grèce ancienne.* Paris

M. JOST (1992) 'Sanctuaires ruraux et sanctuaires urbains en Arcadie', in SCHACHTER (ed.) 1992 [see §6]: ch. V.

§14 D. CASTRIOTA (1992) *Myth, Ethos and Actuality. Official art in fifth-century B.C. Athens.* Madison

K. CLINTON (1992) *Myth and Cult. The iconography of the Eleusinian Mysteries.* Stockholm

C. A. FARAONE (1992) *Talismans and Trojan Horses: Guardian statues in ancient Greek myth and ritual.* Oxford

C. A. FARAONE et al. (1994) 'Review feature' on Faraone 1992: *Cambridge Archaeological Journal* 4.2: 270–89

R. HÄGG (ed.) (1992) *The Iconography of Greek Cult in the Archaic and Classical Periods* (Kernos Supp. 1). Liège

C. SOURVINOU-INWOOD (1991) *'Reading' Greek Culture. Texts and images, rituals and myths.* Oxford

§15 L. P. GERSON (1990) *God and Greek Philosophy: studies in the early history of natural theology.* London & New York

M. L. MORGAN (1990) *Platonic Piety: philosophy and ritual in fourth-century Athens.* New Haven

App.II R. F. RHODES (1995) *Architecture and Meaning on the Athenian Acropolis.* Cambridge

Index

(main entries in **bold** type)